Thomas White and the Blackloists

However often experiment and reasoning may show a man that under the same conditions and with the same character he will do the same thing as before, yet when under the same conditions and with the same character he approaches for the thousandth time the action that always ends in the same way, he feels as certainly convinced as before the experiment that he can act as he pleases. Every man, savage or sage, however incontestably reason and experiment may prove to him that it is impossible to imagine two different courses of action in precisely the same conditions, feels that without this irrational conception (which constitutes the essence of freedom) he cannot imagine life. He feels that however impossible it may be, it is so, for without this conception of freedom not only would he be unable to understand life, but he would be unable to live for a single moment.

L. Tolstoj, War and Peace

Thomas White and the Blackloists

Between Politics and Theology during the English Civil War

STEFANIA TUTINO

ASHGATE

© Stefania Tutino 2008

All rights reserved. No part of this publication may be reproduced, stored in a retrieval system or transmitted in any form or by any means, electronic, mechanical, photocopying, recording or otherwise without the prior permission of the publisher.

Stefania Tutino has asserted her moral right under the Copyright, Designs and Patents Act, 1988, to be identified as the author of this work.

Published by
Ashgate Publishing Limited
Gower House
Croft Road
Aldershot
Hampshire GU11 3HR
England

Ashgate Publishing Company
Suite 420
101 Cherry Street
Burlington, VT 05401-4405
USA

Ashgate website: http://www.ashgate.com

British Library Cataloguing in Publication Data
Tutino, Stefania
  Thomas White and the Blackloists: Between Politics and Theology during the English Civil War. - (Catholic Christendom, 1300–1700)
  1. White, Thomas, 1593–1676. 2. Digby, Kenelm, Sir, 1603–1665. 3. Holden, Henry, 1596–1662. 4. Catholics – England – History – 17th century. 5. Religion and politics – England – History – 17th century. I. Title
  282.4'2'09032

Library of Congress Cataloging-in-Publication Data
Tutino, Stefania.
  Thomas White and the Blackloists: Between Politics and Theology during the English Civil War / by Stefania Tutino.
      p.   cm. – (Catholic Christendom, 1300–1700)
  Includes bibliographical references (p.   ) and index.
  1. White, Thomas, 1593–1676. 2. Christianity and politics – England – History – 17th century. I. Title.
  B1299.W454T88 2008
  192–dc22   2008010403

ISBN 978-0-7546-5817-7

Printed and bound in Great Britain by
TJ International Ltd, Padstow, Cornwall

Contents

Series Editor's Preface — *vii*
Acknowledgments — *ix*
List of Abbreviations — *xi*

Introduction — xiii

1   Thomas White and the Beginnings of the Blackloist Group   1
    1.1 The English Catholic Church on the Eve of the Civil War   1
    1.2 Thomas White's education and background   5
    1.3 Kenelm Digby   7

2   The Blackloists' Natural Philosophy and Theology   15
    2.1 Mixing the Old and the New: between Aristotelianism and Atomism   15
    2.2 'A Natural and New Divinity'   31
    2.3 Catholicism and Natural Philosophy   38

3   The Blackloists' Politics   43
    3.1 The Beginning of the English Civil War: The Blackloists between Politics and Ecclesiology   43
    3.2 Kenelm Digby: A Catholic Political Acrobat   49
    3.3 Henry Holden: A Gallican in England   56
    3.4 Thomas White: A Catholic Political Theorist   59

4   The Grounds of Obedience and Government   65
    4.1 The Text   65
    4.2 The Context   73

5   The Blackloists and the Lord Protector   83
    5.1 Thomas White   83
    5.2 Kenelm Digby   101
    5.3 Henry Holden   106

6   'To Little Purpose': The End of the Blackloist Group   117
    6.1 Thomas White   117
    6.2 Kenelm Digby   136

Conclusion: An Assessment of the Blackloist Experience   143

Appendix — *147*
Selected Bibliography — *195*
Index — *207*

Series Editor's Preface

The still-usual emphasis on medieval (or Catholic) and reformation (or Protestant) religious history has meant neglect of the middle ground, both chronological and ideological. As a result, continuities between the middle ages and early modern Europe have been overlooked in favor of emphasis on radical discontinuities. Further, especially in the later period, the identification of 'reformation' with various kinds of Protestantism means that the vitality and creativity of the established church, whether in its Roman or local manifestations, has been left out of account. In the last few years, an upsurge of interest in the history of traditional (or catholic) religion makes these inadequacies in received scholarship even more glaring and in need of systematic correction. The series will attempt this by covering all varieties of religious behavior, broadly interpreted, not just (or even especially) traditional institutional and doctrinal church history. It will to the maximum degree possible be interdisciplinary, comparative and global, as well as non-confessional. The goal is to understand religion, primarily of the 'Catholic' variety, as a broadly human phenomenon, rather than as a privileged mode of access to superhuman realms, even implicitly.

The period covered, 1300–1700, embraces the moment which saw an almost complete transformation of the place of religion in the life of Europeans, whether considered as a system of beliefs, as an institution, or as a set of social and cultural practices. In 1300, vast numbers of Europeans, from the pope down, fully expected Jesus's return and the beginning of His reign on earth. By 1700, very few Europeans, of whatever level of education, would have subscribed to such chiliastic beliefs. Pierre Bayle's notorious sarcasms about signs and portents are not idiosyncratic. Likewise, in 1300 the vast majority of Europeans probably regarded the pope as their spiritual head; the institution he headed was probably the most tightly integrated and effective bureaucracy in Europe. Most Europeans were at least nominally Christian, and the pope had at least nominal knowledge of that fact. The papacy, as an institution, played a central role in high politics, and the clergy in general formed an integral part of most governments, whether central or local. By 1700, Europe was divided into a myriad of different religious allegiances, and even those areas officially subordinate to the pope were both more nominally Catholic in belief (despite colossal efforts at imposing uniformity) and also in allegiance than they had been four hundred years earlier. The pope had become only one political factor, and not one of the first rank. The clergy, for its part, had virtually disappeared from secular governments as well as losing much of its local authority. The stage was set for the Enlightenment.

Thomas F. Mayer,
Augustana College

Acknowledgments

The research for this book, which is about a group of intellectuals of many different talents and interests, has obliged me to venture outside of familiar intellectual territories and into a series of themes and problems utterly new and foreign to me. And while the many new things learned have provided no small part of my enjoyment in working on this book, I have relied tremendously on the help of many colleagues and friends, and without their scholarly generosity I could have not completed my project. Among them I would like to thank Jeffrey Collins, Barbara Donagan, Mordechai Feingold, Lori Anne Ferrell, Lowell Gallagher, Anita Guerrini, Knud Haakonssen, James Jacob, Margaret Jacob, Marc Lerner, Thomas Mayer, Kirstie McClure, Sears McGee, Peter Reill, Susan Rosa, Jonathan Scott, Debora Shuger, Susan Wabuda. Of course, omissions and errors remain my own.

During the completion of this book I have also benefited from the generosity of many institutions, and in particular UCLA, where I held a Mellon Fellowship from 2003 to 2005, and the William Andrews Clark Memorial Library; the Harry Ransom Center of the University of Texas at Austin; the Huntington Library. I am grateful to the librarians and staff of all these places, who have contributed to make my research trips as pleasant and productive as they could be. I would like to thank Reverend Ian Dickie, who was the archivist of the Westminster Diocesan Archives in London, for his assistance during my visits to the Archives, and many thanks to the staff of the Bodleian Library and British Library. I am also grateful to the librarians and archivists of the Notarieel Archief and Koninklijke Bibliotheek, The Hague, where I went to trace White's movements in the Netherlands. While I could not find what I was looking for, I did find an impressive degree of professional competence and scholarly generosity among the staff of those libraries. I would also like to thank Dr. Daniel Ponziani and Dr. Johan Ickx, respectively the current and former archivist of the Archive of the Congregation for the Doctrine of Faith, as well as Mons. Alejandro Cifres, director of the Archive, for their help during my visits.

While working on the parts of this book concerned with natural philosophy I have enjoyed many stimulating conversations with modern-day scientists, from whom I have learned a great deal about mathematical infinitesimals, Galilean mechanics and the role of science in shaping the way in which we think about the world. Among them I would like to mention in particular Martin Einhorn, Richard Ellis, Elena Gallo, Gordon Kane, Everett Lipman, Carlo Mantegazza and, last but definitely not least, Tommaso Treu, my husband, to whom this book is dedicated.

List of Abbreviations

ACDF	Archivio della Congregazione per la Dottrina della Fede, Rome
AHSI	Archivum Historicum Societatis Iesu
ARSI	Archivum Romanum Societatis Iesu, Rome
BAV	Biblioteca Apostolica Vaticana, Rome
BL	British Library, London
BodL	Bodleian Library, Oxford
DNB	*Dictionary of National Biography*, Oxford 1885–1901
STC	A.W. Pollard-G.R. Redgrave (eds.), *A Short Title Catalogue of BooksPrinted in England, Scotland, & Ireland and of English Books Printed Abroad, 1575–1640.*, London 1976–1991
WING D.G.	Wing (ed.), *Short-title catalogue of books printed in England, Scotland, Ireland, Wales, and British America and of English books printed in other countries, 1641–1700* (2nd edition, 1994)

Introduction

This work aims to analyze the political, intellectual and theological significance of a group of English Catholics, named Blackloists after their leader's *alias*. The core members of the group, with whom this work will be mainly concerned, were three: Thomas White or Blacklo, their leader; Kenelm Digby; Henry Holden.

The Blackloists have received very little attention in current scholarship. Some studies have analyzed parts of the thought and career of individual members of the group. For instance, a rather useful introduction to selected aspects of the thought of Thomas White is Beverley Southgate's recent monograph,[1] the strengths and limitations of which will be discussed in the following pages. Kenelm Digby has been the object of two, almost contemporary, biographies, both of which present Digby as a more or less eccentric *virtuoso*, without taking into account the significance of the political, theological and intellectual context in which he lived and acted.[2] Yet no scholar has attempted an intellectual biography of the group as such. By studying its leading members together, I aim to understand the Blackloists less in terms of their 'originality' and distinctive features, than as a lens through which to offer a novel interpretation of certain aspects of the many theological and political debates in which they took part.

In this respect, the Blackloists are an extremely interesting group for a number of reasons. They engaged themselves in questions of theology (they wanted to propose a rational model of Catholicism, or, as they defined it, a 'new and natural divinity'), ecclesiology (they sketched a program for reformation of the English Catholic Church with important Gallican undertones), natural philosophy (they sought to integrate Aristotelian physics with Galilean science), politics and political theory (they supported Oliver Cromwell's regime on the basis of a peculiar mix of Catholic consent theory and *de facto*-ist arguments). Thus, they were at the core of some of the most important intellectual currents and debates in seventeenth-century Europe.

At the same time, however, they failed to leave lasting traces of their thoughts and theories, mainly because in the dichotomy between antiquity and modernity they systematically ended up supporting the losing side, both in terms of their political fortune and their intellectual enterprises. In a sense, it is safe to say that everything they stood for was to collapse. They supported Galileo even when the Church of Rome considered his case closed. They never ceased to believe in Aristotelian physics even when the new science was completing its work of eradicating it completely and substituting for it the new physics. They tried to create a 'rational' Catholicism when the Court of

---

[1] B.C. Southgate, *'Covetous of Truth'. The life and work of Thomas White, 1593–1676*, Dordrecht-Boston 1993
[2] R.T. Petersson, *Sir Kenelm Digby. The Ornament of England 1603–1665*, London 1956, and V. Gabrieli, *Sir Kenelm Digby. Un inglese italianato nell'eta'della Controriforma*, Roma 1957.

Rome was interested in maintaining papal authority both theoretically and politically. At the height of Counter-Reformation, they sought to integrate the Catholic religion in a Protestant country while affirming their allegiance to the temporal sovereign.

Why study them then? I believe that if we want to understand why certain people, groups, movements, intellectual theories stood the test of time, we need to know the context in which they were born and the intellectual antagonists with whom they were in conversation. A specific example of this is Thomas Hobbes, a 'modern' and 'classical' author on all accounts, whose political theory cannot be properly understood without taking into consideration the context in which he elaborated it. Thomas White and his associates, as I seek to demonstrate in the following pages, were pivotal protagonists of that context. In other words, modernity is not an orphan, and if we want to understand it we need to look at its family history.

Among the many aspects of the Blackloists' contribution to this history, this work focuses on the relation between religion, politics and philosophy. More specifically, it takes into consideration two main themes. The first is the manner in which the Blackloists saw the question of the foundations and nature of the Catholic Church and its relationship to the English state. The second theme analyzed is the Blackloists' attempt to integrate their religious beliefs into the philosophical and scientific discussions of their time from a cross-confessional perspective.

While the Blackloists' manner of interpreting and theorizing the complex set of links between religion, politics and science was indeed novel and distinctive, the centrality of those links, I argue, is not an idiosyncratic aspect of their philosophy and theology, but further evidence that those links did indeed lie at the core of seventeenth-century European intellectual debates. Analyzing the Blackloists, then, can help to analyze these ramifications and to discard the simplistic division between new and old science, Catholic backwardness and Protestant modernity, secular and religious political theories.

Another task I hope to accomplish in this work is to foster further research on those aspects of the Blackloists' thought with which my book does not deal specifically, as, for example, their contribution in the realm of natural philosophy. While I have treated White's and Digby's natural philosophy in so far as this was necessary to understand their political and theological doctrines, I think that an analysis of their role in the Oxford circle could shed light on important questions in the history of science and of the politics of science in mid-seventeenth century England. I hope that this book, by showing the potential fruitfulness of putting the Blackloists in the map of seventeenth-century European history, will serve as a starting point and, in a sense, provide more questions than answers.

CHAPTER 1

Thomas White and the Beginnings of the Blackloist Group

1.1 The English Catholic Church on the Eve of the Civil War

Before examining the implications of the political and theological positions taken by Thomas White in the context of the political and intellectual debate in England between 1640 and 1660, it is necessary to remember that the Blackloists caused a great deal of controversy within the English Catholic Church itself. And this happened not only because of the peculiarities of the Blackloists' view of the relationship between Church and State, or because of their novel and controversial interpretation of central theological issues, but also because of the commotion that White and his followers caused in the delicate balance in the government and structure of the English Catholic Church. In this respect, it seems useful to me to briefly summarize the main events that involved the English Catholic Church during the late sixteenth and seventeenth centuries.

The Elizabethan Settlement of 1559 represented both a solution to, and a manifestation of the many contradictions and ambiguities that the English Reformation presented with respect to the religion of Rome. On the one hand Elizabeth maintained the politically uncompromising stance towards the Papacy that her father had adopted. On the other, however, she allowed the Church of England, whose doctrinal backbone was still rather fluid, to retain a certain 'Roman' flavour in some of its ceremonial manifestations, and she was not too strict in rooting out some Catholic practises and rituals among her Catholic subjects. A clear example of this doctrinal and liturgical ambiguity is the doctrine of the Eucharist in the Elizabethan Church. While transubstantiation was vigorously denied, the 1559 *Book of Common Prayer* did not clearly establish the question of Christ's real presence in the sacrament. Moreover, in an addendum to the 1559 *Injunctions* we read that celebrating the Eucharist on the altar or at the table was to be considered a matter of indifference. In other words, the Queen that in Francis Bacon's opinion did not like to open windows in her subjects' soul seemed not to mind the presence of a certain kind of Catholic residual manifestations, provided that they did not translate into any public political act.[1]

---

[1] For an account of the Elizabethan Settlement see, among the others, N.L. Jones, *Faith by Statute: Parliament and the settlement of Religion, 1559*, London 1982; P. Collinson, *The Religion of Protestants: The Church in English Society, 1559–1625*, Oxford 1982; Id., *The Birthpangs of Protestant England: Religion and Cultural Change in the Sixteenth and Seventeenth Centuries*, Basingstoke 1988.

If this solution allowed the Queen to avoid, for the most part, an open revolt of her Catholic subjects, at the same time it made possible the survival of a distinctive form of Roman religion, mainly confined to English households in which the influence of the central government was for a number of reasons weaker than in London. As John Bossy has highlighted, this kind of Catholicism did not involve acts of non-conformism, but was limited for the most part to a set of social ritual and practises. This situation changed between 1570 and 1580, for a number of factors. In 1570 the Pope excommunicated Elizabeth and consequently released her Catholic subjects from their obedience to a Queen who, as heretic, was therefore illegitimate. In 1580 the Society of Jesus launched its first mission in England: the goal was to revitalize the acquiescent and even rather tepid Catholicism which had survived after Mary's reign, and to implement another model of Catholicism, aggressive on both doctrinal and political issues.[2]

The 1580s, then, saw the development and the affirmation of the 'Jesuitical' model of Catholicism, as led by Father Robert Persons, a participant, with Edmund Campion, in the first mission of 1580. Persons well embodies many of the aspects of such a model: uncompromisingly loyal to the Roman faith to the point of martyrdom, and equally uncompromising towards the English regime. Persons did not want freedom of conscience for the English Catholics; he wanted a Catholic England.

The Jesuits' aggressive stances, combined with the rumours of the many plots – sometimes real and sometimes only imagined – that they were thought to have hatched, and with the all-too-real conflict with Spain that exploded in 1588, heightened the repression by the English regime, which in 1585 declared any priest or missionary found in England guilty of treason against the state. At the same time, the perception of the danger of the Pope and of the Society of Jesus, seen as the Papacy's army, contributed to the formation of the so-called Black Legend around the Jesuits.[3]

Nor was the presence of the Jesuits in England unanimously welcomed within the English Catholic community. In particular, the English secular priests, heirs of the Marian clergy and principal protagonists of the survivalist model of Catholicism, in the 1590s started to become more and more vocal in their opposition to the methods and practises of the Society. There were many issues at stake, but they all stemmed from a basic conflict caused by the very essence of the Society of Jesus, a new, politically and religiously aggressive

---

[2] See J. Bossy, 'The Character of Elizabethan Catholicism', *Past and Present*, n. 21 (1962), pp. 39–59, and Id., *The English Catholic Community 1570–1850*, Oxford 1976 (1975). For a different view see C. Haigh, 'The continuity of Catholicism in the English Reformation', *Past and Present* n.93 (1981), pp. 37–90, and, more recently, Id., *English Reformations. Religion, Politics and Society under the Tudors*, Oxford 1993; E. Duffy, *The stripping of the altars: traditional religion in England, c.1400–c.1580*, New Haven 1992.

[3] On the Black Legend it is still a fundamental reference the work by W.S. Maltby, *The Black Legend in England*, Durham (N.C.) 1971. On the Society of Jesus in England see also T.M. McCoog, *'Our way of proceeding'? The Society of Jesus in Ireland, Scotland and England, 1547–1588*, Leiden 1996.

religious order, who by nature could not blend into the existing structure of the English secular clergy. The Jesuit missionaries were supposed to be mobile, and to overlap, rather than homogenize themselves, with the secular clergy, who, although lacking a proper episcopal government, at the end of the sixteenth century were somewhat stably installed in their households, and used to performing their ministry in the grey zone between conformism and recusancy.

At the end of Elizabeth's reign the conflict exploded and it was centred on the appointment of George Blackwell as Archpriest. The Jesuits strongly approved of Blackwell's appointment, which, in their view, represented a solution to the lack of a formal hierarchy. The regular clergy, by contrast, opposed the appointment, viewing the Archpriest as a puppet in Jesuit hands. In the end, Blackwell was appointed.[4] The clash had also a political edge: the Appellant priests, as they were called because of the formal appeal that they filed to the Pope in 1601 against Blackwell's election, openly condemned the aggressive position that the Society of Jesus held toward Elizabeth's regime, hoping that the Queen, in a sort of *divide et impera* policy, would decide to grant them a form of toleration, while continuing to persecute only the Jesuits.

During the reign of James I the fissure in the Catholic camp did not heal. First the Gunpowder Plot, and then the promulgation of the Oath of Allegiance again raised the question of whether any Catholic could ever be considered a loyal subject, given his or her allegiance to the Bishop of Rome. At an institutional level, Pope Paul V's official condemnation of the Oath in 1606 polarized the English Catholic Church by sparking a heated debate on whether or not the Oath of Allegiance was a legitimate procedure and on whether or not English Catholics should indeed swear it.[5] At the same time, many prominent English Catholics, among whom Lord Wotton, did benefit from a form of toleration on the part of James – a sort of 'don't ask don't tell' kind of policy.[6] All of this, moreover, created a peculiarly delicate situation because of the overall lack of a stable ecclesiological structure within the English Catholic Church, which between the end of Mary Tudor's reign and the end of James's had no form of episcopal government, only an Archpriest, the first of whom was, as mentioned, George Blackwell.

---

[4] A detailed account of the precise stages of the controversy can be found in T.G. Law, *The Archpriest Controversy*, London 1896–98, and J.H. Pollen, *The Institution of the Archpriest Blackwell*, London 1916. For a more general picture of the English Catholic community at the end of Elizabeth's reign see J. Bossy, *The English Catholic Community*.

[5] On the Oath of Allegiance and its impact in the English Catholic Church see, among the others, J.P. Sommerville, 'Jacobean political thought and the controversy over the oath of allegiance of 1606', unpublished Ph.D. Thesis, University of Cambridge, 1981, pp. 23–26, and M.C. Questier, 'Loyalty, Religion and State Power in Early Modern England: English Romanism and the Jacobean Oath of Allegiance', *The Historical Journal*, vol.40 n. 2 (1997), pp. 311–329, at pp. 314–316

[6] A.J. Loomie S.I., 'A Jacobean Crypto-Catholic: Lord Wotton', *The Catholic Historical Review*, vol.III no.3 (1967), pp. 328–345, and K. Fincham-P. Lake, 'The Ecclesiastical Policy of King James I', *Journal of British Studies*, no. 24 (1985), pp. 169–207, pp. 185 and ff.

Finally, in 1623 William Bishop was consecrated Bishop of Chalcedon, and his election marked the beginning of what John Bossy has defined as 'the most eventful years in the posthumous history of the *Ecclesia Anglicana*'. William Bishop's brief episcopate – it lasted just slightly over one year – culminated in the institution of the Chapter, in which the hierarchy of the English clergy was formally represented and could express its will in the election of successive Bishops. But things did not run smoothly after Bishop's death. His successor, Richard Smith, proved to be highly controversial: Smith in fact tried to strengthen in two main areas the authority of the episcopal government by attacking the English regulars, the Jesuits but also the Benedictines, whose presence in England became more and more significant over the course of the seventeenth century. First, he tried to threaten their influence in the administration of pastoral duties, by claiming that the only priest that could effectively bind and loose sins in confession was the parish priest. As John Bossy notices, Smith's claim was especially unsettling for the English Catholic gentry, who, if they opted for a missionary as their confessor, would not be assured of the effectiveness of their confession.[7] The other way in which Smith challenged the regulars was financially: he tried to gain control of the financial resources of the mission, regularly administered by the missionaries themselves.

Rome was asked to intervene in the matter, and in 1631 the Roman hierarchy ruled against Smith, who was obliged to leave his post in England and move to France, where he remained until his death. After Smith's departure, the Chapter remained *de facto* the highest local authority of the English Catholic Church. When Smith died, in 1655, no new Bishop was appointed until 1685.[8]

In the mid-seventeenth century the Chapter split into two factions. George Leyburn, from 1652 on President of the Douai College, a committed Royalist and a firm believer that the Chapter should uphold Smith's leadership even though he had left England, was the most prominent member of the first faction. Thomas White, *alias* Blacklo, was the leader of the other faction.[9] It is with him and his followers that this work will be mainly concerned.

Before continuing, I would like to stress that the Blackloists were by no means a monolithic group. Rather, if it is true that White and his followers shared many intellectual concerns, and elaborated some unified proposals on how the English Catholic Church should be governed, and on how it should approach England's political situation, it is also true that they differed in many important aspects, which I will examine in detail. To approach the Blackloist movement bearing in mind this complexity is, I believe, to follow the most

---

[7] J. Bossy, *The English Catholic Community*, pp. 55–6.

[8] See T.A. Birrell, 'English Catholics without a Bishop, 1655–1672', *Recusant History*, IV (1958), pp. 142–178; and J. Bossy, *The English Catholic Community*, pp. 49–74 (quotation at p. 49).

[9] On the extent and the significance of the division within the English Chapter, and on White's role in it, cf. J. Bossy, *The English Catholic Community*, pp. 60 and ff., and R.I. Bradley S.J., 'Blacklo and the Counter-Reformation: an inquiry into the strange death of Catholic England', in C.H. Carter (ed.), *From the Renaissance to the Counter-Reformation. Essays in Honor of Garrett Mattingly*, New York 1965, pp. 348–370.

cogent methodology when studying the intersections of theology and politics in general, and the English Catholics in particular.

1.2 Thomas White's education and background

Thomas White was born in 1593 in Essex into a prosperous family – his grandfather was Edmund Plowden, the famous Elizabethan jurist and Catholic.[10] White and his siblings were brought up as Roman Catholics: one of White's three brothers, Jerome, followed in Thomas's footsteps by becoming a priest.[11] Following a well established pattern for well-to-do young Catholics, White was sent 'beyond the seas' for his education, first to the English College in St. Omer and then to the English College in Valladolid, which he entered in 1609. Then he moved to Douai, where he completed his studies and was ordained a priest in 1617. He remained there as a professor, first of philosophy and then of theology.[12]

The institution at Douai played a central role in the life of Thomas White and in the development of his thought, and therefore I would like here to briefly illustrate its history, structure and aim. The English College in Douai was founded in 1568 by William Allen, a Catholic priest, theologian and, from 1587, cardinal, who was forced to leave England after the accession of Elizabeth I. The main aim of Allen's institution was to provide a Catholic education to the young Englishmen who, like its founder, had to move to the Continent for their religion.[13] In 1579 the administration of the Douai College was transferred to the Society of Jesus: the following year, the first Jesuit mission to England was launched, and the leadership of the Jesuit Robert Persons began. In this scenario, Persons and his allies successfully transformed the College from an educational institution into a 'training camp' for English priests ready to go back to England as missionaries. The College, then, became an integral part of the Jesuit program to restore Catholicism in England by force.

---

[10] The most recent biography of Thomas White is B.C. Southgate's work, *'Covetous of Truth'*. On White's life see also *DNB sub voce White, Thomas*.

[11] See B.C. Southgate, *'Covetous of truth'*, pp. 3–4. Among his family members, it is here worth remembering that another of his brothers, Richard, was a rather well-known natural philosopher as well. In particular, Richard was a student of Benedetto Castelli's in Pisa, where Castelli was appointed professor of mathematics in 1613 upon recommendation of Galileo Galilei, with whom Castelli had closely worked. On Richard White see *DNB sub voce White, Thomas*. On Benedetto Castelli and his school see G.L. Masetti-Zannini, *La vita di Benedetto Castelli*, Brescia 1961 and M.L. Altieri Biagi-B. Basile (eds.), *Scienziati del Seicento*, Milano 1980, pp. 140–219.

[12] White's academic career can be followed in *The Douay College Diaries, Third, Fourth and Fifth, 1598–1654*, 2 vols., Publication of the Catholic Record Society nn. 10–11, London 1911.

[13] On William Allen see E. Duffy, 'William Cardinal Allen, 1532–1594', *Recusant History*, vol. 22, n. 3 (1995), pp. 265–305. On the origin and first years of the English College in Douai see T.F. Knox (ed.), *The first and second Diaries of the English College, Douay*, London 1878, and Id. (ed.), *The letters and memorials of Cardinal Allen (1532–1594)* London 1932.

At the beginning of the seventeenth century, with the death of Persons and with the accession to the throne of England of James VI of Scotland, the project of re-Catholicizing England by means of a military invasion progressively faded, and with that the Douai College considerably lost its 'Jesuitical' influence, while remaining a fundamental reference point for the education and formation of the English Catholic clergy.[14] As such, the curriculum studiorum remained founded upon traditional Scholasticism, with Aristotle and St. Thomas as the main authors and sources for students' training.[15] For instance, we know that Aquinas's *Summa* was used as a textbook, and we also know that when in 1633 the Inquisition was gathering information against Copernicanism, the leaders of Douai were able to deny that any such doctrine was circulating in the college, which remained a bastion of Scholasticism.[16] White himself, while in Douai, 'profest only rigid Thomistry', as one of his enemies had reported.[17]

In 1624 Thomas White left Douai for Paris to study canon law, but the following year he was sent to Rome by the newly appointed Bishop Richard Smith as an Agent for the English Catholics. We do not have detailed information on White's sojourn in Rome, but we do know that he resigned in 1630, just in time to avoid taking a definite position pro or contra Smith, who would soon be obliged to leave England and move to France.[18] Perhaps more interesting is to consider White's appointment as a sign of his increasing authority within the English Catholic community, given the strategic importance of the Roman position immediately after Charles's ascent to the throne and his marriage with the Catholic Henrietta Maria.

From 1630 and 1633 White moved to Portugal, where he was appointed President of the College in Lisbon. Then he returned to England, where in 1638 he was admitted among the members of the Chapter. In 1643 went back to Paris, and became part of the so-called 'Mersenne circle', which included, among others, Gassendi and Thomas Hobbes.[19] In Paris White, who by this time was a professor of theology and philosophy of a quite traditional Scholastic background and a man with some limited diplomatic and political experience, also renewed his acquaintance with a fellow Catholic of an entirely different background, whom he had met sometime during the late 1630s[20] and who would become a central figure in the Blackloist group: Sir Kenelm Digby.

---

[14] In 1613, three years after Persons' death, the College at Douai was put in the hand of Matthew Kellison, an opponent to the Jesuitical faction: see J. Bossy, *The English Catholic Community*, p. 48.

[15] See B.C. Southgate, *'Covetous of Truth'*, pp. 25 and ff.

[16] See Ibid., pp. 26–27, and D.Berti, *Il processo originale di Galileo Galilei*, Rome 1876, pp. 130–1.

[17] See R. Pugh, *Blacklo's Cabal*, s.l. 1680, 'The Epistle to the Catholick Reader', unfoliated.

[18] R.I. Bradley, 'Blacklo and the Counter-Reformation', pp. 357–8.

[19] On Mersenne and his collaborators see P. Dear, *Mersenne and the Learning of the Schools*, Ithaca 1988.

[20] On the circumstances that brought Digby and White together see J. Henry, 'Atomism and Eschatology: Catholicism and natural philosophy in the Interregnum', *The British Journal for the*

1.3 Kenelm Digby

Kenelm Digby was born in 1603 to a Catholic family: his father, Sir Everard, was executed in 1606 among the participants to the Gunpowder Plot.[21] After the death of Digby's father, the family remained committed to the Roman faith while vocally and ardently supporting the King: during the Civil War, John Digby, Kenelm's brother, would die fighting on the Royalist side.[22]

After a brief sojourn in Spain as a member of a diplomatic mission sent by James I, in 1618 Digby went to Oxford, where he studied natural science and alchemy with the rather well-known mathematician and natural philosopher Thomas Allen. Digby left Oxford in 1620 without a degree, and from there went to France and to Italy, where he remained for two years, studying natural philosophy with Italian Catholic scholars.[23] In 1620 he was in Siena, where he was invited to give some lectures to the Accademia dei Filomati. We know the text of three of them: the first one was on the superiority of writing over speaking, the second was on the virtue of parsimony, and the last one was a panegyric of Plato as the founder of the Academy, to which Digby connected the Accademia in Siena.[24] It is worth paying some attention to the first lecture, centered on the argument that the written language was of a superior quality than the spoken one. The reason for this superiority, Digby argued, was that through words one could express not only visible things, but also 'sublime mysteries' and God himself. A long section of the text, in fact, is devoted to explain the different forms of 'scrittura occultissima', in particular what Digby calls 'Ghemantria', a form of geometry-based occult scripture that is:

> the most spiritual and inventive, and used in the profound meditations of the Kabbalah, of Magic and of Alchemy; that is, of the elementary science, of the heavenly science and of the super-worldly and intelligible science, so called because it deals with intelligences and separate substances, and thus it is above the others the most worthy of being considered to be the one that concerns the knowledge of the Creator, which is the greatest perfection that men can boast.[25]

History of Science, XV (1982), 211–239, at pp. 216–217.

[21] Kenelm Digby wrote an autobiography, rather romanticized, published in London in 1827 with the title of *Private Memoirs of Sir Kenelm Digby written by himself*, and more recently edited by V. Gabrieli as *Loose fantasies*, Florence 1968. For more details on Digby's biography see R.T. Petersson, *Sir Kenelm Digby*, and V. Gabrieli, *Sir Kenelm Digby*.

[22] Information on John Digby's life can be found in *Life of John Digby*, Camden Miscellany, vol. XII, London 1610, and in *Private Memoirs*, p. 60.

[23] On Digby's Italian years see V. Gabrieli, *Sir Kenelm Digby*, pp. 20–36.

[24] The texts of the orations can be found in BL, Add. Mss.41846, ff.118r–141v. On the Italian part of Digby's journey see R.T. Petersson, *Sir Kenelm Digby*, pp. 53 and ff.

[25] [...e' la piu' spirituale e la piu' ingegnosa, ed impiegata nelle profonde meditationi della Cabala, della Magia, e dell'Alchimia; cio e', della scienza elementare, della celeste, e della sopramondana o intelligibile, cosi' chiamata percioche tratta delle intelligentie e delle substanze separate, e percioche e' piu' degna sopra tutte le altre d'esser intesa come quella che si raggira intorno alla notitia del creatore, che e' la maggior perfettione della quale l'huomo gloriarsi possi], BL, Add.Mss. 41846, f.119v.

This passage, aside from the verbose and slightly irritating style that was typical of Digby's early writings, is interesting because of the connections that the Catholic made between alchemy and religion. Indeed, for Digby alchemy, the 'super-worldly' science, was the only one that could allow men to explore the knowledge of the divine. This link between alchemy and religion, not uncontroversial in early modern science, will be developed by Digby more systematically after 1660, as we will see.

In addition to traveling through Europe, in the 1630s Digby began corresponding with Venetia Stanley, the granddaughter of Thomas Percy, seventh Earl of Northumberland, whom he married in 1625 – Digby's love for Venetia is at the core of the his autobiography.[26] In 1623 Digby was in Spain again, where he participated in the negotiations for the Spanish match: at his return to England James knighted him. Under Charles I Digby was appointed as a Gentleman to the Privy Council, and soon after the King gave him permission 'to take in hand a voyage by Sea'[27]: Digby's privateering expedition in the Mediterranean ended rather successfully in 1629.[28] In 1630 he completed his *cursus honorum* in the Stuart diplomatic corps by converting to the Protestant religion.[29]

The 1630s were a turning point in Digby's life: in 1633 his wife died; in 1635 he decided to reconvert to Catholicism[30] and moved to Paris, where he would remain for the greater part of his life, while alternating long trips back to England and to Italy.[31] After a brief period of moral asceticism, Digby returned to two of the main interests of his previous life: diplomacy and natural philosophy.

As for the first, in the 1630s and early 1640s Digby tried to combine his newly re-embraced Catholic faith with his loyal service to the King and Queen: in 1635 in fact he became Henrietta Maria's Agent in Rome. Even if the most important events involving Digby's activities in Rome will not take place until 1645 (a point we will return to), the 1635 appointment deserves attention. More specifically, it is worth noticing that Digby's role as Agent of the Queen in Rome, together with his conversion to Catholicism, did not seem to cause a breach in the relationship between the Catholic and the English Protestant establishment. In particular, in the 1630s Digby cultivated scholarly relations with prominent members of the English Protestant Church. Among those, Digby seemed to have a particularly close relationship with George Hakewill. Hakewill is an interesting figure in this context: a committed Calvinist, he

---

[26] On the literary aspects of Digby's romance as he narrated it in the *Memoirs* see Gabrieli's Introduction to *Loose fantasies*.

[27] The text of the Royal Commission granted to Digby in 1627 for his expedition can be found in BL, Egerton Mss. 2541, ff.86–95 (quotation at ff. 86–7).

[28] See R.T. Petersson, *Sir Kenelm Digby*, pp. 74–82, and V. Gabrieli, *Kenelm Digby*, pp. 37–62.

[29] See R.T. Petersson, *Sir Kenelm Digby*, pp. 93–5.

[30] R.T. Petersson highlights the importance of the religious experience in Digby's life (pp. 109–112), while Gabrieli considers Digby's conversion as a result of his intellectual reflections (pp. 143–4).

[31] See V. Gabrieli, *Kenelm Digby*, pp. 144–173.

was appointed in 1616 by James I to refute the work written by Benjamin Carrier, James's former chaplain, in which Carrier defended his own recent conversion to Catholicism. Impressed by Hakewill's work, James granted him the archdeaconry of Surrey in 1617, but the Protestant's promising career was fatally wounded by his Calvinist positions, which put him at odds with the Arminian establishment. In 1622 Hakewill wrote a treatise against the Spanish match, and presented it to Charles without James's knowledge. The king, infuriated, put Hakewill briefly in prison, and the Protestant clergyman, who died 1649, would never regain presence at court.[32]

Hakewill and Digby seem to have been frequent and cordial correspondents. In 1635 Hakewill sent to Digby a copy of the new edition of his major work, *An Apologie...of the Power and Providence of God*, published for the first time in 1627. Digby replied immediately, thanking Hakewill for sending 'your learned book and your excellent additions in the last impression'.[33] Digby's judgment of Hakewill's work was utterly positive:

> I must as a well wisher to the Republike of letters contribute unto you my ...thankes, acknowledging ingenuously that I have not in any language upon any particular subiect mett with so large a body (and so well featured and composed a one) of naturall Philosophy, History, various erudition, with Metaphysicall and Theologicall reflections, as in this piece of yours, wherein with pregnant reasons drawne out of all these stores you vindicate the worlde from the vulgarly received opinion of decay or deterioration.[34]

Even in the year of his formal conversion, then, Digby did not think that his religious confession should get in the way of his interests in philosophy and theology. Or, to put it differently, confessional allegiance, for Digby, should not prevent anybody from being a 'well wisher to the Republike of letters'. In addition to this, Digby's letter to Hakewill contains also the embryonic form of a theme that is to be central in Digby's own natural philosophy and theology, namely the relationship between faith and 'pregnant reasons'. In another passage of his letter Digby praised Hakewill's treatment of the immortality of the soul, and added that together with the Calvinist's 'Metaphisicall and Theologicall reflections' one could also seek to deal with the topic in a different way:

> out of a Philosophicall consideration of the naturall operations of a humane soule, one may peradventure by undeniable reason conclude the immortality of it; for they will prove that although the principle of perfect cognition be in matter, yet it selfe is immateriall; and being so it, must be incorruptible.[35]

The immortality of the soul, then, could 'peradventure' be demonstrated by 'undeniable reason' stemming from an analysis of 'naturall operations'.

---
[32] On Hakewill see *DNB*, *sub voce Hakewill, George*.
[33] Digby to Hakewill, London 13 May 1635, BL, Harleian Mss. 4153, ff. 6r–13v, at f.6r.
[34] Ibid., ff. 7r–v.
[35] Ibid., f. 7v.

And it is to this 'reasonable' demonstration that Digby will dedicate his most ambitious work later on.

Another key figure of the Caroline Church with whom Digby corresponded was none less than William Laud, with whom the Catholic courtier seems to have had, once again, a close scholarly collaboration. In 1634 Laud sent to the University of Oxford a series of books and manuscripts given to him by Digby to donate to the Bodleian Library,[36] and in the accompanying letter he reminded the governing body of the University to write 'a letter of thanks to Sir Kenelm Digby, whose love thus and divers other ways expressed deserves it abundantly'.[37]

Digby's conversion to Catholicism did not compromise Laud's esteem and favor. When Digby decided to convert, he wrote personally to Laud to inform him of his decision. Laud replied to the 'open and clear account' of Digby's religious considerations by discussing some of the theological points raised by the Catholic in his explanations, in particular the mark of antiquity which for Digby gave certainty to the Catholic faith in the midst of many disputations and 'mistaking of both sides'. Apart from the frank theological discussion, however, Laud praised Digby's way of handling his conversion, 'full of discretion and temper, and so like yourself, that I cannot but love even that which I dislike in it'.[38] The Archbishop ended his letter worrying about the consequences that Digby's conversion might have had for his relation with the King – a concern that was to be proved, to a certain extent, wrong.

Digby, in fact, remained loyal to the sovereigns, at least for the next decade. In 1639 Digby and Walter Montague were actively involved in the fundraising to organize an army in Scotland to support the King. In particular, Digby and Montagu were in charge of securing the donations: they wrote a letter to the English Catholics in which they asked them to nominate 'such persons as shall in your opinions be agreed of for the ablest and best disposed in every severall County, not onely to solicite, but to collect such voluntarily contributions, as every bodies conscience and duty shall proffer'.[39] It should be noted that at this time not only did Digby not find any source of conflict between his political

---

[36] In 1634 Digby donated all of his manuscripts to the Bodleian Library: the collection was mainly composed of medieval religious tracts, works of the Latin and Greek Fathers, and treatises on astrology and natural philosophy, part of which belonged to Allen, Digby's mentor at Oxford. For a complete catalogue of Digby's manuscripts see R.W. Hunt-A.G. Watson, *Digby Manuscripts*, Oxford 1999.

[37] Laud to 'my very loving friends, the vice-chancellor, the doctors, the proctors, and the rest of the convocation of the university of Oxford', 19 December 1634, in *The Works of the Most Reverend Father in God, William Laud, D.D. sometime Lord Archbishop of Canterbury*, 7 vols, New York 1975 (reprint of the Oxford 1847–1860 ed.), vol. V, pp. 104–106.

[38] Laud to Digby, 27 March 1636, in Ibid., vol. VI pp. 447–455. Digby's letter, to which Laud replied, appears to be lost.

[39] The letter, together with other documents related to the 1639 fundraising – including a list of the Catholic nominees in charge of the collection of the money – is printed in *A copy of I The letter sent by the Queenes Majestie concerning the collection of the Recusants Mony for the Scottish Warre…5.The Message sent from the Queenes Majestie to the house of Commons by Master Controller the 5 of Febr. 1639*, printed anonymously in London in 1641, at pp. 3–5.

and religious allegiance, but he firmly believed that the Catholic cause was inextricably linked with the King's. In the aforementioned letter he insisted that:

> It will easily appear to every body how much it imports us, in our sence of her Majesties desires to presse every body to straine himselfe even to his best abilities in this proposition, since by it wee shall certainly preserve her graciousnesse to us, and give good Character of our devotion to the King and State; of whose benignitie wee have all reason to give testimonies, and to indeavour to produce arguments for the prosecution and increase of it.[40]

The Parliament discovered the Queen's maneuvers to collect money, and the Queen apologized for Digby and Montagu's actions, which she defined as 'mistakes and errors of her servants', and promised 'not to exceed that which is convenient and necessary for the exercise of her Religion', avoiding any form of proselytizing.[41]

Digby did not escape easily the resentment of Parliament: in 1641 he was summoned under a charge that he had tried to convert to Catholicism the young Thomas Pope, second Earl of Downe. Digby's accuser was John Dutton, Pope's guardian and later elected to represent Gloucestershire in the Long Parliament.[42] In the draft of the speech Digby wrote in preparation to defend himself before Parliament, he started by not denying his Catholic faith, but added that he had always professed his religion with 'moderation', so 'that I was never offensive to the lawes of the kingdome, nor troublesome to any private person'.[43] By contrast:

> for matter of practise in morall and civill regards…under that consideration are comprised two severall duties which concerne every man: The one a publike, the other a private one. This latter I conceive to be alike in all men of what persuasion soever they be in matter of religion; and is summed up in being an honest man. The other importeth their duty and obedience to the Prince and lawes where they live. Now in this particular, I conceive my bond of allegiance to the King my Master and my duty of obedience to the lawe of this kingdome, to be so firme and strong as no power on earth can absolve me from it. But whenever any attempt should be made against it upon pretence of any authority whatsoever I would readily draw my sword, and expose my life, and spend my fortunes in opposition of it.[44]

This passage is interesting for a number of reasons. First and foremost, it is noteworthy how carefully Digby excluded the topic of confessional allegiance when addressing questions of 'morall and civill regards'. The private sphere of those regards is limited to the moral category of 'honesty', which Digby

---

[40] Ibid., pp. 3–4.
[41] Ibid., pp. 11–12.
[42] On Pope and Dutton see *DNB*, *sub voce*, respectively, *Pope, Thomas, second early of Downe* and *Dutton family*.
[43] Digby's draft can be found in BL, Additional Mss. 41846, ff. 113r–117v, at f.114r.
[44] Ibid., f. 115v.

insisted had nothing to do with one's religious profession. As for the public sphere, Digby reiterated his uncompromising loyalty to his King, and denied to 'any power on earth', included the Pope as a political, rather than spiritual, leader, the authority of absolving him from such loyalty. That meant that Digby's profession of the Catholic religion was neither a 'morall' nor a 'civill' issue, but a purely religious and spiritual matter. Indeed, Digby affirmed that he had professed and was going to profess Catholicism only insofar as this did not break any law: since there was no law that 'commanded absolutely' to attend Protestant services, it was allowed for him not to do so. But since 'the law doth absolutely and peremptorily command me that I shall not goe about to persuade any Protestant from their religion', he declared to have always refrained from doing so, and therefore he proclaimed himself innocent of the accusation that Dutton had made against him. The real cause of Dutton's calumnies, Digby remarked, was that he had tried to protect the earl from his guardian's attempt to rob him from his estate.[45]

Digby's explanation must have been satisfactory, for the case against him was dropped. A year later, however, after the outbreak of the Civil War, Digby was arrested and kept in a rather comfortable detention for almost a year. In 1643 he was released and went to France, where Queen Henrietta Maria had set up her household and where in 1644 Digby was appointed her Chancellor.[46]

Before momentarily leaving Digby's political career to concentrate on his natural philosophy, I would like to offer some considerations. The correspondence between Digby and various prominent Protestant divines, as well as Digby's relation to the King and Queen at this date, is important, in my view, for a number of reasons. First, understanding Digby's relation with the Protestant establishment between 1630s and 1640s can shed some light on the theological debate within the Church of England on the nature of the Church of Rome and on its relationship with English Protestantism. From this perspective, while Digby's relation with Laud does not pose particular problems, his correspondence with George Hakewill, who in 1616 had powerfully argued that Catholicism was to be considered akin to heathenism, is perhaps more interesting. The intellectual debate between a conformist Calvinist and the Catholic Digby – of whose conversion to Catholicism Hakewill might have not been aware yet, but who nevertheless had never expressed any interest in defending or even discussing Calvinist theology – over 'super-confessional' questions such as the immortality of the soul represents a good example of the complexity of the theological and polemical issues that the relation between the Church of England and the Church of Rome originated.[47]

---

[45] Ibid., ff.115v–117v

[46] See R.T. Petersson, *Sir Kenelm Digby*, pp. 212 and ff., and V. Gabrieli, *Sir Kenelm Digby*, pp. 181 and ff.

[47] On the theological debates concerning the nature of the Church of Rome and its relation with the Church of England see the seminal work by A.Milton, *Catholic and Reformed. The Roman and Protestant Churches in English Protestant Thought, 1600–1640*, Cambridge 1995. On Hakewill's role in this debate see in part. pp. 173 and ff.

Secondly, and more importantly from the standpoint of the questions that concern me here, the way in which Digby managed – at least until the mid-1640s – to combine the profession of Catholicism with his loyalty towards the King, as well as to maintain the favor of the Roman hierarchy in the process, demonstrates first how complex the intersection between theology and politics was, and then how much room there existed for compromise. At the same time, however, the religio-political equilibrium was extremely fragile. The interests of the English Catholics, those of the Roman Curia and finally those of the King were not coincident, as Digby still thought at this date. Nor was it possible to link rigidly theology and politics, and, as Digby came to understand later, the King's cause and the Catholic religion were not linked by an intrinsic affinity, but only by a temporary convergence of interests, which would soon shift dramatically. The evolution of Digby's own political positions is a perfect illustration of this.

On a different level, we need to remember that the other Blackloists did not by any means share Digby's attitude either towards his faith or his political allegiance. Thomas White and Henry Holden, who together with Digby were the most prominent members of the Blackloist faction, had different ways of interpreting their religious and political allegiance, different opinions on the possibility of combining the two, and, finally, an utterly different set of priorities.

CHAPTER 2

The Blackloists' Natural Philosophy and Theology

2.1 Mixing the Old and the New: between Aristotelianism and Atomism

In Paris in the late 1630s Digby entered the circle of Marin Mersenne, in which he met Pierre Gassendi and other leading Catholic natural philosophers of the period; it was to prove the ideal setting for him to elaborate his own scientific theories. Among the English émigrés in Paris Digby found also Thomas White as well as an old friend, Thomas Hobbes, with whom he had been corresponding in the 1630s, and who was then gravitating around the circle of William Cavendish, future Duke of Newcastle.[1] Indeed, from Paris in 1637 Digby had written to Hobbes informing him of the political situation in France and the country's relationship with England:

> For news lett me tell you; this state is now upon new uncertainties & dependeth more of the future than when you were here and that the Spanish army was at their gates. They are oppressed with poverty & want at home, threatned by the Enemy abroad, & in distresse of whom to trust within; so that all is destruction. It is surmised Monsieurs party is stronger & his designes more stedely than at the first was conceived. It is whispered the King will go towards him.[2]

After returning to England, Digby wrote to the English philosopher again, excusing himself for his long silence: 'This is the first time I have bin able to govern a penne these 6 weekes: And very badly now, as you will perceive by my scribbling: for it is so long since a fall from my horse rendered my arme uselesse'.[3] In the same letter Digby asked Hobbes to send him 'any piece of your Logicke', since 'I exceedingly value all that cometh from you; for you ioyne nature and solide reason together; whereas others that are accounted learned, beget Chymeras & build castles in the aire'.[4] From here

---

[1] On the Newcastle circle and the importance of Thomas Hobbes's French sojourn see Q. Skinner, 'Thomas Hobbes and His Disciples in France and England', *Comparative Studies in Society and History*, vol. 8 (1965–6), pp. 153–165; L.T. Sarasohn, 'Motion and Morality: Pierre Gassendi, Thomas Hobbes and the Mechanical World-View', *Journal of the History of Ideas*, vol.46 (1985), pp. 363–380; Id, 'Thomas Hobbes and the Duke of Newcastle. A Study in the Mutuality of Patronage before the Establishment of the Royal Society', *Isis*, vol.90 (1999), pp. 715–737.
[2] Digby to Hobbes, Paris 17 January 1637, in BodL, Rawlinson Mss. D1104, ff,12v–13v, at ff.13r–v.
[3] Digby to Hobbes, London 11 September 1637, in BodL, Rawlinson Mss. D1104, f. 11v–12v, at f.11v.
[4] Ibid., ff. 12r–v.

a very important feature of Digby's natural philosophy emerges, namely, his insistence on unifying 'nature and solide reason together', a concern that will inform his future works.

Less than a month after, Digby wrote to Hobbes again, this time sending him a copy of Descartes' *Discourse on Method,* which Digby judged 'a production of a most vigorous and strong braine', although he complained of a lack of 'accuracy' in the 'metaphysicall part', compared to the experimental passages, which he found more convincing.[5]

In the 1640s then Digby, Hobbes and White were together in Paris. Even though there is no evidence of a direct correspondence between Hobbes, White and Digby, they were engaged in a close scientific debate: Hobbes read and replied to White's treatise entitled *De Mundo,* his first attempt to combine Galilean physics with Aristotelian philosophy, and a work that aroused vivid enthusiasm in the circle of Mersenne.[6] Many more cross-references among White, Digby and the rest of Mersenne's circle, Hobbes included, could certainly be adduced here. My point, however, is not to prove and explain the 'influences' of one theorist on the others, a task whose perils have been already extensively illustrated by Quentin Skinner.[7] I would like simply to emphasize that the role of Digby and White in the Parisian circle of which Thomas Hobbes was part needs to be taken into a greater account, for it can give us a more historically accurate picture of the theories and career of many better-known theorists, as Jeffrey Collins has recently demonstrated in his work on the importance of Thomas Hobbes's Erastianism and its link with the Blackloist ecclesiology to explain Hobbes's political allegiance.[8]

To return to the scientific theories of the Blackloists, both White and Digby were immensely interested in the new Galilean scientific method, as well as in atomism, the object of great revival in early seventeenth-century Europe. The reasons why so many natural philosophers between the end of the sixteenth and the start of the seventeenth century turned to atomism are rather complex. Among the many issues that need to be addressed to explain the interest in atomism on the part of early modern European natural philosophers, it will suffice here to mention the Humanistic interest in classical texts and theories, which prompted a revival of ancient atomists as Democritus and Lucretius, the manuscript of whose *De Rerum Natura* was discovered by the Italian Humanist

---

[5] Digby to Hobbes, London 4 October 1637, in Ibid., f. 12v.

[6] See T. White, *De Mundo, Dialogi Tres,* Paris 1642, and B.C. Southgate, '*Covetous of truth*', pp. 7–9 and pp. 104 and ff. Hobbes's treatise written in reply to White's remained unpublished until 1973: see J. Jacquot-H.W. Jones (eds.), *Thomas Hobbes: Critique du 'De Mundo' de Thomas White,* Paris 1973; and the English translation by H.W. Jones, *Thomas Hobbes: Thomas White's 'De Mundo Examined'*, London 1976. On the implications of the debate over White's *De Mundo* on Hobbes's theory of desire and on his explication of the reasons why men decide to move from a state of war to a state of peace see N. Malcolm, 'Hobbes and Spinoza', in N.Malcolm, *Aspects of Hobbes,* Oxford 2002, pp. 27–52, at p. 30.

[7] Q. Skinner, 'Meaning and Understanding in the History of Ideas', *History and Theory,* vol. 8 n. 1 (1969), pp. 3–53, in part. pp. 25–27.

[8] J.R. Collins, *The Allegiance of Thomas Hobbes,* Oxford 2005. See especially pp. 115–206 on the relation between the Blackloists, Thomas Hobbes and Oliver Cromwell.

Poggio Bracciolini in 1417.[9] Another significant factor for the development of early modern atomism was the need to find a theory compatible with the mechanical experiments then being carried on, especially on motions of gross bodies and on the vacuum.[10]

To give some background on atomism in seventeenth-century Europe, traditional scholarship has mainly distinguished between two camps of theorists interested in re-discovering and developing the theories of Lucretius and Democritus: the first in England, the other in France. The first venue in England in which atomism was discussed was the circle formed around Henry Percy, third earl of Northumberland. A great patron of the arts and sciences in Elizabethan England, and kinsman of Thomas, one of the participants in the Gunpowder Plot, Henry Percy was himself suspected of having participated in the Plot. For this reason Percy was imprisoned in 1606, and he remained in jail until 1622. During his long confinement in the Tower of London, he had his books and instruments sent to him, and from there he continued his scientific inquiries, together with a group of disciples. Among them there was Thomas Allen, Digby's old mentor from Oxford, Francis Bacon, John Dee and Thomas Digges. The group's interest in atomism was to a certain extent secondary to other currents in the circle, namely, Copernicanism, Platonism, alchemy, and a new emphasis on experiment. Bacon, for instance, in his *Novum Organum* rejected atomism, whose validity he had previously upheld, because it did not stand the test of the 'laboratory', according to which motion was to be explained not with atoms, but with the interaction between visible parts of matters and invisible spirits.[11]

Among the members of the Northumberland circle there was also Walter Warner: aside from his contribution to the development of atomism in England, a topic which has been treated extensively by Richard Kargon,[12] Warner is here important as a link between the first and the second generation of English atomists. Among Warner's closest scientific associates, in fact, were Thomas Hobbes and Sir Charles Cavendish, brother of William and member of the Newcastle group, which inherited, so to say, the interests and findings of the Nurthumberland circle.

In France, at the same time, another group of atomist philosophers was taking shape: probably its most prominent member was the Catholic priest and natural philosopher Pierre Gassendi. The historiographical debate on the reasons for Gassendi's interest in Epicurus and his atomism continues to this day,

---

[9] See M. Boas, 'The establishment of the mechanical philosophy, *Osiris* vol.10 (1952), pp. 412–541, at p. 423.

[10] On the development of atomism in early modern Europe see M. Boas, 'The establishment of the mechanical philosophy'; on the history of English atomism see F.R. Johnson, *Astronomical thought in Renaissance England*, Baltimore 1937, and, more recently, R.H. Kargon, *Atomism in England from Hariot to Newton*, Oxford 1966.

[11] On the complex attitude of Bacon towards atomism see M. Boas, 'The establishment', pp. 439–441 and R.H. Kargon, *Atomism in England*, pp. 43–53.

[12] Ibid., pp. 31–42

and no convincing explanation has yet been provided.[13] Historians of science agree, however, that among the many factors that must be taken into account in explaining Gassendi's relationship with Epicurean atomism there are his Humanistic background, his religious beliefs and his complex relationship with Aristotle. During the early stages of his career, when Gassendi was a professor of philosophy (his first appointment was at the University of Aix en Provence in 1616), his teaching was limited almost exclusively to Aristotle's works and Scholasticism. In the 1620s Gassendi became more and more interested in the humanistic tradition of criticism of Aristotle, which made him question the validity of his philosophy tout court. A passage in his 1624 *Exercitationes Paradoxicae adversus Aristoteleos* clearly shows the tension between Scholasticism and his Humanistic studies. While the latter, for Gassendi, could provide the tools for an ethical system of philosophy, Scholasticism seemed to be limited to a sort of 'dry' metaphysical elaboration:

> I had decided to apply myself to philosophy because I had saved in the back of my mind from my humanistic studies that praise by Cicero: 'it is impossible to praise enough that philosophy of which whoever is a follower could live for ever without suffering': It appeared sufficiently to me that I had to recognize that this was not to be expected in that Philosophy transmitted in the Schools.[14]

In addition to the dissatisfaction with the ethical component of Aristotelian and Scholastic philosophy, Gassendi also questioned its epistemological validity by following another of the traditional Humanistic arguments against Aristotle, that is to say, Phyrronian skepticism. After reading Pyrrho and his followers, he wrote:

> It was possible to see how much separation there is between Nature's Genius and men's: what else could I do but realize that the profound causes of the natural effects escape human understanding? So, I began to feel pity and shame for the superficialities and the arrogance of the dogmatic philosophers, who claim to have understood them, and who so rigidly assert that they know nature.[15]

---

[13] Cf. B. Rochot, *Les travaux de Gassendi sur Épicure et sur l'atomisme, 1619–1658*, Paris 1944, B. Brundell, *Pierre Gassendi: From Aristotelianism to a New Natural Philosophy*, Dordrecht 1987; L. Sumida Joy, *Gassendi the Atomist: advocate of history in an age of science*, Cambridge 1987; M.J. Osler, *Divine will and the mechanical philosophy. Gassendi and Descartes on contingency and necessity in the created world*, Cambridge 1994.

[14] [...me enim ad Philosophiam applicandum decreveram, quod alta mente reposuissem, ex studio usque humaniore, illud Ciceronis elogium, "Numquam satis laudari digne poterit Philosophia: cui qui pareat, omne tempus aetatis sine molestia possit degere": videbar satis agnoscere non esse id expectandum ex tradita illa in Scholis Philosophia] P.Gassendi, *Exercitationes Paradoxicae adversus Aristoteleos*, in *Opera Omnia*, Lyon 1658, 6 vols, vol. IV, p. 99.

[15] [...pervidere licuit quantis Naturae Genius ab humano ingenio diffideret intervallis: quid aliud potui, quam existimare effectorum naturalium intimas causas prorsus fugere humanam perspicaciam? Miserere proinde, ac pudere coepit me levitates, & arrogantiae Dogmaticorum Philosophorum, qui & glorientur se arripuisse, & tam severe profiteantur naturalim rerum scientiam] Ibid., pp. 99–100.

While the use of skepticism against Aristotle proved rather effective, it was dearly bought: to what extent could Gassendi, as a Catholic priest, fully endorse skepticism, since its questioning of the certainty of any form of human knowledge necessarily included the knowledge of God? In 1625 Gassendi met the Minim Marin Mersenne, who in those years had actively written against skepticism and in defense of Aristotle. The meeting greatly influenced Gassendi, who decided to interrupt his anti-Aristotelian works and to devote himself instead to writing on the history of philosophy.[16]

In the course of his studies Gassendi stumbled across Epicurus's writing, and, intrigued by his life and theories, he decided to write a historically accurate biography of him, and to translate into Latin the Greek text of Epicurus's life written by Diogenes Laertius. In this same period Gassendi also became interested in the new experiments of, among others, Galileo, whose new science of motion he defended in a text entitled *De motu impresso a motore translato,* published in 1642. In this context, it is not surprising that Gassendi found Aristotelianism, which already in the 1620s had seemed heavily flawed, utterly unable to explain the new mechanic: Epicurus's doctrine of the atoms, by contrast, was the perfect solution, and so Gassendi dedicated the remaining part of his career to explicating and interpreting it. Epicurean philosophy was far from perfect, however, with two particularly troubling consequences for Gassendi, namely, the notion that the soul, also composed by atoms, was mortal, and the denial of the existence of God. Unlike in his early career, when Gassendi tried to substitute Aristotelianism en bloc with Phyrronism, he now decided to 'correct' Epicurus, or, to borrow Margaret Osler's apt term, to 'baptize' his philosophy,[17] maintaining that Epicurus was wrong in denying God's existence, which could, by contrast, perfectly fit with an atomistic explanation of physical phenomena: even if there is no reason why the atoms must have been necessarily created by God, the product of those atoms, that is to say, the world, is nevertheless too complex and perfect for having been created merely by chance.[18] If men do not understand why God wanted the world to be constituted by atoms, Gassendi wrote, it is no wonder: 'What kind of Creator would God be, if this work, in which all of the works of God and of everything is comprehended, could be measured by the little man, and be comprehended by his little mind?'[19]

As for the immortality of the soul, Gassendi argued that it could be deduced from many factors observable 'by experience' – for instance, the human capacity for self-reflection as a sign of immateriality, or the ability to form

---

[16] For the influence of Mersenne's anti-skepticism on Gassendi in the 1620s see L. Sumida Joy, *Gassendi the atomist*, pp. 30 and ff.
[17] M.J. Osler, *Divine Will*, pp. 36 and ff.
[18] P. Gassendi, *Animadversiones in Decimum Librum Diogenis Laeartii*, Lyon 1649 pp. 706 and ff.
[19] [et qualis Artifex esset Deus, si posset homuncio metiri, comprehendereque ingeniolo suo id opus, quo opera omnia & dei, & rerum omnium comprehenduntur?] Ibid, p. 647.

and understand universals[20] – and he demonstrated that it was compatible with Epicurean atomism on the basis of a voluntarist understanding of theology. In other words, since God had no necessity to create the world, and to create it as it is, i.e. composed of atoms, even if in the material world there is nothing that proves incontrovertibly the existence of an incorporeal soul, it does not mean that God could not create it anyway, since God is an 'agens sapientissimus, potentissimus ac liberrimus'.[21] In this way, Gassendi was able to modify Epicurus's atomism to make it compatible with Christian religion, and to avoid any materialistic and skeptical consequences.

The same need to build a mechanical system that could explain natural phenomena while also accounting for the existence of God and of an incorporeal soul without giving way to any form of epistemological and theological skepticism, was the starting point of Descartes, who had, as is abundantly known, a central role in the philosophic debate in France in mid-seventeenth century. I do not wish to explain in detail Descartes' mechanical theory of matter, which differed from Gassendi's in many important points.[22] I am interested, rather, in pointing out the similarities between the two, for these can well exemplify the main elements present in what for the sake of simplicity I would define as the 'French current' of seventeenth-century atomism. On the one hand, then, the elaboration in France is centered on how to separate atomism from mechanical philosophy *stricto sensu*, in order to be able to combine atomism with Christianity, and to purge it of any skeptical outcomes. At the same time, and closely linked, there was a lively debate on Aristotelianism, which to some – like Mersenne – had seemed the most efficacious barrier against skepticism, and as such a still necessary complement of the 'new' science.[23]

At the same time, the English atomism presented somewhat different characteristics. Again, to put it roughly, in England there was less concern with anti-skepticism and with combining mechanism and theology, so that in the Newcastle circle the question of Aristotelianism was, in a sense, less central. This is not to say that English atomists rejected Aristotle speedily and easily, and as speedily and easily embraced a fully mechanical and atheist view of philosophy – in this respect Hobbes's materialism represents an exception

---

[20] Ibid., pp. 549 and ff., and Id., *Syntagma Philosophicum*, in *Opera Omnia*, vol. II, pp. 237 and ff. *passim*. For a discussion of Gassendi's proofs for the incorporeity of the soul see M.J. Osler, *Divine Will*, pp. 59 and ff.

[21] P. Gassendi, *Animadversiones*, p. 721.

[22] On Cartesianism and the debate between Descartes and Gassendi see, among the others, B. Rochot, 'Les véritées éternelles dans la querelle entre Descartes et Gassendi', *Revue philosophique de la France et de l'ètranger*, vol. 141 (1951), pp. 288–298; Id., 'Gassendi et la "Logique" de Descartes', *Revue philosophique de la France et de l'ètranger*, vol. 80 (1955), pp. 300–308; O.R. Bloch, 'Gassendi critique de Descartes', *Revue philosophique de la France et de l'ètranger*, vol. 91 (1966), pp. 217–236; L.T. Sarasohn, *Gassendi's Ethics. Freedom in a mechanist universe*, Cornell 1996, pp. 76 and ff.; M.J. Osler, *Divine Will*, pp. 153 and ff.

[23] On the relationship between Mersenne and Aristotelianism see R.H. Popkin, *The History of Scepticism from Erasmus to Spinoza*, Berkeley 1979 (1960), pp. 129 and ff.; P. Dear, *Mersenne and the Learning of the Schools*, pp. 48–79.

rather than the rule –, but it is true that the kind of scientific elaboration of the Newcastle circle focused more on the question of how to explain matter in motion, rather than on how to build a coherent and systematic philosophy that encompassed, without being limited to, a mechanical explanation of that motion.[24] Gassendi and his associates, by contrast, started out precisely with the problem of how to replace Aristotelianism with a comparably solid and systematic theory, in which atomism was but a part, however important.

According to this account, then, in Paris in the 1640s these two 'currents' of atomism met and merged, so to say, and English atomism was modified by incorporating many notions from the French group. Robert Boyle is considered as the best, if not necessarily the first, representative of the 'new' English corpuscularism, transformed after the encounter with the French; not much attention has been devoted to either White or Digby.[25]

More recent historiography has insisted on the important role of alchemy in this story. Since the pioneering studies by Paolo Rossi on Francis Bacon and Frances Yates on Giordano Bruno, historians of early modern science have fruitfully analyzed the alchemical practices of many of the canonical pillars of the 'new science', from Boyle to Newton, and have found that these scientists did not see their 'scientific' interests in mathematics, physics, astronomy, either contradictory to or separated from their alchemical activities. Regarding Boyle in particular, William Newman argued persuasively that his corpuscular philosophy owed a great deal to the theories of earlier Continental 'chymists', chiefly among them the German atomist Daniel Sennert.[26]

Among the French atomists, alchemy had been strongly condemned for its atheistic implications by Mersenne, in a heated controversy that opposed the Minim to Robert Fludd, expressed in a series of treatises written by Mersenne with the help of Gassendi during the 1620s.[27] This is not to say, however, that the French atomists had no interest whatsoever in alchemy and high magic:

---

[24] See R.H. Kargon, *Atomism in England*, pp. 18–42.

[25] See M. Boas, 'The Establishment', pp. 460 and ff., and R.H. Kargon, *Atomism in England*, pp. 93 and ff.

[26] For a survey of this body of scholarship see, among the others, P. Rossi, *Francis Bacon: from magic to science*, English trans. London 1968 (1957); F. Yates, *Giordano Bruno and the Hermetic Tradition*, Chicago 1964; A.G. Debus, *The Chemical Philosophy: Paracelsian Science and Medicine in the Sixteenth and Seventeenth Century*, 2 vols, New York 1977; C. Webster, *From Paracelsus to Newton: Magic and the Making of Modern Science*, Cambridge 1982; B.J.T. Dobbs, *The Janus Faces of Genius: The Role of Alchemy in Newton's Thought*, Cambridge 1991.

On the role of alchemy in the history of atomism its implications in the development of Boyle's corpuscularism see, among the others, A. Clericuzio, 'A redefinition of Boyle's chemistry and corpuscular philosophy', *Annals of Science*, vol. 47 (1990), pp. 561–589; W.R. Newman, 'Boyle's debt to corpuscular alchemy', in M. Hunter (ed.), *Robert Boyle Reconsidered*, Cambridge 1994, pp. 107–118; Id., 'The Alchemical sources of Robert Boyle's Corpuscular Philosophy', *Annals of Science* vo.53 (1996), pp. 567–585; L.M. Principe, *The Aspiring Adept: Robert Boyle's Alchemical Quest*, Princeton 1998; W.R.Newman-L.M.Principe, *Alchemy tried in the fire. Starkey, Boyle, and the fate of Helmontian chymistry*, Chicago and London 2002, pp. 6–34.

[27] On the controversy see P. Dear, *Mersenne and the Learning of the Schools*, pp. 109–116; A.G. Debus,'Chemists, Physicians, and Changing perspectives', in *Isis*, vol. 89 n. 1 (1998), pp. 66–81, at pp. 74 and ff.

a chapter of Gassendi's own *Syntagma Philosophiae*, for instance, is devoted to explaining the transmutation of metals, and current scholarship is more and more interested in the relationship between alchemy and Descartes, with interesting results.[28]

As historians of science are offering a more historically accurate account of the context in which 'modern' chemistry has to be put by drawing attention to the importance of its alchemical past, and are indeed vigorously reconsidering the boundaries between 'pre-modern' and 'modern' science, I think that a careful study of Digby's and White's contribution to atomism can add important elements to this story.

Kenelm Digby's atomism embodies a sort of synthesis between Aristotelianism, religion, mechanist philosophy and alchemy, to which Digby had devoted himself in the early 1620s while enrolled at Oxford, and later after his wife's death in 1633.[29] In order to understand Digby's highly interesting synthesis I would like to analyze his most ambitious work and the most scientifically relevant product of his Parisian sojourn, the *Two Treatises*.[30] The work was divided into two parts, the first dedicated to explaining the nature of bodies, and the second the nature of souls. For Digby the two activities were not to be considered at the same level. Rather, the former was but ancillary to the latter, as he explained in the text's dedicatory epistle, and addressed to his son: 'in my first Treatise of the Nature of Bodies…I ayme no further, then to shew what may be effected by corporeall agents. There, possibility serveth my turne, as well as the determinate indivisible point of truth. I am obliged to that, onely in my maine great these; which is the soule'.[31]

On the one hand then, for Digby explaining the nature of the body was only useful insofar as it could lead to explaining the nature of the soul. This set of priorities directly derived from Digby's profound religious beliefs: as he wrote, before thinking about any kind of theory one must realize that the end of men's actions is beatitude, and in order to understand which path is better to lead men to that goal, one must determine first 'whether the Beatitude we speake of, do belong to this life, or be not to be attained, till we come to the next: or rather, whether or no, there be an other life besides this, to be happy in'.[32] It would be a mistake, however, to consider Digby's religion as a dogmatic

---

[28] See P. Gassendi, *Syntagma Philosophiae*, vol. II pp. 135–143, 'De metallis et eorum transmutatione'; J.C. Darmon, 'Les clairs-obscurs d'une critique: quelques enjeux épistémologiques de la querelle entre Gassendi and Fludd', in F. Greiner (ed.), *Aspects de la tradition alchimique au XVIIe siècle*, Milan-Paris 1998, pp. 67–84; J.F. Maillard, 'Descartes et l'alchimie: une tentation conjurée?', in Ibid., pp. 95–109; S. Matton, 'Cartisianisme et alchimie: a propos d'un termoignage ignore sur les travaux alchimiques de Descartes. Avec une note sur Descartes et Gomez Pereira', in Ibid., pp. 111–184.

[29] On Digby's early studies in alchemy see B.J. Dobbs, 'The natural philosophy of Sir Kenelm Digby. Part II. Digby and Alchemy', *Ambix*, vol. xx n. 3 (1973), pp. 143–163.

[30] The complete title is *Two Treatises: in the one of which, the nature of bodies; in the other, the nature of mans soule; is looked into: in way of discovery, of the immortality of reasonable soules*, Paris 1644.

[31] Ibid., Dedicatory Epistle 'to my Sonne, Kenelm Digby', unfoliated.

[32] Ibid.

one, to which science is simply subordinated. Continuing in his discussion of whether or not there is life after death, Digby explains that there are two means by which we can be sure of this, 'eyther infallible authority, or evident science'. And of the two, it is clear that Digby believes that the second is better than the first, for 'they that rely on the first, depend on others: and they onely who know, are absolutely complete of themselves'.[33] Here, then, we have the first instance in which Digby's natural philosophy appears in his complexity: it is surely *ancilla theologiae*, but the *theologia* in question is a rather strange kind of theology, since it can be demonstrated by 'evident science'.

Digby, on the other hand, believed that his attempt to produce a unifying theory of body and soul that in the end could prove the immortality of the latter was only possible by employing two different methods. If studying bodies required the knowledge of the 'corporeall agents' that affected matter, souls, being of a different nature, 'can not be reduced into those principles, by which all corporeall actions are affected'.[34]

Let us start with bodies then. The main difficulty for the natural philosophers of his time, Digby thought, was that they ended up creating 'prodigious conceits and impossibilities in nature', which 'doe spring out of theire mistake in framing Metaphysicall and abstracted notions, instead of contenting themselves with those plaine, easy and primary notions, which nature stampeth a like in all men of common sense, and understanding'.[35] But what are exactly these 'plaine, easy, and primary notions?'

The 'roote of all the rest' of the notions about the universe is for Digby Quantity, which he defines as 'the plainest and the first, that nature printenth in us, of all the thinges we see, feele and converse with all'.[36] Matter, then, is composed of quantity, and the only notion that 'reacheth the nature of it' is divisibility.[37] Therefore, for Digby, it is a mistake to attribute different natures to different things, and in so doing multiply different entities: rather, in nature 'a body is a mere passive thing, consisting of divers partes, which by motion can be diversly ordered'.[38] The Aristotelian four elements for Digby are not distinguished by different qualities, but only by the different degrees of rarity and density combined with the action of gravity.[39] The atomistic nature of matter is proved for Digby by the experiments of many philosophers, among whom Digby often refers to Galileo, 'unto whom we owe', as he wrote, 'the greatest part of what is knowne concerning motion'.[40] Indeed, Digby believes in the absolute validity of the 'experimental method', if correctly applied,[41] only he does not find any contradiction between the results of Galileo and

---

[33] Ibid.
[34] Ibid., p. 342.
[35] Ibid., p. 7.
[36] Ibid., p. 8.
[37] Ibid., p. 18.
[38] Ibid., p. 342.
[39] Ibid., pp. 32–38.
[40] Ibid., p. 79.
[41] Ibid., p. 198.

the others, and Aristotle's theories. By contrast, Aristotelianism is precisely what the likes of Galileo need in order to make sense of their experience. For instance, when writing on Galileo's theory of gravity, Digby did not agree with Galileo's conclusions that gravity was independent of the mass of the falling object. The conclusion was not, however, that Galileo's experiment was a mistake, but that it needed Aristotle's theory to make sense of it:

> But we can not passe this matter without noting how himselfe [i.e. Galileo] maketh good those arguments of Aristotle, which he seemeth by no meanes to esteeme of: for since the gravity doth overcome the resistance of the medium in some proportion; it followeth that the proportions between the gravity and the medium, may be multiplied without end...which no man will sticke att confessing to be very absurd.[42]

In this instance, it is easy to see that Digby, apart from not endorsing, did not really understand the principles of the physics of Galileo, of whom he only admired the method. As far as atomism is concerned, however, Digby accomplished a different intellectual operation. While Digby was by no means a 'true' Galilean, he was a 'true' atomist, in that he believed that the only characteristic that distinguished matter was quantity. How did he reconcile this with Aristotelianism? For Digby the question was, as it were, of a philological nature: in other words, one needed to distinguish between the true doctrine elaborated by Aristotle, and the one introduced by 'the latter sectatours, or rather pretenders of Aristotle'. As for the former, for Digby Aristotle too was a 'true' atomist:

> Lett any unpartiall Aristotelian answere, whether the conceptions we have delivered of Quantity, of Rarity and Density, of the foure first Qualities, of the combinations of the Elements, of the repugnance of vacuities, be not exactly and rigorously Aristotles? Whether the motion of weighty and light things, and of such as are forced, be not by him, as well as by us, attributed to externe causes? In which all the difference betweene us is, that we enlarge ourselves to more particulars that he hath done. Lett any man reade his bookes of Generation and Corruption, and say whether he doth not expressely teach, that mixtion (which he delivereth to be the generation or making of a mixt body) is done per minima; that is in our language and in one word, by atomes; and signifyeth, that all the qualities, which are naturall qualities following the composition of the Elements, are made by the mingling of the least partes or atomes of the said Elements; which is in effect to say, that all the nature of bodies, their qualities, and their operations, are compassed by the mingling of atomes: the shewing and explicating of which, hath beene our labour in this whole Treatise.... The same do Hippocrates and Galen: the same, their Master Democritus; and with them the best sort of Physitians: the same so Alchymistes, with their Master Geber; whose maxime to this purpose, we cited above: the same do all naturall Philosophers, eyther auncient commentatours of Aristotle, or else moderne inquirers into naturall effects, in a sensible and

---

[42] Ibid., pp. 84–5.

understandable way: as who will take the paines to looke into them, will easily perceive.[43]

For Digby, if one read Aristotle 'in a sensible and understandable way', one could not fail to realize that what he termed 'minima naturalia' were the atoms, only expressed in another language. From this perspective, Digby can draw a genealogy of atomists that starts with Aristotle, and then goes on to Galen, Democritus, the 'Alchymistes', and, finally, the 'moderne inquirers' and himself. By contrast, Aristotle's alleged followers had misunderstood the master:

> for whereas he called certaine collections or positions of thinges, by certain common names...terming some of them Qualities, other actions...or the like: these his latter followers, have conceited that these names did not designe a concurrence of sundry thinges, or a diverse disposition of the partes of any thing...but have imagined, that every one of these names had correspondent unto it, some reall positive entity or thing, separated (in its own nature) from the maine thing or substance in which it was.[44]

In reality then, Aristotle, his ancient commentators – in particular Avicenna, whom Digby cites often –, the alchemists and Digby himself said essentially the same thing. The problem was that the 'latter followers' of Aristotle had created different entities where there was only a difference in quantity. We will go back to Digby's inclusions of alchemists in this group, but now I would like to address another question. Simply put, why was Digby so invested in Aristotelianism? What did Aristotle's doctrine have, that for Digby was so necessary and impossible to abandon?

As we have seen, Digby's whole work was devoted to a single aim: to prove that the soul was immortal, just as Aristotle had done. As Digby summarized, 'we proposed unto our selves to shew that our soules are immortall: whereupon, casting about to find the groundes of immortality, and discerning it to be a negative, we conceived that we ought to beginne our search, with enquiring What Mortality is; and what be the causes of it'. The treatise on the nature of the bodies was therefore, to borrow one of Digby's metaphors, 'the porch' that leads the way to the 'house', that is the treatise on the soules.[45] For Digby Aristotelianism, which contained both a physical explanation of nature and a demonstration of the immortality of the soul, had already built the core of the system, and were it not for Aristotle's alleged followers, who had misunderstood what the Master had said about matter, there would not have been any need for Digby to dwell at such length on the nature of bodies; but it would have been enough to 'touch up' Aristotelian physics with the new experimental findings. Now that the misunderstanding was cleared up, Digby could safely go back to the main point of the treatise, for which Aristotle was

---

[43] Ibid., pp. 343–4.
[44] Ibid., p. 344.
[45] Ibid., p. 350.

once again the main reference.[46] In fact, Digby began his work on the nature of the soul by quoting the initial passage of Aristotle's *De anima*, and throughout the treatise he followed closely the Aristotelian discussion of the immortality of the soul, as it has been extensively demonstrated by Bruce Janacek.[47]

Together with linking physics and metaphysics, the doctrine of the immortality of the soul provided Digby with a way to add his Catholic belief to the mix. More specifically, given that matter is passive, and but the sum, differently organized, of parts, what was men's role in all this? Men cannot be composed of the same matter, for if they were, they would be subjected to the same mechanical law of motion, which would thus deny them any free will. The Catholic Digby could not accept such an outcome, and so there must have been another substance, different than matter, which 'must necessarily be of a noble straine, and of a different and higher nature than it; and consequently, can not be a body, or be composed of Quantity…which we express by calling it a spirituall thing'.[48] This 'spirituall thing' is precisely the soul, which can be both joined with the body while men are alive, and separated from it after death. The Cartesian notion of Ego is, so to say, the vestige of the soul that presents itself to us while it is joined with the body.[49]

To summarize, then, Aristotelianism represented a necessary reference for Digby for many reasons: first, it proved the immortality of the soul, which for the Catholic was the most important element. Secondly, from Aristotle's discussion of the soul Digby could start to elaborate on the relationship between that and the body, in a way that could guarantee the 'scientific' demonstration of men's free will, a central point of the Catholic doctrine in which he believed. Finally, Aristotelianism, if understood 'in a reasonable way', could account for atomism and the mechanical view of nature, that Galileo and other philosophers of Digby's time were testing and upholding 'by experience'.

As I have said, Digby's philosophy of nature doubtless had a theological origin, yet it is important to remember that his theology had nothing to do with dogmatism (one manifestation of which was the Scholasticism practiced by those whom Digby considered to have misunderstood the Master's theory of *minima naturalia*). Rather, it was a highly original synthesis of physics and metaphysics in which Digby's alchemical interests were prominent.

Alchemy entered Digby's theory of bodies and souls at two levels. First, and more specifically, in the *Two Treatises* there are many traces of alchemical language and alchemical procedures that Digby would develop later in his career. One particularly interesting example is the chapter on 'How a Plant

---

[46] Ibid., pp. 350–4.

[47] See B. Janaceck, 'Catholic Natural Philosophy: Alchemy and the Revivification of Sir Kenelm Digby', in M.J. Osler (ed.) *Rethinking the Scientific Revolution*, Cambridge 2000, pp. 89–118, at pp. 93 and ff.

[48] K. Digby, *Two treatises*, p. 411.

[49] Ibid., pp. 417 and ff. *passim*. On significance of Descartes' theory in demonstrating men's free will see M.J. Osler, 'Eternal Truths and the Laws of Nature: The Theological Foundations of Descartes' Philosophy of Nature', *Journal of the History of Ideas*, vol. 46 (1985), pp. 359–362, and Id., *Divine Will*, pp. 219 and ff. *passim*.

or an Animal cometh to that figure it hath', in which Digby explains the generation of plants and animals by referring to the 'first temperament that is in the seed', which 'the ordered series of naturall causes' develops into the different creatures.[50] In 1661, after a period of intense alchemical activities – in the mid-1650s he was a member of the 'universal laboratory' of Hartlib's kitchen[51] – Digby took up once again the topic of the generation of plants and described it in alchemical terms. To this topic he devoted a treatise entitled *A Discourse concerning the vegetation of plants*.[52]

More generally, and perhaps most importantly in the context of the present study, Digby used alchemy also to glue together atomism and Aristotelianism, or, in other words, his physics and his metaphysics. Although the study of the bodies was different from the study of the soul, this did not mean for Digby that the two were rigidly separated. Rather, the knowledge of the bodies and souls was a unified process, and one that much resembles an alchemical one:

> ..none of natures greatest secrets, whereof our senses give us notice in the effects, are so overshaded with an impenetrable veyle, but that the diligent, and wary hand of reason, might unmaske them, and shew them to us in their naked and genuine formes, and delight us with the contemplation of their native beauties.[53]

Therefore just as the soul appears to be the 'purified' matter, as opposed to the gross matter of the body, the process of knowledge as well consists of a purification of sorts, from the secrets of nature to the 'naked and genuine form' of the spirit.

Aside from being necessary to explain Digby's mixture of Aristotelianism and atomism, his alchemical interests are interesting here for another reason. Recent scholarship has been revisiting the relationship between alchemy and politics: in particular, J.Andrew Mendelsohn has taken issue with the link between alchemy and the Puritan Revolution, that was highlighted by historians such as Christopher Hill, Keith Thomas and Charles Webster.[54] Against these historians' view of alchemy as a central component of radical ideas, Mendelsohn has demonstrated that alchemy was practiced both by radicals and by Royalists before and after the Restoration, and he has

---

[50] Ibid., pp. .226–230.

[51] For an accurate analysis of Digby's role in Hartlib's laboratory see B.J. Dobbs, 'The natural philosophy of Sir Kenelm Digby. Part II', pp. 151 and ff.

[52] See K. Digby, *A Discourse concerning the vegetation of plants. Spoken by Sir Kenelme Digby at Gresham College, on the 23. Of January, 1660*, London 1661, pp. 11–48, and B.J. Dobbs, 'Studies in the Natural Philosophy of Sir Kenelm Digby: Part II'.

[53] K. Digby, *Two Treatises*, p. 340.

[54] J.A. Mendelsohn, 'Alchemy and Politics in England 1649–1665', *Past and Present*, n. 135 (1992), pp. 30–78; and C. Hill, *Intellectual Origins of the English Revolution*, Oxford 1965, pp. 122 and ff. *passim*; Id., *The world turned upside down. Radical ideas during the English Revolution*, London 1991 (1972), pp. 387–305 and *passim*; K. Thomas, *Religion and the Decline of Magic*, London 1971, pp. 227 and ff.: C.Webster, 'English Medical Reformers and the Puritan Revolution: A Background to "Society of Chymical Physitians"', *Ambix*, vol. 14 (1967), pp. 16–41.

convincingly concluded that 'the political meanings of alchemy were multiple', even if alchemy seemed 'naturally associated' with each of the divers political agendas with which it was linked.[55] The alchemy practiced and studied by Kenelm Digby contributes to demonstrate the validity of Mendelsohn's thesis. No one, I believe, can serve as a better case-study to argue for the impossibility of intrinsically linking alchemy with any political agenda in mid-seventeenth century England than Kenelm Digby, a Protestant Royalist in 1631, a Catholic Royalist in the early 1640s, a Catholic supporter of Cromwell in the 1650s, and, finally, a Catholic Royalist after the Restoration, and throughout all of this an 'adept'.

If for Digby Aristotelianism and atomism were two parts of the same quasi-alchemic process, Thomas White also found no contradiction between an atomistic view of nature and Aristotle's theories, albeit his trajectory differed somewhat from Digby's.

White started working out his natural philosophy in his 1642 *De Mundo*, to which Digby referred to in many instances in his *Two Treatises*, and in 1646 he published a *summa* of his natural philosophy under the title *Institutionum Peripateticarum*.[56] From the work's very title, White demonstrates his firm belief in the validity of Aristotelianism, which he had absorbed during the long course of his studies in Douai and which, like Digby, he saw as perfectly compatible with the 'new science'. When introducing his methodological approach in the *Institutions*, White explained: 'I call them Peripateticall, because, throughout they subsist upon Aristotle's Principles; though the conclusions sometimes dissent'.[57] The dissent arose precisely out of the findings of 'experiences' of natural philosophers like Galileo, whom White quoted often and always admiringly. Far from undermining the validity of Aristotelianism, for White Galilean experiments represented an enrichment of it, as he declared in his long discussion of the problem of the divisibility of quantities ad infinitum.[58]

As for atomism in particular, White acknowledged the debt he owed Digby, from whose doctrine, to the development of which he greatly contributed, he heavily borrowed.[59] Like Digby, White too believed that the world was composed of elements that differed only quantitatively from one another. Therefore, the traditional four elements (earth, water, air and fire) which according to Aristotle were the bulk of matter, differed for White only in quantity 'and, because Divisibility is the very nature of Quantity, the rare

---

[55] See J.A. Mendelsohn, 'Alchemy and Politics', pp. 75–77.
[56] On the significance of the *Institutionum*, published in Latin in 1647 and later translated into English as *Peripateticall Institutions in the way of that eminent Person and excellent Philosopher Sir Kenelm Digby. The theoricall part. Also a theologicall Appendix of the beginning of the world*, London 1656, see J. Henry, 'Atomism and Eschatology; pp. 223 and ff.
[57] T. White, *Peripateticall Institutions*, 'The Author's Design', sig. a4 r–a5 v.
[58] Ibid., pp. 28–29.
[59] In the preface of his *Peripateticall Institutions* White acknowledged to have written his text 'in the way of that eminent Person and excellent Philosopher Sir Kenelm Digby…. because, since, in that so justly-to-be-envy'd Book, Of the Immortality of the Soul, he has dissected the whole composition of Nature, from the first notion of Body, to the very joynts and articles of an invisible spirituall Soul' [sign. a5 r].

will have more, the dense lesse of Quantity'.[60] Thus, according to White the difference between the elements was purely a difference in quantity, or in the various 'degrees' of density.

If Digby insisted that 'the number of Elements assigned by Aristotle, is truly and exactly determined by him; and that there can be neither more nor lesse of them',[61] that is to say, that the different combination of density and rarity and gravity could produce only four different results, i.e. fire, water, earth and air, White, in contrast, felt the need to underline that the combinations of elements were in fact infinite. Once again, however, for White Aristotle's theory of the four elements should not have been discarded, for it represented a compromise between the logical consequences of atomism, and the deficiency of men's intelligence: 'Men do not determine this kind of things, according to the fruitfulnesse of Nature; but, by grosse and sensible differences, according to the slownesse of our Apprehension'[62].

This difference between White's and Digby's explanation of the four elements is significant, for it exemplifies clearly the different approach that they both adopted towards Aristotelianism. For Digby, as we have seen, the main advantage that upholding Aristotle's theory presented was a proof of the immortality of the soul, or, better, a system in which the immortality of the soul was presented as the core of both metaphysics and physics: as Digby had written to Hobbes many years earlier, he found in Aristotle a way to unify 'nature and solide reason' together. Therefore, in a sense, Digby was less interested in Aristotelianism as a logical system than in Aristotelianism as the surest way to prove the link between body and soul, and between mechanical physics and Catholic metaphysics.

Thomas White, by contrast, had a much deeper relationship with both Aristotelianism and Scholasticism as a logical system. He did not cut the Gordian knot by distinguishing between the two and condemning the latter as a 'pretended' Aristotelianism, as Digby had done, but he wanted to save Scholasticism too by purging it from its dogmatism and maintaining its internal logic. For this reason White felt the need to correct slightly Digby's doctrine of the four elements: because considering fire, water, air and earth as the only possible combination of rarity, density and gravity was precisely illogical.

Once again, the question here is why White had so much stake in Aristotelianism as a system. Unlike Digby, whose main concern was to prove the immortality of the soul, for White the most important and truly necessary merit of Aristotle's theory was its systematical and logical character. As a true disciple of Mersenne's in this respect, White needed the Aristotelian system to deny what he saw as the main danger that natural philosophers of his days could run in, i.e., skepticism: 'The main fault seem'd to me to lye at their doores, who neither do themselves nor can endure others should expect

---

[60] T. White, *Peripateticall Institutions*, p. 43.
[61] K. Digby, *Two Treatises*, p. 30.
[62] T. White, *Peripateticall Institutions*, p. 52.

any certainty from It [i.e. Philosophy]'.[63] White's philosophy, then, was to be understood as an antidote to skepticism, which remained a troubling concern for him until his death and to whose denial he dedicated many of his later works, as Beverley Southgate has analyzed.[64]

Historians of science, with the exception of John Henry[65] and few others, have generally overlooked the contribution of White and Digby to the history of atomism in England. The main reason for this is that the Catholic natural philosophers developed their views within the Aristotelian framework, whose validity they never ceased to uphold. More specifically, in his survey of atomism in England, R.Kargon denies to Kenelm Digby any significant role in the development of mechanist theories precisely because of Digby's Aristotelianism, which Kargon seems to reduce to the fact that Digby decided to call his atoms by the Aristotelian name of *parva* or *minima naturalia*.[66] Despite the terminological coincidence, however, Digby and White's *minima* did not differ in quality, like the Aristotelian ones, but only in density. Once we realize this fundamental difference, therefore, the reputation that the Catholic natural philosophers enjoyed among the English mechanist philosophers is *not* 'difficult to explain'.[67] Indeed, there are many reasons why Robert Boyle praised Kenelm Digby and his circle as being among the few philosophers who 'in our less partial & more inquisitive times ... so luckyly reviv'd & so skillfully celebrated ... the Atomicall Philosophy invented or brought into request by Democritus, Leucippus, Epicurus & their Contemporaries'.[68] Also, in this respect it is also worth noting the high opinion that John Locke had of Digby and White: Locke in fact owned several of the Catholic natural philosophers' books, and he made some annotation on the link between physics and metaphysics that White's and Digby's theory presented.[69]

The significant role played by Digby and White in the development of atomism suggests to us that further work needs to be done on the relationship between new science and Aristotelianism. As Richard Westfall put it, if it is undeniably true that for the natural philosophers who embraced the new mechanical philosophy Aristotelian philosophy of nature 'had become untenable', it is also true that the task of replacing the old with the new was

---

[63] T. White, *Peripateticall Institutions*, 'The Author's Design', sign. A 3 v
[64] On White's position against skepticism see B.C. Southgate, '"Cauterising the Tumor of Pyrrhonism": Blackloism versus Skepticism', *Journal of the History of Ideas*, vol. 53 n. 4 (1992), pp. 631–645.
[65] See his already cited 'Atomism and Eschatology'.
[66] R.H. Kargon, *Atomism in England*, pp. 71 and ff.
[67] Ibid., pp. 72–3.
[68] See R.S. Westfall, 'Unpublished Boyle Papers relating to scientific method', *Annals of Science*, vol. 12 n.2 (1956), pp. 103–117, at pp. 111–112. See also M. Boas, *Robert Boyle and Seventeenth Century Chemistry*, Cambridge 1958, p. 25. On the link between Digby and Boyle on the grounds of their common alchemical interests see also W.R. Newman-J.L. Principe, *Alchemy tried in the fire*, pp. 261–2.
[69] See BodL, Ms.Locke F. 14, ff. 8, 46, 96, 270.

'an intellectual labor of enormous dimensions'.[70] White and Digby, I argue, greatly contributed to this labor.

2.2 'A Natural and New Divinity'

The logical and rational character of White's mixture of Aristotelianism and atomism, as opposed to the 'alchemical' one of Digby's, had highly interesting implications in the realm of theology, which was one of the main interests of White's throughout his life. Unlike Digby, who had never attempted to create a systematic theology, White sought to build an all-encompassing system of philosophy, in which natural science and theology could complement each other: indeed, for White natural philosophy was essential to improve one's devotion to divinity.[71] To this aim, White had attached a 'Theological Appendix' to his *Peripateticall Institutions,* in which through a close reading of the initial chapters of the *Genesis*, he sought to demonstrate that theology and natural philosophy said essentially the same things.

For instance, whereas in the philosophical part of his treatise White had embraced and demonstrated the validity of heliocentrism,[72] in the theological appendix, by contrast, White argued that there was no contradiction between this and the Biblical account:

> From the whole Story [of the first Chapter of Genesis] 'tis evident that our Earth is situated in the very middle of the Universe…Which I would not have so understood, as if the Centre of the Earth were the very middle point; but, that the Great Orbe, (that is, all that Orbe, which the Earth makes with its circle about the Sun) has the notion of a Centre: for, that is scarce makes a visible Magnitude, in respect of the rest of the world, Astronomers find by experience.[73]

The validity of the *Genesis* account could go undoubted, therefore, if we interpret it correctly: for White the Holy Scripture stated that the whole orbit of the earth, and not only the planet, was at the center of the universe.

Another interesting example concerns the nature of matter. As we have seen, White argued that matter was composed of four elements, which differed only in density. Fire was the most mobile and the least dense among them, and therefore it was the 'operation of Fire' and its action on the other elements that produced motion. This is confirmed, according to White, in the *Genesis* account of God's creation of fire, or light, after the other elements:

> Again, because neither materia prima nor any other part of a Thing, but only Physicall Compound, is apt to receive Existence: and, of Physicall

---

[70] See R.S. Westfall, 'The Scientific Revolution Reasserted', in M.J. Osler (ed.), *Rethinking the Scientific Revolution*, pp. 41–55, at p. 45.
[71] T. White, *Peripateticall Institutions, The Theological Appendix*, 'Epistle to the Reader', Unfoliated.
[72] Ibid., pp. 174–190.
[73] Ibid., pp. 364–5.

> Compounds the most simple and, as it were, most potential, that is, next above mere possibility, are the Elements: and something must, of necessity, have flow'd instantaneously from God: It follows, that some one or more of the Elements were, by Creation, call'd by God out of the common Abysse of nothingnesse...Yet not all the four [elements]: Since FIRE we call an Element that makes it self be seen, which implyes Action; but corporeall action is not without motion; nor motion from pure Creation. But, of the other three Elements no one could be conveniently omitted: For EARTH and WATER are those we see mixt by Fire through the whole course of Nature; and Fire is immediately generated and nourished by AIRE: If any one, therefore, of these had been wanting; the matter had been unfit for Angelicall operation.[74]

In White's text, therefore, the temporal succession of the *Genesis* account of the creation follows the rules of natural philosophy: God needed to create some elements, because without elements there was nothing to receive existence. Not all elements were created at the same time, since fire is the 'action-element', which needs something to act upon. The three remaining ones, however, were all needed to explain the creation of the world. And the examples of this method of proving the Scripture in support of natural philosophy could be multiplied here.[75]

In the context of the historiography on the relationship between theology and science during the scientific revolution, current scholarship has admirably complicated what once seemed to be a clear-cut passage from the former to the latter. The work of, among the others, Betty Jo Dobbs, James Jacob, Margaret Jacob, Margaret Osler, has shown how religion and science coexisted at a very profound level in the intellectual production of some of the 'pillars' of the new science, such as Robert Boyle and Isaac Newton.[76] It remains true, however, that the relationship between the two domains changed over the course of the seventeenth century. As Richard Westfall has argued, when Bellarmine condemned heliocentrism, he did so because it was in conflict with the Bible: in other words, natural philosophy needed to be validated by the Scriptures. Sixty-five years later Isaac Newton defended the truth of *Genesis* precisely because it was validated *by* the truth of science, and not the other way around.[77] If we accept Westfall's definition of the shift in the relationship between science and theology as one of the marks of the scientific 'revolution', then Thomas White represents something in between Bellarmine and Newton, and in this respect the study of his thought could shed some light on the transition from the former to the latter. At the beginning of his *Peripateticall Institutions,* White wrote that:

> Since Philosophy has then attain'd its Dignity, when, apply'd to Action, it renders Man better, that is, more Man; and Christians are initiated to this

---

[74] Ibid., pp. 343–344.
[75] See B.C. Southgate, *'Covetous of truth'*, pp. 104 and ff.
[76] A good synthesis of the new acquisition of this scholarship can be found in M.J. Osler (ed.), *Rethinking the Scientific Revolution*.
[77] R.H. Westfall, 'The Scientific Revolution', p. 50.

by Divinity: this, evidently, is the highest pitch of Philosophy, to wait on and be subservient to the Traditions deriv'd from God.

Yet later in the same passage he added that:

> ...since in the ancient Theology, we had this [i.e. 'the Notions of Nature'] accurately decyphered, beyond the Attempts of Philosophers; but untraceable, because the Paths of Nature were unknown: It seem'd to me, a more express Seal of Theologicall Approbation could not be desir'd, then that the Institutions should carrie a Torch before the Mysteries of Genesis; and, from those so discover'd, receive themselves, with advantage, the Glody and Splendor of Authority.[78]

Also, when White decided to send to Kenelm Digby a copy of the theological appendix of the *Institutions*, he reminded his friend to bear in mind that 'the notes *de Origine mundi* are not a treatise, but an *appendix* added to shew how Divinity depends on Philosophy'.[79] Natural philosophy, then, is surely 'subservient' to the 'highest pitch of Philosophy', that is to say, subservient to theology. However, natural science also does 'carrie a Torch' that enlightens the 'Mysteries of Genesis', which cannot be fully understood without the knowledge of the 'Paths of Nature', or, as White said to Digby, 'Divinity depends on Philosophy'. And it is in this ambiguity regarding the relationship between natural philosophy and theology, in which it is unclear which one needs the other more, but it is clear that both need to be verified by each other, that White's position acquires its significance in the history of science.[80]

But once we explain the link between natural philosophy and theology in White's thought, it remains to be seen just what kind of theology the Catholic author was referring to. When Thomas White, later in his career, synthesized the foundations of his natural philosophy, he declared:

> ...when looking into my life they should find...that I have written the Principles of Philosophy, and divinity upon this intention, to shewe that Christian religion is conformable to reason, and to cast out of the church such erronious Opinions seemed to make it contrary to reason, and to draw all rationall men to the verity of Christian belief.[81]

---

[78] T. White, *Peripateticall Institutions, The Theological Appendix*, 'Epistle to the Reader', Unfoliated.

[79] White to Digby, January 1647, in *Blacklo's Cabal*, p. 10.

[80] Here I disagree with Ruth Jordan, who has argued that in White's work reason outgrew its role as *ancilla theologiae* and became instead the center of the Catholic's elaboration (see R.A. Jordan, 'The Blackloists 1640–1668. Ecclesiastical, Theological and Intellectual Authority in English Catholic Polemic', unpublished Ph.D. Thesis, University of Cambridge 1999). While I think that Jordan's reflections are indeed extremely useful to understand White's theology, as I show below, I believe that White's natural philosophy cannot be understood without recognizing its central theological aspects.

[81] T. White, *Apology for the Treatise of Obedience and Government*, Westminster Diocesan Archives, Old Brotherhood Mss. II.130, ff.529–531, at f. 531.

In this respect, it seems interesting to report an anecdote that John Sergeant, one of White's disciples, narrated in a pamphlet written in 1659 to criticize certain points of his master's doctrine:

> I have heard from a very Learned and Worthy Friend of mine, that he himself being present at a Conference between Master White and another eminent Scholar of our Nation, divers years before Master White appeared in Print: among other things then discoursed of, Master White advanced a Phylosophical Position which the other denied, as inconsistent with our holy faith of the Blessed Sacrament: to which Master White replied, "Let us find out the Truth in Phylosophy, and the Mysteries of our Faith will square well enough with them": to which the other "Nay, Sir, by your favour, let us in the first place presuppose the establisht verities of faith, and then square our Philosophy to them".[82]

And here is Sergeant's assessment of the question:

> I have often entertained my self with these thoughts, what a dangerous method Master White prescribed, and as now appears followed? what a natural and new divinity it would prove, which should be squared to those Phylosophical truths, which our weak understandings should be able to establish, independent of divine revelation? And at last Master White hath brought forth this his issue, and made it publick to the world.[83]

White, however, did not only bring the question 'to the world', he actually tried to build and theorize this 'natural and new divinity' that could 'be squared to those Phylosophical truths'. His quest for a rational doctrine did not only produce a theology that was compatible with, and indeed validated by the truth of mechanical physics, but one that also led the Catholic theologian to make some very controversial statements in the realm of Catholic dogmas.

Two are the main lines along which White tried to build a rational theology. First, he sought to combine Catholic doctrine with his mechanic natural philosophy. A good example of this is his theory of transubstantiation, which he elaborated in a manuscript work devoted to the topic.[84] White thought that while reason had no business in proving the truth of transubstantiation, since this was granted by faith, nevertheless its task was 'to shew that tis Possible, without violating any Maxim, either of Logick, Nature, or Christianity, which may I conceive be thus manifest'.[85] The way to prove this is by use of the atomic natural philosophy. More specifically, for White Christ's flesh, like any matter, could be divided into 'Particles', or atoms, every one of which contained 'the Whole Nature of Flesh': Therefore,

---

[82] [John Sergeant], *A Vindication of the Doctrine contained in Pope Benedict xii, his Bull, by S.W. a Roman Catholic*, Paris 1659, p. 5. On John Sergeant see D. Krook, *John Sergeant and his circle. A study of three seventeenth-century English Aristotelians*, Leiden 1993.

[83] J. Sergeant, *A Vindication*, p. 6.

[84] The title of the undated manuscript work is 'On Transubstantiation', and it can be found in BodL, Gough Norfolk Ms. 15, ff. 246r–249r.

[85] Ibid., f. 246r.

> since all the Corpuscularian & best Philosophers do grant that Particles laid together on the same Fashion do work the same effect, & make the same Impression on our sense, therfore those least Particles of Flesh being postured as the least Particles of Bread were, will work in the same maner on our senses as Bread did formerly.[86]

In other words, the atoms of Christ's flesh are 'rearranged' to form bread. And the reason why they remain in the form of bread both before and after the consecration, without ever 'turning' into proper human flesh, is that 'the Ordainer of this Mystery aymed only at the encreasing, & heightening our Devotion by the reall & true Presence...to wich tis altogether...insignificant on what manner the parts of his [i.e. Christ's] Flesh were postured'.[87]

The second pivotal element of White's rational theology was the way in which he defended the principle of tradition against the Protestants' *sola Scriptura*. As Ruth Jordan has recently explained, White's and his associates' emphasis on tradition did not only represent the reformulation of a common argument in the Protestant-Catholic controversy, but it also signified the shift that the Blackloists operated from the 'content' of faith to its 'method of transmission'.[88] In other words, if the content of faith, i.e. the truth of the Catholic religion revealed by Christ, could be subject to a rational scrutiny only to a certain extent, by contrast the transmission of this faith from Christ to the Catholic Church of White's day could logically and, as it were, 'scientifically' be demonstrated. The procedure for this demonstration is fully Aristotelian in its methodology: for White, in fact, reasoning by deduction, 'since 'tis confessed the Catholik Church goes upon this Maxim, that Her Doctrine is received from Christ, and still handed along to the present generation; they who cavil at this assertion, should assign some Age when they conceive an errour crept in'.[89] But since mankind is 'naturally inclined to truth', and there is no reason for the fathers to lie to their sons, it is illogical, and thus impossible, to think that an entire age had first corrupted Christian doctrine, and secondly transmitted it in its entirety to the following generation, thus corrupting the transmission of the true faith of Christ.[90]

The emphasis on tradition, together with representing a vivid example of White's belief in the possibility of producing a rational theology, led to some highly problematic consequences with respect to some of the most central elements of Catholic ecclesiology and doctrine. Since the Catholic Church had to test and validate accurately its doctrines against both tradition and

---

[86] Ibid., f. 246v.
[87] Ibid,
[88] See R.A. Jordan, 'The Blackloists 1640–1668', pp. 122 and ff.
[89] See T. White, *An Apology for Rushworth's dialogues*, Paris 1654, at p. 8.
[90] Ibid., pp. 8–14 *passim*. The same concern for the centrality of tradition in the context of 'rational' proofs of the truth of Catholicism can be found in Kenelm Digby: see his manuscript letter to Frances Viscountess of Purbeck, dated 13 January 1636 and written in Paris, and later published in Paris in 1638 with the title *Conference with a Lady*, to be found in BL Add. Mss. 10575, ff. 3r–91v, at ff. 29v–65v, and his *A Discourse concerning Infallibility in Religion*, Amsterdam 1652, pp. 177 and ff. *passim*.

Scripture, the logical consequence of this operation was to eliminate all the doctrines of dubious origin. One of the first doctrines to go was for White the Papal infallibility, which, since it did not pass the Blackloist test, should not be believed *de fide*.[91] Another of those controversial statements was White's position on the incorporeal nature of Purgatory, expressed in his 1653 treatise *Villicationis suae de medio statu animarum,* published contemporaneously in England and on the Continent, and later translated into English as *The middle state of souls*. In this work White wanted to maintain the validity of the doctrine of Purgatory, granted by tradition, but also to dispute what he called the *sententia vulgaris* according to which the souls who are in Purgatory suffer from corporeal punishment. On the contrary, White reformulated, with some variations, the notion of the incorporeal state of souls after death, and consequently he opposed the legitimacy and value of indulgences, a central theme in the European confessional debate since at least the time of Erasmus and Luther.[92]

John Henry has interpreted White's opinion on Purgatory, transubstantiation and the doctrine of Papal Infallibility as a sign of his 'ecumenism': in other words, since White and his circle were working, so to speak, shoulder to shoulder with Protestant natural philosophers, they were 'making a deliberate effort to develop a reformed Catholic theology which was close to, or amenable to, English Protestant thought'.[93] I think that 'ecumenism' is not the best way to describe either White's theology or his and his circle's involvement with the Protestants. We need to remember that White's argument on the necessity of using tradition as a criterion to distinguish the doctrines that were to be believed *de fide* from those that were not, out of which White's denial of the Papal infallibility and his doctrine of Purgatory sprang, was elaborated precisely as a tool to uphold the truth of Catholicism against Protestantism. For White, as for Digby, there was no doubt that the Catholic religion was the only true one, and that both the Puritans and the English Protestants were simply wrong. Indeed, when Digby wrote about the English Protestants, 'or common prayer men', he affirmed that while they can be 'neerer truth then the Presbyterian', their doctrinal foundation, or 'discourse', as Digby put it, was 'even more irrationall than the puritans proceeding', for while they thought that admitting the authority of the Fathers together with the Scripture should mitigate the Puritans' emphasis on the personal interpretation of the Bible, in reality '[the Protestant] maketh himselfe iudge which of the fathers are to be received; and when; and what of them to be reiected; and how to be understood'.[94] Moreover, as far as ecclesiology was concerned, White's ideas

---

[91] See T. White, *Tabulae Suffragiales*, London 1655 *passim*.
[92] T. White, *The middle state of souls*, 5–6. See also *De medio statu animarum*, 3: 'Non itaque locum uspiam tartareis oppletum ferculis cogitamus, quibus Animae ab extrinseco tortore lanienam patiantur, sed intimam & viscitus ingenitam affectuum contra ratione rabiem & furias horrescimus. Hanc peccatis propterea proportionatam esse, quia ab iis prognatam', and the dedicatory epistle to the English translation, to the Reader, unfoliated.
[93] J. Henry, 'Atomism and Eschatology', p. 217.
[94] K. Digby, *A Discourse of Infallibility*, pp. 187–189.

on how the structure and hierarchy of the Catholic Church should be reformed cannot be reduced to an attempt to please the Protestants. Instead, White re-elaborated a series of complex issues and different ecclesiological models, *in primis* the Gallican one, in order to elaborate an ecclesiological structure that could be compatible with this peculiar kind of theological baggage, as we will see below.

Rather than 'ecumenism', then, I believe that White's theological elaborations have to be put in a theological and philosophical context in which on both the Protestant and the Catholic side the fideistic arguments to prove the truth of one's religion were more and more often accompanied by a rational examination of one's religious tenets. Or, to put it differently, the language and rhetoric of confessional polemics encouraged readers to examine critically matters of faith. This is not to say that 'rational' Protestants and 'rational' Catholics were working towards elaborating a sort of 'common theology', but it means, as Ruth Jordan put it, that 'whatever their rhetoric, the Anglicans were as fideistic or as unfideistic, as rational as irrational, as their Catholic adversaries'.[95]

I do not intend to elaborate on the Protestant fideistic arguments, which have been explored in detail by James Jacob, Margaret Jacob and Barbara Shapiro among the others.[96] As far as Catholic theologians were concerned, I would like to point out, as Susan Rosa has demonstrated, that Scholasticism was the necessary background for rational arguments, given the intellectual legitimacy that St. Thomas had given to the Church as the institution in charge of establishing what had to be believed *de fide*.[97] Moreover, in the case of White specifically, as we have seen, Scholasticism was necessary to validate the truth of a rationally intended Catholicism not only against the Protestants, but also against skepticism.

In this respect, the link between anti-Protestantism and anti-skepticism in White's theological and ecclesiological stances clearly emerges if we examine a text that White wrote in 1651 against the *Discourse on Infallibility* written by Lucius Cary, second Viscount of Falkland and published for the first time in 1645.[98] Against Falkland's statements on the impossibility of solidly

---

[95] R.A. Jordan, 'The Blackloists', p. 12. I would like to thank Susan Rosa for the insightful suggestions she gave me on this topic.

[96] On the question of 'rationality' in English Protestantism see, among the others, M.C. Jacob, *The Newtonians and the English revolution*, Ithaca 1976; J.R. Jacob and M.C. Jacob, 'The Anglican origins of modern science: the metaphysical foundations of the Whig constitution', *Isis*, vol. 71 (1980), pp. 251–267; B.J. Shapiro, *Probability and certainty in seventeenth-century England. A study of the relationships between natural science, religion, history, law, and literature*, Princeton 1983.

[97] S. Rosa, 'Seventeenth-Century Catholic Polemic and the Rise of Cultural Rationalism: An Example from the Empire', *Journal of the History of Ideas*, vol. 17 n.1 (1996), pp. 87–107.

[98] On Falkland's *Discourse* and on its interpretation in the context of the Great Tew Circle see the insightful, if problematic, essay by Hugh Trevor-Roper, 'The Great Tew Circle', in Id., *Catholics, Anglicans and Puritans. Seventeenth Century Essays*, London 1987, pp. 166–230. Falkland's text was reprinted in 1651, together with the replies of Thomas White and Walter Montagu, in *Sir Lucius Cary, late Lord Viscount of Falkland, His Discourse of Infallibility*,

demonstrating the infallibility of the Church of Rome, White once more defended the notion of the method of transmission of tradition as an infallible and reasonable mark of the true church. As he wrote, 'if we consider, that Faith is a Science, and Science a thing whose parts are so connexed, that if one be false, all must needs be false, we shall easily see that contrarily'.[99] And since the 'Spirit of God' makes sure that His Church remains infallible, 'that we may have some guide',[100] it follows that there must indeed be a way to 'connect rationally all the parts', which is precisely the Catholic notion of tradition. The confessional perspective is, once again, clear: tradition is the validation, and a rational kind of validation, for the Catholic Church as opposed to the Protestant one. But the stakes are higher: encouraging such doubts, in White's opinion, meant not only questioning the Catholic Church, but questioning the certainty of any religious belief. As White wrote,

> If…[any one or more of them]…light upon some book of an Arrian, Trinitarian, or other Sect, so wittily written, that he putteth probable solution for the places of Scriptures, sheweth slight wayes, how our well-meaning fore-fathers may have slipped into such an error; what is there to retain these men, from….breake[ing] themselves to the Arrians: And when the heat is passed, light upon some Rabbi, who shall cunningly exaggerate the absurdities (as he shall terme them) of the Trinity…what shall hinder this to become a Jew, and at last to prove himselfe so great a Clerk, as to write De Tribus Impostoribus.[101]

The outcome of such a process, in White's opinion, is dangerous: 'Take away the power of the Church (which every man doth, who taketh away the Infallibility) what can retaine any man, why he should not yeeld to that discourse, which seemeth fairest, seeing nothing is certaine?'.[102] The Catholic notion of tradition defended through Scholasticism, therefore, can both constitute an unshakable defense against such an outcome and satisfy the requirement of reason.

2.3 Catholicism and Natural Philosophy

Having examined the profound link between science and theology in Thomas White, I would like to offer now some considerations on the confessional background in which the seventeenth century science has to be placed, and White's role in it. More specifically, after the seminal and much-debated work of Christopher Hill, who reformulated the 'Merton-thesis' by arguing that Puritan

---

London 1651. Falkland's text is reproduced without the page-numbers, while White's text is at pp. 1–49.

[99] Ibid., p. 25.
[100] Ibid., p. 32.
[101] Ibid., pp. 41–42. Mersenne also mentioned the *De Tribus Impostoribus* in the first edition of his *Quaestiones in Genesim*, but he erased the references when he revised the work after publication in 1623: for a discussion of the significance of this see W.L. Hine, 'Mersenne Variants', *Isis* vol.67 n.1 (1976), pp. 98–103.
[102] Ibid., p. 42.

ideology gave the development of new science its impetus,[103] new scholarship has fruitfully complicated and sharpened the link between Protestantism and natural philosophy. Further work, however, remains to be done in order to assess and explain the relevance of the contribution made by Catholic natural philosophers.[104] Among the many issues concerning the relationship between Protestant and Catholic theology and mechanist philosophy, I would like to briefly explore the role of the doctrines of predestination and free will in the context of the new science.

As far as the Protestant doctrine is concerned, Gary Deason has recently argued that while it is incorrect to affirm that the Reformation 'caused' the scientific Revolution, nevertheless 'Protestantism possessed qualities of thought and practice that had significant affinities with early modern science'. Among those 'qualities of thought', Deason underlines the Protestant notion of 'radical sovereignty' of God, which, in his view, provided an important background for the new mechanist philosophy. In other words, the fundamental assumption that the mechanist philosophers held against Aristotelianism, the fact that matter was passive, was not only compatible with, but was also reinforced by the Protestant theological view that God did not cooperate with Nature and with mankind.[105]

However, it has to be noted that during the seventeenth century a group of important natural philosophers, Gassendi, Mersenne, and White and Digby among them, tried to demonstrate with numerous and interesting arguments that the new mechanical science could find a 'naturally' fertile ground in *Catholic* theology, and, in particular, that it was perfectly compatible with the Catholic doctrine of free will.[106] As we have already seen, Digby introduced the question of free will as an important link between the world of physics, which works in a mechanical way, and the world of metaphysics, or the realm of the immortal souls. Men are somewhere in between the two worlds: they are part of matter, and yet they have a soul, and this double nature is the cause of both man's battle with his beastly instincts, and his capability to attain salvation. Moreover, men's capability of actually reflecting upon nature and their own soul makes them agents of that quasi-alchemical process of discovering the truth of the soul.

---

[103] C. Hill, *Intellectual Origins*.
[104] On the significance of the Catholic contribution to the new science, see for instance W.B. Ashworth Jr., 'Catholicism and Early Modern Science', in D.C. Lindberg and R.L. Numbers (eds.), *God and Nature. Historical Essays on the Encounter between Christianity and Science*, Berkeley 1986, pp. 136–166; W.A. Wallace, *Galileo, the Jesuits and the Medieval Aristotle*, Hampshire-Brookfield 1991; M. Feingold (ed.), *Jesuit science and the republic of letters*, Cambridge (Mass.) 2002; Id. (ed.), *The new science and Jesuit science: seventeenth century perspectives*, Dordrecht-London 2003. Concerning more specifically Thomas White's group see, together with B. Southgate's *'Covetous of the truth'*, also J. Henry, 'Atomism and Eschatology'.
[105] Gary B. Deason, 'Reformation Theology and the Mechanist Conception of Nature', in D.C. Lindberg and R.L. Numbers (eds.), *God and Nature*, pp. 167–191.
[106] For the significance of the relationship between mechanical philosophy and the doctrine of free will see also the considerations made by M.J. Osler on Gassendi's and Descartes' philosophy in her *Divine will and the mechanical philosophy*, pp. 80 and ff.

Thomas White concerned himself with the question of the free will in an even deeper way, and his belief in men's free will is one of the main pillars not only of his theology and natural philosophy, but also of his political theory, as we will see below. In his *Peripateticall Institutions* White explained the link between free will and mechanist theory by recourse to a version of the same voluntarist theology that we have seen in Gassendi:

> ….neither the Contingency of naturall causes, nor the Liberty of rationall Creatures is infring'd by this government of God. For, since Contingency is nothing else, but that the nature of the cause is such that it may and uses to be hundred, by other causes; and Liberty, that a Creature, upon the consideration of more proceeds to action: and, 'tis so manifest, that both these are in nature, and no waies touched by the operation of God (as that operation is explicated) that it needs only the remembring: 'tis clear, that the government of God is sweet, and offers no violence to the natures of naturall causes.[107]

According to White then, as God does not meddle with the 'Contingency of naturall causes', so he does not govern mankind directly and 'violently', but his 'sweet' government is reduced to men's 'remembring' that they were created 'to the Image of God, and to the Similitude of Angels', and therefore as free rational creatures, not subjected to the same natural causes to which nature is subjected.[108] Moreover, the very account in *Genesis* of the creation of Eve demonstrates that man had some sort of agency from the beginning:

> The sacred Authour adds, "But to Adam there was not found a helper like him": the primitive expression is, "And to the Man he found not a help as it were before him", or, as others explicate, "as it were against him". It appears, therefore, that the WOMAN was made, not out of the necessity of nature alone, but by the consent and will of Adam: God governing Man, a Reasonable Creature, by perswasion and induction, not by force and command; that is, according to the nature which he had given him.[109]

If we link all these elements of White's natural philosophy and natural theology together, we end up with a world that works according to the 'second causes' of mechanical philosophy. Since God willed it to be this way, and his government on the world is a 'sweet' one, there is no conflict between nature and theology, which remains the only way to understand what natural philosophy cannot and should not interpret. Moreover, in this world man is created by God as a rational creature, 'free' to act according to reason in order to attend the eternal Beatitude, and this again presents no contradiction with the providence of God, who created men 'to his image'.

In conclusion, it is not my intention here to revisit the debate over the confessional background in which the birth of the 'new science' took place; rather, I would like simply to emphasize that the notion of the passivity of matter did not necessarily require God's 'radical' sovereignty, or his lack

---

[107] T. White, *Peripateticall Institutions*, pp. 320–1.
[108] Ibid., pp. 373.
[109] Ibid., pp. 375–6.

of cooperation with nature *and* with man. In fact, Thomas White and his associates sought to build a system in which God could avoid meddling with nature, without ceasing his relationship with mankind altogether. White's natural philosophy and voluntarist theology, then, granting God a 'sweet sovereignty', save both the passivity of matter and the agency of human beings in their own salvation. The case of White's mix of theology and mechanist philosophy suggests to us that a promising way to look at the question of the theological background of the new science beyond the 'Merton thesis' could be to abandon a rigid confessional perspective, and to consider instead the different approaches and debate within each denomination. In other words, it seems potentially more fruitful for scholars to cease to oppose Protestantism to Catholicism tout court, and to look more carefully at the 'rational' theology of certain groups of both Catholics and Protestants, together with the debate that originated both within and across confessional boundaries.

CHAPTER 3

The Blackloists' Politics

3.1 The Beginning of the English Civil War: The Blackloists between Politics and Ecclesiology

During the 1640s Thomas White and the Blackloists were taken up not only with natural science and theology, but also with politics, in matters of both ecclesiology and secular policy. Together with Thomas White, the other member of the Blackloists most interested in the problem of Church government, and a central figure in those years, was Henry Holden.[1]

Holden was born in 1596 or 1597 to a well-to-do Catholic family. In 1618 he entered the College at Douai, and there he met Thomas White. Holden was ordained a priest in Cambrai in 1622, and left Douai the following year to join a small community founded by Richard Smith at Arras. In 1626, however, Holden asked Smith permission to take a post in the household of Michel de Marillac, Richelieu's finance minister. Among Marillac's friends and associates was also François de Harlay de Champvallon, the Gallican Archbishop of Rouen, with whom Holden was to collaborate later in his career. With Marillac's death, in 1633, Holden returned to Arras. Soon after, Holden returned to England, where he lived in Digby's house and where he met frequently with his old mentor White. In 1636 White and Holden traveled back to Paris together: Holden was to remain there for most of his career, first as a professor of divinity at the Sorbonne, and after 1659 as the first superior of the convent of the Order of the Immaculate Conception of Our Lady of Paris, to which he left most of his possessions upon his death, in 1662. While Paris was Holden's main geographical and intellectual reference point, he made frequent and important trips elsewhere in Europe. In the second half of the 1630s he was in Rome, where he was involved in the discussion over the status of the English Chapter, and over the question of Smith's succession. In the 1640s Holden returned for a while to England, and there he found once again White and Digby.

Up until the early 1640s, then, Holden's intellectual profile was shaped by two main influences. First, we need to take into account the impact on the English Catholic of the theology of Thomas White, who was his mentor in Douai and with whom he remained in close contact later on. Holden was specifically interested in the ecclesiological consequences of White's notion of tradition as a 'rational' and certain manner of establishing the rule of faith. If we assume that the most important mark of the truth of the Catholic religion

---

[1] I borrow this passage on Holden's biography from A.F. Allison, 'An English Gallican: Henry Holden, (1596/7–1662), Part I (to 1648)', *Recusant History*, n. 22 (1995), pp. 319–349, which remains the best account of the Catholic's early life and career.

is indeed the self-evident certainty of its continuity with the *primitiva Ecclesia* through transmission of tradition, a logical corollary is that the authority of the Pope, and, to a certain extent, the authority of the General Councils as well, lose their value in the context of the dogmatic complex of the Roman credo. The Blackloists however decided to concentrate their ecclesiological effort in limiting the authority of the Pope, which Thomas White did not merely shrink from an ecclesiological point of view, but which he questioned in some of its most central doctrinal aspects, as the Papal infallibility.[2]

Secondly, together with absorbing those theological and ecclesiological notions, which Holden was to interpret and systematize a decade later in his main theological work,[3] he gained first-hand experience of the politics of the Roman Court during his mission to Rome in the 1630s. While he was trying to negotiate for a suitable successor to Bishop Smith, Holden realized with extreme dissatisfaction that the Pope's authority was less an instrument to be used for a better government in the Church than a system of patronage and petty politics.[4]

Before theoretically systematizing their ecclesiological stances, the Blackloists had occasion to express them in the realm of secular politics, in a most interesting way.[5] While White and Holden were reflecting on the proper model of government for a Church whose foundational aspect, so to say, was its distinctive notion of tradition, the political turmoil of the English Civil War befell them. In this context they adapted their ecclesiological views to reach an agreement with the Independents between 1647 and 1648. In 1647 Holden, together with White, Digby and Peter Fitton, a Catholic theologian in Paris, drafted and proposed to the Independents an Oath that the English Catholics would have to swear in exchange for toleration.[6] At the beginning of the document, Holden stated clearly that the aim of the proposal was for the Catholics 'to live with the same freedom & enjoy the same liberty which the other free borne subiects of the Kingdom do, & which their naturall birth right seemes to challeng as due unto them'.[7] In Holden's perspective, therefore, the Parliament had to recognize the 'natural rights' of the Catholics, which were no different than those of a Protestant Englishman. But the Catholics had something that no Protestant had, namely, a fundamental allegiance to the Pope, which, as the history of England since at least Elizabeth's excommunication proved, was understood ambiguously as both a spiritual and a political bond.

---

[2] On this point see R.A. Jordan, 'The Blackloists', pp. 122 and ff., and A.J. Brown, 'Anglo-Irish Gallicanism, c.1635–1685' unpublished Ph.D. Thesis, University of Cambridge 2004, pp. 165–166.

[3] This is Holden's *Analysis Divinae Fidei*, published in Paris in Latin in 1652, and translated into English in 1658.

[4] See A.F. Allison, 'An English Gallican', pp. 325–327.

[5] Some of the points made in the following pages have been treated more extensively in S. Tutino, 'The Catholic Church and the English Civil War: the case of Thomas White', *The Journal of Ecclesiastical History* vol. 58 n. 2 (2007), pp. 232–255

[6] The text of the Oath can be found, among other documents related to the Blackloists, in R. Pugh, *Blacklo's Cabal*, pp. 36–40.

[7] Ibid., p. 36.

Therefore Holden wanted to reassure the Parliament that the political loyalty of the English Catholics was not in question, and in the very first paragraph of his proposal he declared:

> First let no forrain King, nor state be suffred to intercede or medle in the behalf of Catholicks, to the end the Catholicks may see their freedome doth only proceed from the Parliaments gratious disposition & willingnesse to settle universall liberty, & consequently that they are not to depend, nor hope, nor be obliged to none but them for their freedome.[8]

A declaration stating the English Catholics' unquestionable political allegiance to England, and excluding the possibility of asking for, and accepting any form of interference by any foreign state, addressed the political side of Holden's view of the role of the Catholics in England. Nevertheless, for the Catholic theologian, issues of foreign policy were not the only ones that needed to be addressed concerning the role of the Papacy for the English Catholic community. More profoundly, the relationship between the English Catholic Church and the Pope needed to be specified by reconsidering the hierarchical structure of the government of the Church of Rome. In other words, if the English Catholics wanted to separate themselves from the influence of Rome, they needed not only to swear their political allegiance to the English government, but also to define their ecclesiological position with respect to the authority of the Pope within their Church. In order to address this question, the proposal drafted by Holden introduced a drastic ecclesiological change. He and White suggested that English Catholics were to be governed by 'six or eyght Bishops more or less, by whom they may be governed in matters of Religion & conscience'. These Bishops were to be ordained by Parliament, and 'the Pope can have no Power over them to the preiudice of the state'. The Bishops, moreover, would have to 'acknowledge the Pope the first Bishop, & head of the Church; but not receive any of his commands without the leave of the state'.

Now for Holden there was nothing to prevent Parliament from accepting the English Catholics, once they had eliminated Papal authority both from their political horizon and from their ecclesiological structure. The Blackloists' proposal, however, was never discussed in Parliament, and in Rome it seemed to have been condemned, although no disciplinary action was taken against the Blackloists.[9]

John Bossy recognizes the ecclesiological relevance of Holden's plan, which in his view represented an attempt to 'effectively...sever the connection between the envisaged Catholic Church and the Pope'.[10] In Bossy's opinion, however, the fact that Holden and White were addressing the Independents is only a 'superficial' modification of the Catholic loyalist tradition, since they were not the only Catholics who tried to come to terms with the new regime. At the

---

[8] Ibid.
[9] See A.F. Allison, 'An English Gallican', pp. 335 and ff.
[10] J. Bossy, *The English Catholic Community*, p. 66.

same time as the Blackloist proposal was being drafted, another effort was being made by a section of the Catholic clergy to convince the Independents to grant a measure of toleration. The group included two members of the Society of Jesus – Henry More and George Ward – and a group of Catholic laity. As Thomas Clancy has outlined,[11] in 1647 these Catholic laymen and clergy elaborated two slightly different proposals for another Oath to be taken by English Catholics in exchange for toleration. In this formula English Catholics were to swear that the Pope had no power to release anyone from their obedience to the Civil Government, no matter whether or not the sovereign was Catholic. In addition to that, the version of the Oath proposed by the clergymen contained a preface in which it was specified that the Oath was conditional upon the Parliament granting toleration.[12] The proposed Oath, in other words, denied the doctrine of the *potestas papalis in temporalibus*, both *directa* and *indirecta:* for that reason it was condemned by the Roman hierarchy before it could actually reach and be discussed in Parliament.

We do not know exactly what happened to the clergy involved in the proposal, but we do know that they were severely punished.[13] In particular the two Jesuits, Henry More and George Ward, were sent into exile in the Low Countries. On 4 April 1648 the Nuncio in Bruxelles wrote to the Holy Office that after he had communicated Rome's decision on the Oath to Henry More, who was at the time in Ghent, the Jesuit, after trying to justify himself, 'submitting himself with the utmost prudence, said he would obey and humbly conform himself to that decree'.[14] More's submission does not seem to have been successful, for he remained in Ghent until at least 1649.[15]

On the 8th of October the same Nuncio in Bruxelles communicated to the Holy Office that William Penry *alias* Father Eliseus, the Carmelite who had signed the Oath, submitted himself to the decision of the Inquisition. The Nuncio enclosed a petition from the Superior of the Carmelites (who had given Eliseus a pardon for his involvement) to Cardinal Spada, a member of the commission that eventually condemned the Oath, in order to obtain an additional pardon from Rome for Penry.[16] We do not know what the Roman See decided in Penry's case.

In my opinion, however, Holden and White's approach to the Independents is utterly different in scope and nature from More and Ward's. As I have mentioned, the proposal of Ward and More was careful to stress the fact that the formula denying the Pope the authority to exonerate a subject from his

---

[11] T.H. Clancy S.J., 'The Jesuits and the Independents: 1647', *AHSI*, vol.xl (1971), pp. 67–89.

[12] Ibid., pp. 76–8.

[13] For a discussion on the fate of the seculars see A.F. Allison, 'An English Gallican', pp. 339 and ff.

[14] [massime essendosi con molta prudenza sottomesso, et detto di obbedire et conformarsi a quel Decreto con ogni humilta]: see ACDF, St. St., SS 1-e, ff. 524r–v.

[15] See Clancy, 'The Jesuits and the Independents', pp. 85–6. The correspondence between Henry More and Vincenzo Carrafa, the Jesuit General, during More's exile can be found in ARSI, Provincia Angliae, Epp. Gen. II, 1 (1642–1698), ff. 105 and ff.

[16] ACDF, St.St. SS 1-e, ff. 528r–534v.

civil allegiance was conditional upon Parliament agreeing to grant toleration, in which case there would have never been an actual possibility of conflict between the Pope and the English government.[17] Besides, when More and Ward themselves appealed their sentence, they repeated that their proposed Oath was intended to be taken *after* toleration had been granted.[18]

Even the reaction of the Holy See to the Jesuit proposal shows its 'contingent' nature. In autumn 1647 a commission of theologians was appointed to examine the Oath, and ended by approving it. Particularly telling in this respect are the reasons for approval given by Antonio Perez:

> Since no external profession contrary to the Catholic faith is demanded of Catholics, and they are not required to perform any action that they cannot legitimately perform, nor are they required to cease performing any action that they are supposed to perform, *especially in these circumstances, in which a great danger is imminent*, I do not doubt that Catholics can approve these propositions. And it is not difficult to show parallel cases from Scriptures, and from antiquity and the custom of the Church. Even Jesus Christ himself was silent on many matters, leaving discussion of them to a more appropriate time... Popes themselves have prohibited public disputations of matters of Faith, even to learned laymen. Indeed a general proclamation of our faith demands a proper calculation to negotiate its places, times, persons, and the like, around which prohibitions and pledges can be made without harm to our faith.[19]

Perez, in other words, was allowing the text of the Oath to be interpreted in an 'equivocal' sense[20], given the dangerous situation. The text did not impose any external profession openly contrary to the Catholic religion, and 'in his circumstantiis', in a moment of great necessity, that was enough ground to allow Catholics to swear it, since even Christ is said to have 'equivocated', reserving some matters for more appropriate times. Less than a month after the approval, another commission of the Inquisition, under the direction of Cardinal De Lugo (one of the participants in the previous commission, which had approved the Oath) reversed the initial approval and decided to condemn

---

[17] T.H. Clancy, 'The Jesuits and the Independents', p. 78.
[18] Ibid., p. 85.
[19] [Cum nulla his exigatur a Catholicis professio externa contraria professioni fidei Catholicae, neque ulla actio, quam licite praestare non possint, neque cessatio ab ulla actione, quam teneantur praestare, *praesertim in his circumstantiis, in quibus imminet maius periculum*, non dubito, quin possint Catholici has admittere conditiones. Neque esset difficile ostendere ex sacra scriptura et ex antiquitate et usu Ecclesiae, similia esse observata. Ipse etiam Christus multa tacuit, reservans eorum declarationem ad tempus opportunius ... Ipsi etiam Pontifices prohibuerunt Laicis etiam doctis disputationes publicas de rebus fidei. Nam publicatio nostrae fidei mixta rectam rationem petit sua loca, tempora, personas et modum agendi, circa quae possunt fieri prohibitiones et obligationes sine detrimento fidei] ARSI, Anglia 34, ff. 119v–120v, at f. 120r–v. My italics. Hereafter, unless otherwise noted, all italics are in the original text.
[20] On the doctrine of equivocation see J.P. Sommerville, 'The "new art of lying": equivocation, mental reservation, and casuistry', in E. Leites (ed.), *Conscience and Casuistry in Early Modern Europe*, Cambridge 1988, pp. 159–184; and P. Zagorin, in *Ways of Lying. Dissimulation, Persecution, and Conformity in Early Modern Europe*, Cambridge (Mass.) 1990, pp. 163–185.

the Oath. The reason was that, notwithstanding the present emergency, the proposed Oath was very similar to the Oath of Allegiance of 1606, which had been condemned by the Holy See: concluding any agreement in such a way was prejudicial to the authority of the Pope.[21] Finally, the attempt by More and Ward was largely forgotten, and it had no impact on the future story of the English Civil War.

By contrast, behind the Blackloist attempt there were much more important issues at stake. Their proposal represented an attempt to unify their anti-papalist – if not properly Conciliarist – model of government of the Catholic Church together with an original interpretation of the Gallican model of relationship between Church and State.

In a nutshell, the central principle and starting point for Gallicanism was, in Bouswma's definition, 'that Christendom properly consisted not of a unified, hierarchically organized system, but of discrete and parallel entities'.[22] That meant that the government of the Church was not centred hierarchically on the Papacy: rather, the localized and independent authority of the Bishops constituted the true source of authority. On a different level, since the main concern of the Gallicans was precisely to distinguish between ecclesiological and spiritual issues, another important corollary was the sharpening of the separation between secular and temporal jurisdiction. In other words, the Papacy could not influence the politics of the French sovereign state, because the Pope was only the chief spiritual authority of the Catholic Church. It was up to the Bishops, then, to negotiate with the state.[23] As for Holden's proposal, on the one hand it represented a mix between the Blackloists' theology of tradition with its anti-papalist consequences, and the Gallican concern for the need of distinguishing the areas of jurisdiction of the State and the Church. On the other hand, Holden and White had adapted those Gallican themes in the English context, in which since at least the Pope's excommunication of Queen Elizabeth in 1570, the question of Papal authority had been the main point of contention for those who declared it impossible to grant any form of toleration to the English Catholics, since their allegiance to the Pope precluded their loyalty as subjects to any temporal sovereign. The Blackloist plan, then, represented both the practical result of their mixture of theology and ecclesiology, and a uniquely English solution – albeit with a French twist – to the uniquely English problem of how to integrate the Catholic minority into the English state.[24]

---

[21] ARSI, Anglia 34, ff.186r–189v. The condemnation was ratified again in another meeting of the Congregation of the Holy Office, on the 10th of January 1648: see ACDF, St.St. SS 2-b, unfoliated.

[22] W.J. Bouswma, 'Gallicanism and the Nature of Christendom', in A. Molho and J.A. Tedeschi (eds.), *Renaissance. Studies in Honor of Hans Baron*, Florence 1970, pp. 809–830, at p. 815. See also V. Martin, *Le Gallicanisme et la réforme catholique*, Paris 1919, and Id., *Les origines du Gallicanisme*, Paris 1939.

[23] See W.A. Bouswma, 'Gallicanism', pp. 818 and ff.; and A.G. Martimort, *Le Gallicanisme de Bossuet*, Paris 1953, pp. 84 and ff.

[24] On this point see the consideration made by A.J. Brown, 'Anglo-Irish Gallicanism', pp. 48 and ff. *passim*.

Even if the Blackloists' proposal was never discussed in Parliament, Oliver Cromwell did seem to take them seriously in the late 1640s. As Jeffrey Collins has recently demonstrated, there is evidence of a 'Blackloist conspiracy' in 1648–1649: the Blackloists were negotiating with Cromwell, offering their help with the Irish situation in exchange for toleration. The negotiations ended in 1649–50, when Cromwell decided to deal with Ireland by force, thus needing no further help from the Blackloists.[25] Nonetheless, the relationship between Cromwell and the Blackloists did not end in 1650; rather, White and his associates had an important role during the Protectorate as well, as we will see below.

Once we establish that the Blackloists' dealings with the Independents were profoundly different in nature from those of the Jesuit More and Ward, and once we demonstrate their significance in the realm of the history of ideas, i.e. the novelty of their mixture of French Gallicanism and anti-papalism in the English context, it remains to be seen whether or not the fact that the Blackloists were proposing their interesting mixture to the Independents is indeed significant. In other words, is there a reason why the Blackloists saw in the Independents, and later in Cromwell, the most fitting counterpart for their model of 'Catholicism without the Pope'? Could they have acted in the same way with the King? The answer to this question is extremely complex, for not every member of the Blackloist group approached the Independents for the same reasons. And that is why I am going to proceed by examining the motivations of Thomas White, Henry Holden and Kenelm Digby separately, in order to understand more profoundly the differences among them, but also the elements that brought them together in their political involvements. Incidentally, a close scrutiny of the Blackloists' individual motives and distinct intellectual, religious and political concerns, as well as of the elements that can be correctly ascribed to the whole group, is a way of proceeding that, I believe, should always be used when dealing with the English Catholics, and more specifically, when dealing with the political role of the English Catholics in England.

3.2 Kenelm Digby: A Catholic Political Acrobat

Let us start with Kenelm Digby, who, among the three Blackloists, had more 'hands-on' political experience. We left Digby in Paris in 1644, when he was part of the household of Queen Henrietta Maria. How and why did he go from there to flirting with the Independents?

In 1645 the Queen sent Sir Kenelm Digby to Rome, in an effort to convince the Pope to confirm the English Chapter and to help the King financially. In order to obtain the much-needed financial aid, Digby argued his case by claiming that 'his [i.e. the King's] request would benefit the Catholic faith not only in that realm, but in all Europe, since the King's gains and losses are

---

[25] J.R. Collins, 'Thomas Hobbes and the Blackloist conspiracy of 1649', *Historical Journal*, vol.xlv (2002), pp. 305–331.

very strictly connected with the gains and losses of the true religion'.[26] On the one hand, Digby's arguments were based on the link between Parliament and anti-Catholicism. For instance, Digby had stated that the war against the King originated with the rumour that Charles wanted to introduce the Roman religion in England, and he reported that the King himself had never tried completely to eradicate Catholicism, as Parliament intended to do. On the other hand, Digby referred to the link between Catholicism and absolutism in a 'quasi-Machiavellian' manner: 'it is easier to convert a Monarchy to the faith than a Republic, for the former depends upon the will of one man, which is easier to bend, and the latter upon the will of a multitude'.[27]

Unfortunately for Digby, the Roman hierarchy did not share his belief in the link between Catholicism and the King's cause. In an anonymous report[28] on Digby's attempts to lobby in favour of the Queen and on the Roman reaction to the mission, we read that Thomas Courtney,[29] a member of the Society of Jesus and from 1620 Praefectus Studiorum at the English College in Rome, had advised Digby to proceed with caution: in a time of persecution it was dangerous for Rome to do anything openly in favour of the King and of the hierarchy of the English secular clergy. As for Parliament's supposedly aggressive attitude towards the Catholics, this was only a strategic move needed to gain public support against the King, 'in order to lead the people to believe that the King was going to convert, so as to confirm them [the people] in their rebellion'.[30] In this scenario, in conclusion, it would have been better 'd'andar adaggio et aspettare congiunture piu' opportune' [to go slowly and to wait for more propitious times]. The Pope himself, when he had to take a decision on Digby's request, asked the same Courtney for advice, and, convinced by the Jesuit's argument, suggested Digby to wait before taking any action to see how the situation evolved.[31]

Digby went back to England empty-handed, but in 1647 he returned to Rome again: this time the situation looked much worse for the English monarchy, and the Queen desperately needed money. This time, however, Digby used very different arguments to plead his case. If in 1645 helping the Queen meant for Digby helping the philo-Catholic Royalist faction to overcome the viscerally anti-Catholic Parliament, this time helping the Queen meant favouring a peaceful resolution of the conflict. As Digby explained to the Pope in an

---

[26]   [.. la sua richiesta tornerebbe in benefizio della fede Cattolica, non solo in quei Regni, ma in tutta l'Europa, essendo gli avantaggi, e perdite del Re strettissimamente collegati con l'avantaggi, e perdite della vera religione]; ARSI, Anglia 34, Letter from Digby to the Pope, s.l., 1645, ff. 22r–28r, at f. 24r.

[27]   [e' piu' facile che si converta alla fede una Monarchia, che una Repubblica, dipendendo quello dalla volonta' di uno solo, che agevolmente si muta, e questa dalli pareri di molti]; Ibid., f.25r.

[28]   ARSI, Anglia 34, ff. 31r–35v, undated, but written before 1647.

[29]   On Courtney see T.M. McCoog S.J. (ed.), *Monumenta Angliae: English and Welsh Jesuits*, 3 vols, Roma 1992, vol. ii, p. 277.

[30]   [per far credere al popolo, ch'il Re volesse mutar religione, e confermarlo nella ribellione], ARSI, Anglia 34, ff. 32r–33v.

[31]   Ibid., ff. 33r and ff.

address that he presented at the end of his mission,[32] a profound rift seemed to have opened within the Parliamentarians between the Independents and the Presbyterians:

> At the time of the Revolt of the Army under the command of General Fairfax, the two most potent and contrary Factions of the Independents and Presbyterians came to clash and fall foul upon each other, both of them casting an eye upon the English Catholic party, and upon the Confederats of Ireland, considering in them, the forces they had intrinsecall and proper, or rather intrinsecal and foreign with intention to grant them a free and secure exercise of the Catholic faith, in case they cou'd make them sound assurances that they were able to be of use to then, and wou'd prove their faithful friends in this conjuncture. The Queen concluded, that having obtain'd a considerable summ of money, and being strongly upheld by the Apostolic See, she might under the forces of the Catholics so considerable, that instead of receaving, she might in a short time give Laws and conditions to the sayd Factions, with all cautelous provisions and security which human Reason cou'd consider.[33]

Both the Queen and the Pope, for Digby, had to take advantage of this scenario in which both factions were 'casting an eye upon the English Catholic party'. In practice, that meant that the most desirable strategy, toward which both the Queen and the Pope should have been working, was to conclude 'a new treaty of accommodation…with the inclining Independents', and if the Pope had agreed to invest a reasonable amount of money in the English affairs, he would have succeeded in rendering 'the King and the Catholic party the more considerable to the sayd Independents'.[34] The outcome of a direct and financially significant participation of the Pope, in Digby's opinion, would have been both the re-establishment of peace in England, and liberty of conscience for the English Catholics.

In 1647 then Digby started to see the practical impossibility of both the triumph of the Royalist cause, and the conversion to Catholicism of the King and the English nation. In this situation, the scenario that Digby thought most desirable was a form of toleration granted to the English Catholics by a sort of coalition formed by the Queen and the Independents, financed with the Pope's help. In order for the English Catholics to be granted 'a free and secure exercise' of their faith, however, the Pope's money was not the only thing needed. Most importantly, the English Catholics needed to reassure the political establishment of their loyalty to their nation. As Digby wrote to the Pope in his 1647 relation, Queen Henrietta Maria had done everything that she could to root out the link between Catholics and treason:

> From the first moment her Majesty sett foot in England, she understood that the most rigorous Laws made in the times of the predecessors of the present King Charles her husband and my sovereign against the Catholics

---

[32] The document, entitled 'The negotiation of Sir Kenelm Digby in Rome, 1647', can be found in Westminster Archives Mss., vol. XXX, document n.100, ff. 315–334.
[33] Ibid., ff. 321–22.
[34] Ibid., f. 331.

were founded on a vehement suspect and jealousy …That the Popes of Rome had no other aym, than under the pretense of Religion, to maintain and countenance a party of English Catholics within that Kingdom, which shou'd be ready on all occasions to lend an hand to foreign forces which shou'd be ready to be emploid, under color of restoring the ancient Faith, to despoil the natural Prince of his Dominions. Thereupon the Queen my Mistresse us'd her best endeavors, and the most favorable conjunctures to efface from the mind of the King and the principal of his Council, those sinister Conceits, and to perswade them that the Popes of Rome and English Catholics were most averse from such thoughts'[35]

Now it was time for the Pope to help the Queen, by contributing to eradicate any suspicion against the political loyalty of the English Catholics. First of all, according to Digby, the Pope needed to cease to foster division in Britain. In particular, Digby asked the Pope to intervene in Ireland, where the Papal Nuncio, Monsignor Rinuccini, instead of working towards 'an establishment and securing of liberty of Conscience for the Irish Confederats & together with it, a meliorating the condition of the English Catholics', 'has infus'd a belief into the world that he had some private and occult instructions to change the government in Ireland, and to separate that Island from the Crown of England'.[36]

In addition to removing Rinuccini, there was another decision that the Pope needed to make in order to facilitate the integration of the English Catholic Church: the confirmation of the Dean and Chapter of the English clergy, which would have contributed to 'the well ordering and subsistence of a body so illustrious and deserving as is that of the English clergy'. And the reason why the Pope, in Digby's opinion, needed to strengthen the Chapter was that the seculars, unlike the Jesuits, did not 'under pretence of Religion' try to subvert the political state, but could fit with any political regime, since they did not threaten any.[37]

From the analysis of this document there are two elements that shed some light on Digby's political involvement. First of all, there is an undeniable element of political opportunism. In the space of two years, from 1645 to 1647, Kenelm Digby had seen the balance of power shift, and the cause of Parliament become stronger. In this situation, he found he needed to change his own position, and to support the possibility of an agreement with Parliament. That is why in 1647, as an Agent of the Queen, he was presenting a possible treaty with the Independents as the best solution for both the English Catholics and the Queen. But we have to remember that in parallel with his Roman mission, Digby was directly involved in the proposed draft of an agreement between the Independents and the Catholics which White and Holden were preparing and which the Queen knew nothing about. In a letter that Digby wrote to Holden in 1647, immediately after seeing the draft of the Oath, the Catholic had suggested to his associate to 'close with the Independents. Make them see

---

[35] Ibid., ff. 317–318.
[36] Ibid., ff. 323–326.
[37] Ibid., ff. 331–334.

their interest to strengthen themselves, by union with Catholick party, which may adhere with them, when after the Parliament & Army dissolved, the Presbiterian will grow too hard for them'. As for the Queen, Digby continued, 'under your [i.e.Holden's] direction I should hope, that the interest I have with the now ruling persons, & such little knowledge as I have in affaires of the world, & particularly of this nature myght produce some good'.[38] Digby, therefore, considered his service to her less as his first and foremost priority, than as a means to obtain that agreement with the Independents. To a certain extent, therefore, Digby felt committed to the Queen as long as this proved feasible. And in 1647 he thought that an agreement with the Parliament was both feasible and desirable for both himself and the Queen. This does not mean that once the interest of the Queen diverged from his own, Digby would have necessarily decided to remain loyal to Henrietta. At the end of the 1640s Digby's trapeze act was a dangerous one, and in fact events moved too fast for Digby to avoid a free fall. After 1649, the Parliament, who saw Digby as irreparably compromised with the Crown, sent him into exile and confiscated his property. In these circumstances the Catholic did not show any scruples in begging for Cromwell's favour, which he eventually obtained, by downplaying the nature of his service to the Queen – he explained that his post as Agent in Rome was an employment taken because of 'extreme necessity, to be able to live himselfe, and to give his Children bread'.[39]

However, if Digby was certainly an opportunist as far as his political allegiances were concerned, it would be a mistake to reduce his political experience to personal ambition. Even when changing masters, in fact, Digby remained constant in one matter, that is to say, his commitment to the Catholic cause, which he did not deny even in the 1650s, after he had gained Cromwell's favour and was allowed back into England. We have seen that in 1647 the Catholic diplomat urged Holden to 'close with the Independents', and declared himself willing to use his contacts with the Crown in order to 'produce some good'. But of what good was he speaking? Not only his own: rather, Digby thought that a treaty with the Independents was the best solution also for the English Catholic community. As he wrote in the same letter, 'I should not care whom I displeased, so I compassed the Catholicks just endes'.[40]

While Digby's commitment to the Roman faith remained constant between the end of the 1640s and the 1650s, the model of Catholicism that he defended did, however, change. As Digby became more and more influenced by the Blackloist ecclesiological model, he became convinced that it was not Parliament that was the main enemy for the possibility of granting toleration to the Catholic Church à la Thomas White, but the Papacy. During his Roman sojourn Digby had in fact experienced, like the rest of the Blackloists, that the Papacy, instead of providing for a better government of the Catholic Church,

---

[38] Digby to Holden, Rome 7 October 1647, in *Blacklo's Cabal*, p. 53.
[39] See the declaration for the Parliament which Digby sent from Paris, 27 March 1652, in Ibid., pp. 83–88, at p. 85.
[40] Digby to Holden, Rome 7 October 1647, in Ibid., p. 53.

and of the English Catholic Church specifically, was instead trying to promote its own political agenda. As Digby put it in 1647, 'In such cases they [i.e. the members of the Court of Rome] consider not us, but their owne sordid ends'.[41] If Rome had had the interest of the English Catholics in mind, the Pope would not have refused the proposal of agreement between the Queen and the Independents that Digby presented in 1647, nor would the Pope have refused to grant confirmation to the English Chapter.

It is precisely Digby's religious agenda, together with his career ambition, that can explain how he could almost effortlessly transform himself from a staunch Royalist until the mid-1640s, to somebody in favour of the compromise in 1647, to somebody very comfortable in Cromwell's regime during the 1650s. In other words, the peculiar kind of Catholicism in which Digby had come to believe did not require a distinctive form of political government, but could easily fit into either monarchy or republic. For this reason, Digby did not see any contradiction in his dealings with the Crown and the Parliament for the sake of the English Catholics. And this kind of Catholicism which Digby upheld was the mixture of the Blackloists' ecclesiological positions we have examined, and of Digby's own personal understanding of a 'rational', 'scientific' religion. All this needs to be put in a confessional perspective insofar as for Digby there was no doubt that the Catholic religion was the only true one. Nevertheless, Digby's long and close collaboration with important Protestant philosophers and theologians – not to mention his own, although brief, experience as a Protestant convert between 1630 and 1635 – led him to believe in the possibility of coexistence of the true religion with other, albeit less true, ones.

In this respect a very interesting document, left in manuscript, is Digby's outline for a political treatise he was never to write.[42] In it Digby indicated the main theses and arguments that he intended to present in the twenty-two chapters the treatise was supposed to comprise. The text's main thesis, and possibly title, was 'that it belongeth in chiefe unto the office of a supreme Governour, to make his subjects bee of good life'. The secular perspective, however, immediately shifts, for the very first chapter was to argue 'that, if there be a life beyond this life; the government is mainely defective, which aymeth not to make the people fitt for it'. By this Digby meant that the governor had to encourage the pursuit of those activities which 'made people fit' for the next life as well as for this one, and to discourage those who did not. As for the former, the only necessary element that the governor needed to enforce was what Digby simply defined as 'Vertue': 'if vertue maketh mans life in this world sweete unto him; the government is mainely defective, which aymeth not to make the subiect vertuous'. By 'vertue' Digby did not mean a theologically specific set of notions, but rather the understanding that every institution, decision, activity in this life needed to be considered in light of the next one. Without this transcendent perspective, in fact, most of the things

---

[41] Digby to Fitton, Rome 30 October 1647, in Ibid., pp. 45–46.
[42] The document, entitled 'Outline of a tract by Digby', can be found in BL, Additional Mss. 41846, ff. 178r–179v.

that made this life pleasurable lost any significance, as for instance 'eating, women, sporting'.[43] The same virtue was necessary, in Digby's mind, for one to be 'a good Common-weale man', because it was virtue that suggested that every individual subject employ himself in those distinctive activities that were needed in society. Among those activities, 'the inventions, arising from Geometry, Physikes, or Alchymy and Agriculture, are the greatest defence and utility to the common wealth, that is imaginable'.[44]

Digby was not by any means a political theorist, and it would be incorrect to ascribe to him any sort of systematic political thinking, nevertheless this fragment clearly shows some of the features that I have underlined before. It was not the task of the governor to enforce any distinctive confession, but rather he needed to instil in his subjects' minds the certainty of a life after this one, and to make it possible for them to reach it. 'Vertue', then, is not only the most important task of a ruler, but also the only criterion by which he should be judged. Also to be noted in this outline is Digby's emphasis on the role of natural science in contributing to the good of the commonwealth, and furthermore, the mention of alchemy in this context. And this demonstrates not only the depth of Digby's alchemical interests, but also the extent to which the Catholic's notion of religion owed to his interests in the realm of philosophy and natural science. Again, while Catholicism was the true faith, many other confessions shared the same interest for a religion that was not necessarily in conflict with alchemy.

In conclusion, Digby's political experience is a complex mixture of personal ambition and religious concerns. The religion in question was obviously Catholicism, but a peculiar kind of Catholicism, which, even if it remained the only true faith, was nevertheless open to the possibility of coexistence with other religions, provided that they manifested the same 'rational' character that Digby's Catholicism had. From a political point of view, Digby came to believe that Catholicism was not intrinsically tied to either the English Crown, or the Parliament: Henrietta Maria was surely Catholic, but that did not mean that even a Protestant member of Parliament could not find possible and desirable an agreement with the Catholics. And that because for Digby English Catholics had a proper political space in the English political debates, and a highly valuable one at that, because of their 'international network', so to say, which was part and parcel of the very nature of the *catholic* religion. Digby, who had occasion to travel through the Mediterranean in his youth, and to discover the world of maritime trade, was convinced of the importance of the Catholics in this respect, and also of the importance of an alliance with England for the Pope. As he explained to the Pope, on the one hand any Protestant faction in England could have used the international cachet that came of an alliance with Rome: 'the Pope appearing and interesting himself in this affair as the vicar of Christ, rever'd of all the Princes of Christendom, They [i.e. the Parliamentarians] might justly fear he wou'd overwhelm them with

---

[43] Ibid., f. 178r.
[44] Ibid., f. 178v.

Warres on every side'.[45] On the other hand, maintaining a close relationship with England could prove extremely useful for the Pope,

> for England being so vastly powefull at Sea, and by Land also, when it enjoys the benefit of its own forces (the violent and distracted condition under which it now groans, not being likely to continue always) it may at its own pleasure (as it has always bene) ballance the forces of other Monarchies and States, yea and turn the Seale to what side soever it inclines. And as we have seen the King of Denmark elected one of the Mediators of Peace at the Treaty of Munster, so may it also happen to the Crown of England; and in that case of how great iportance wou'd a good correspondence with it prove, for the establishing of an universall peace with honor and advantage to the Apostolic See.[46]

This friendly and mutually beneficial relationship between Rome and London was possible precisely because it was inserted in the realm of foreign politics: in other words, the Papacy and England were two sovereign states, and the former had no right to claim any jurisdiction over the latter by means of the faith of the English Catholics. Rather, it was as if the English Catholics had a special line of communication with Rome, while being as faithful subjects to the English regime as any Protestant could be. Conversely, any trace of the 'Jesuitical' way of proceeding needed to be erased from the mind of the English Catholics: their Church was not in any sense antagonist to the English state, only tremendously helpful.

3.3 Henry Holden: A Gallican in England

If Digby was especially invested in the question of how to find a place for the English Catholics in the English political scenario – and in the process Digby tried to find a place for himself as well –, Henry Holden's motivations for approaching the Independents were significantly different. Unlike Digby, Holden had no personal investment in England: he did not want to move there, because he was happy in Paris, where he had found a profoundly congenial intellectual environment. He was not even particularly interested in the English politics as such, as we will see in a moment. Rather, the question that interested Holden then, and that will continue to interest him for the rest of his life, concerned the internal dynamics of power within the Catholic Church.

In the correspondence between Holden and the rest of the Blackloists, in fact, Holden's impatience towards the complicated political game of chess that his associates were playing with the Queen and the Parliamentarians appears clearly. In 1647 Holden wrote to the Digby that he was not in a position to make a sound judgement on England's political situation and its outcomes: 'The Presbiterians may make a head, the Independents may be divided, & many

---

[45] 'The negotiations of Sir Kenelm Digby', f. 320.
[46] Ibid., f. 322.

other things may be which I fore see not, I can only confesse my ignorance'.[47] By contrast, Holden considered it his task to move against the 'court of Rome', and in particular the Pope, who by claiming an illegitimate authority over the English clergy was sabotaging any attempt at improving the situation of the whole Catholic community in England. The question of the government of the English clergy, and of its relationship with political authority, was for Holden less a matter concerning the delicate political circumstances in England, than the local manifestation of a deeper and wider ecclesiological clash within the Catholic Church. He and his associates were fighting against the usurped authority of the Pope in matters that were of exclusive competence of the Bishops: they were the ultimate source of authority within the 'national' Church, and, as such, the only ones who should be dictating conditions in negotiations with political power. On the other side of this war there were the Blackloists' enemies, neither the King nor the Independents, but those among the English clergy who supported the (according to Holden usurped) prerogatives of the Papacy. Indeed, those English priests were so much dependent on Rome that '[they] will never dare to close stool without a Breve from Rome'.[48]

If for Holden the problems of the English Catholic Church were part of a larger question involving the whole ecclesiological structure of the Roman Church, the solution to those problems could also be found outside of England. The same year in which he drafted the proposed Oath, in fact, Holden wrote a question to be proposed to the faculty of theology of the Sorbonne, in which he complained that the Pope was systematically refusing to appoint a Bishop to England notwithstanding the many requests received in this respect. The excuse that the Pope was providing for not appointing Bishops, Holden declared, was that such an appointment would have constituted a testimony of alliance with the Parliament of England, whereas in reality the lack of a stable local hierarchy in England in effect meant that the Pope had decided to neglect the interests of 'saecentum & amplius Sacerdotibus saecularibus, & millium aliquod Catholicis Laicis'. In this situation, Holden asked the Sorbonne whether or not it was lawful for the English Catholics to ask to the French Bishops to do the job, in the name of the interests of the universal Church.[49] Even if Holden's question did not seem to have been formally discussed at the Sorbonne, nevertheless it prompted a significant reaction in France. Indeed, Harlay the Champvallon, the Gallican Archbishop of Rouen and Holden's friend since the 1630s, had proposed his own candidacy for the post, and Mazarin, who was then interested in maintaining a friendly relationship with the Pope Innocent X, had declared himself ready to help the Pope in his dealings with the English Catholics by making sure that no Frenchman collaborated with them.[50]

---

[47] Holden to Digby, 6 September 1647, in *Blacklo's Cabal*, pp. 26–7, at p. 27.
[48] Ibid.
[49] The text of Holden's question was included in a letter that he sent to Digby on August 30th 1647, in Ibid., pp. 24–5
[50] For details on Holden's question and on the reaction that it provoked in France see A.F. Allison, 'An English Gallican', pp. 334 and ff.

In the context of the present study, Holden's question to the Sorbonne is a useful document in that it shows clearly the extent of the influence of Gallicanism in the English Catholic. From a theoretical point of view, Holden's document was based on the Gallican principle according to which the Pope was in charge of appointing Bishops on behalf of the universal Church, by whose consent he was granted the authority of appointing them in the first place. On a different level, by actually inviting the French Bishops to take charge of the Church in England, Holden was in practice applying directly the French solutions to the English Catholic Church.

In conclusion, if Digby had absorbed and modified some of the central issues of the Gallican-influenced ecclesiology of the Blackloists by including them in a different package, which was influenced by his peculiar theological views and his direct involvement in the specific dynamics of English political struggle; for Holden, on the contrary, the English situation was but a reflection of the same questions which the Catholic Church in France had to face, and to which Gallicanism had provided the answer. Holden's proposal of actually having French Bishops sitting in for the English ones is, as it were, a concrete symbol of precisely this operation. In this respect, Allison is certainly correct in defining Holden an 'English Gallican': he thought that what the English Catholic Church really needed was French Bishops, who could have then made sure to negotiate with the political power in the terms that Holden had already envisioned in his proposal.

On a different level, Holden's view of the political situation of the English Catholics as a part of a larger question involving the ecclesiological structure of the Catholic Church had some interesting cross-confessional consequences. In particular, during the negotiations with the Independents Holden collaborated with William Grant, a Protestant Churchman who at the beginning of the 1640s had gotten into trouble for his vocal anti-Puritanism and for the 'Papistical' flavour of some of the ceremonies that he performed.[51] Holden asked Grant for his opinion on what the Protestant government really needed in order to grant toleration to the Catholics, and, as Allison shows, he incorporated some of

---

[51] We do not know much about William Grant, aside from the accusations made against him while he was vicar of Istleworth. In 1641 Grant was accused by his parishioners of accepting £10 per year for a lecturer, whom he later fired without returning the payment, and also for being openly anti-Puritan, maintaining the book of Sports, speaking against the doctrine of predestination, and for allowing some 'Papist' practices such as encouraging confessions and having images of saints in the church. In his reply to his parishioners' petition, Grant denied some of the allegations (for instance he denied speaking against the doctrine of predestination and maintaining the lawfulness of images in church) and mitigated some others. For example, on his alleged opinion against clerical marriage, he replied: 'Not unlikely but I have; neither know I, as yet any reason, why should I recant it: for, for my part, I know not (as yet) any thing that makes more to the undoing of Clergy men, or other ...that will bring more misery upon them, than the estate of wedlock rashly runne into, before there be sufficient meanes to support it': see W. Grant, *The vindication of the Vicar of Istleworth, in the County of Middlesex*, s.l. 1641, pp. 9–10. On Grant see C. Hill, *Society and Puritanism in Pre-Revolutionary England*, London 1964, pp. 111, 485.

Grant's suggestions in his 1647 proposal.[52] Holden's relationship with Grant was not dictated simply by the contingencies of the political situation, but it was founded upon Grant's interest for Holden's ecclesiological stances, as is demonstrated by the fact that Grant was the author of the English translation of Holden's *Divinae Fidei Analysis,* which was published in 1658.[53]

Grant's interest in Holden's Gallicanism is highly significant: the prerogatives of the Gallican Church had been in fact a central argument in the theological and ecclesiological debates within the Church of England in the 1620s and 1630s. Some important figures of the Laudian Church, most notably Richard Montagu, had used the Gallican Church as both an example of Catholicism that had successfully separated itself from Rome and as a possible model of the relationship between the Church of Rome and the Church of England. Montagu's use of the Gallican case, therefore, was on the one hand a polemical tool used to highlight the dichotomy between the 'bad' Catholics, i.e. the Jesuits, and the 'good ones'. On the other hand, it was used as a 'positive' example of a Church which had succeeded in being both 'Catholic and Reformed', as well as an indication of a possible way for the Church of England to reconcile itself with Rome while retaining its own ecclesiological and doctrinal independence.[54]

Now, to see the Gallican Church once again on the map of Protestant debate well into the 1650s is a testimony of how profound for the Church of England was the question of its relationship with Rome, and it would be worth investigating how the political climate of the Protectorate influenced this. As for Holden and the Catholic side, his seeking a Protestant audience for his Gallicanism does not, in my view, point to any sort of ecumenism or reunification between the Catholic and the Protestant Churches – after all, for Holden, as for the rest of the Blackloist, Catholicism remained the only true church. His was an attempt to demonstrate that an English Catholic Church governed according to the Gallican ecclesiological model could perfectly coexist with any other confession in any political regime, and in this respect it was important for him that not only his coreligionists, but also the Protestants recognized this. All in all, if Holden manifested 'tolerant and irenic attitudes towards Protestants',[55] it was a kind of irenicism more like Bodin's than Castellio's.

3.4 Thomas White: A Catholic Political Theorist

If, roughly put, among the Blackloists Digby was the one more specifically interested in the political maneuvers in England and Holden the one more

---

[52] A.F. Allison, 'An English Gallican', pp. 332–3.
[53] Ibid., p. 332.
[54] For an analysis of Montagu's use of the model of the Gallican Church see A.Milton, *Catholic and Reformed*, pp. 229–269 *passim.*
[55] These are some of the characteristics that Anthony Brown identifies as part of the Blackloist experience: see his 'Anglo-Irish Gallicanism', pp. 260–1.

invested in the ecclesiological debate within the Church of Rome, the manner in which Thomas White and the Independents crossed their path is altogether different.

In the complicated phase of the negotiations between the Blackloists, London and Rome, it is clear that Digby, Holden and Fitton regarded White as their leader and theoretical inspiration. They kept referring to him as their philosophical mentor,[56] they kept him posted on the various steps of the negotiations,[57] and they also found the time to follow the publishing and the distributing of White's books, as well as to monitor the reactions that these provoked.[58] Yet, it is remarkable that in White's own letters to his associates we can see very little interest on White's part about the actual developments of the negotiations.

In 1646 White sent a brief letter to Digby, together with the first part of one of his work, probably his *Institutionum Peripateticarum*.[59] At the beginning of 1647 White wrote to Digby again: apart from a line in which White generically wished that 'God reward you for what you labour for the Clergy', the rest of the letter is taken up by a long philosophical discourse on the work that he had sent before. In particular, White reminded Digby to 'consider that the notes *de Origine mundi* are not a treatise, but an *appendix* added to shew how Divinity depends on Philosophy, & so hath all its grounds in the former work; without memory wherof it is not well understandable'.[60] Again, in July 1647, and thus in the height of the negotiation, White wrote again, this time to let Digby know about his intended journey to Douai: 'my intention, White writes, is to see whither I can plant any impression of my doctrine in that colledge for I conceive it may in time gett a great root, if it were sett constantly on foot therein'.[61] In September and October White wrote again: he did mention the political dealings – in particular he expressed skepticism on the possibility of getting help from Rome –, but the bulk of the letters is still on his books, and on the reactions that they provoked.[62]

At first sight, White's attitude seems to be a reflection of a well-known feature among academics of every time, namely a hearty dose of egotism. On further examination, White's reiterated interest for his own doctrine suggests something more important than that. In 1645 White wrote a letter to Holden to express the opinion that the English Catholics should not exploit the conflict between England and Ireland, but should rather keep in mind the interest of

---

[56] For instance, in a letter to Holden, Digby asked him to avoid condemning his method of negotiating because 'to censure an important action without knowing its principles, mr Blacklow says tis french Levity': Digby to Holden, 26 October 1645, in *Blacklo's Cabal*, p. 3.

[57] See Holden's letter to Digby, 6 September 1647, in Ibid., p. 26.

[58] See Holden to Digby, 15 October 1647, in Ibid., p. 32; and Digby to Holden, Rome 7 October 1647, in Ibid., p. 54.

[59] White to Digby, 25 October 1646, in Ibid., p. 6.

[60] White to Digby, January 1647, in Ibid., p. 10. I believe that White was here referring to the theological appendix of the *Peripateticall Institutions*.

[61] White to Digby, 4 July 1647, in Ibid., p. 18.

[62] White to Digby, 19 September 1647, in Ibid., pp. 41–2, and Id. ad Eund., 31 October 1647, in Ibid., pp. 65–66.

the Queen, which was precisely what Digby, Henrietta's Agent in those years, was doing. In uncertain times such as the ones that England was living in, the main danger that White saw was a 'perpetuall war' between Ireland and England, and in this perspective 'both England and Ireland will be ruined'.[63] There are, White wrote, Catholics who thought it better to take advantage of the political turmoil by controlling Ireland, but if this was an understandable decision 'for the Pope, or strangers…for an Englishman, I know not how he can do it with maintaining his duty to his country, that is, to God'. Behind this statement, there is not only a certain 'patriotic' feeling of an Englishman who did not want to see his country ruined by war, or a reflection of the Blackloists anti-Papalist stances in the context of Rinuccini's operations in Ireland. Nor is this simply a version of the well-known Pauline maxim on the need for Catholics to recognize that authority comes from God. Rather, White here was trying to say something different.

In the letter he continues: 'God hath set divers degrees in our country, and having given the charge of governing to some *eo ipso* hath taken it from the rest who are to promote their Religion all they can, under and not oppositely to the steeringe of the common'.[64] In other words, White here is not simply saying that men are subject to authority, but that men are subject to 'the steeringe of the common'. Indeed, acting 'under' that steering represented for White the only expression of one's duty to one's country, that is, one's duty to God.

The key point here is that acting under the steering of the common and obeying the King or Queen are not the same thing. Even Robert Pugh, White's archenemy and publisher of the Blackloists' correspondence, realized the main theoretical implication of White's letter, together with its – for him – troubling consequence. In his own comments, which he printed immediately after White's letter, Pugh remarked that 'Mr Blacklo…was a Patriot even ultra aras, beyond Iustice and without due regard to ryght'.[65] And by 'ryght', Pugh meant 'the King's ryght to his Crown'. In 1645 the steering of the common and the King's right pointed to the same direction, but when they did diverge, in White's opinion there was no doubt about which side one had to take.

Going back to White's letters from 1646 and 1647, the reason why he was not interested in the nitty-gritty aspect of the political situation in England was that he, unlike the rest of the Blackloists, wanted to isolate the question of the connections between Catholicism and political authority from the political and ecclesiological contingencies of England. In the 1645 letter White was expressing a still embryonic attempt at theorizing the relationship between religion and politics, he was not interested in describing, analyzing, and suggesting the best way to operate.

For White the duty of a Catholic was not to 'dispose of Kingdomes…under pretence of religion', but to profess his or her religion 'under the steering of the common', wherever that might lead. And when it led to Cromwell, White gave

---

[63] White to Digby, 29 May 1645, in Ibid., pp. 1–2.
[64] Ibid., p. 2
[65] Ibid., pp. 2–3.

him his support, and elaborated these ideas into a coherent political theory, which he expressed in a treatise entitled *The Grounds of Obedience and Government*, published in London in 1655.[66] Before turning to the analysis of this extraordinary text, I think that the differences and the similarities of the three most important members of the Blackloist group suggest some insightful, if preliminary, conclusions.

First of all, the diversity of the approaches, aims and methods with which Holden, White and Digby decided that the English Catholics needed to find an agreement with the Independents suggest to us that it is probably not very useful to talk about the English Catholics as a coherent and homogeneous group. As far as their political position is concerned, the analysis of the Blackloists' position demonstrates that they saw no intrinsic political character in the religion of Rome. All of them, from different angles, thought that the English Catholics were entitled to a proper space in the political discourse in England precisely because they were not supposed to support either the King or the Parliament *a priori*. Rather, they needed to play their cards according to where the game was going, as like many other factions in England were doing in those years. The Catholic hierarchy in Rome, on its part, did not deny this principle: when Digby was looking for money in 1645 the Pope thought that Rome should not commit to the King's cause immediately, but that it would have been better to wait and see. And the reason why the Pope looked with suspicion at the Blackloists' dealings in the second half of 1640s has more to do with the dangerous implications of their ecclesiology, rather than with the political consequences of their allegiance.[67]

But it is also true that ultimately White, Holden and Digby decided to support the Independents first, and Cromwell later. What do we need to make of that? The Blackloists, that is to say, a part of the English Catholic community, decided that the King was not necessarily the only hope for the Catholic Church, nor were the Parliamentarians its main enemy. Yes, there was an element of political opportunism in that – after all the King's cause looked more and more desperate as time went by –, but there are also other considerations. Just as the Blackloists thought that there was nothing inherently 'monarchical' in the Catholic religion, by the same token none of them thought that a republican regime had to be necessarily preferred to a monarchical one. However, the victory of the Parliamentarians brought about a great advantage. As Digby said in 1645, it was easier for a monarchy to convert than for a

---

[66] T. White, *The Grounds of Obedience and Government*, London 1655. Two different editions were printed in the same year by the same press, although the only difference between them concerns the correction of several typos. On the problems related to the date of the first edition see B.C. Southgate, 'Thomas White's *Grounds of obedience and government*: a note on the dating of the first edition', *Notes and Queries*, vol.28 (1981), pp. 208–9. For an analysis of the text see also B.C. Southgate, '"That Damned Booke": *The Grounds of Obedience and Government* (1655), and the downfall of Thomas White', *Recusant History*, vol. 17 n.3 (1985), pp. 238–253.

[67] For a more detailed analysis of the Roman reaction to the Blackloists see S. Tutino, 'The Catholic Church and the English Civil War'.

republic. In other words, if we have the perspective of religious uniformity in mind, a monarchy is better than a republic. Conversely, if in order to govern England the political leaders were forced to find allies and to strike agreements with the diverse factions, then those political leaders would have been forced to grant a measure of liberty of conscience, so as to establish peace and avoid a civil war. In this context, the Blackloists, who had experienced for themselves the benefits of living, discussing and thinking shoulder to shoulder with the Protestants, saw it as their task to elaborate a theological and ecclesiological model for the Catholic Church that could allow every English Catholic to enjoy some of those measures of toleration. To be sure, the Blackloists cannot be said to have elaborated anything remotely similar to a kind of government by parties of modern democracies. However, they recognized that if the English Catholics hoped to be integrated in England, they had to abandon the logic of religious uniformity, and substitute that with a scenario in which many different confessions coexisted within the same state. By the same token, the Blackloists were not interested in ecumenism: they wanted the only true Church, that is to say, the Church of Rome, to be able to prosper under any regime.

As for White in particular, he went beyond this: by reflecting on the English political turmoil and on the role of the Catholic Church in this, he elaborated a coherent theory of the nature and aim of secular government, or 'the steeringe of the common', and on the place of religion 'under' it. To this theory it is now time to turn our attention.

CHAPTER 4

The Grounds of Obedience and Government

4.1 The Text

It is time now to turn to the text of *The Grounds of Obedience and Government,* which represents White's (and the Blackloists') main contribution to the debate over the nature and scope of government.

After a dedicatory epistle to Kenelm Digby, the text begins with a quotation from Xenophon's *Cyropaedia* on the difference between governing men and governing beasts, and on the reasons why 'few men are so intelligent as to be fit to govern men', while every man is capable of governing an animal. White's reply to Xenophon and the starting point of his reflections is that

> …the very question seems to beare the solution in its owne bowells. For, when one asks, why man is hard to be governed since he governes other creatures, hee asks, why one, who hath the power to rule others, is himselfe so difficult to be mastered. And the answer is, because the powers, by which he reduceth others to his obedience, makes *[sic]* him apter to resist them who seek the conquest of himself, and so renders it a higher taske to weild and manage him, then those creatures which he hath power over.[1]

For White, the reason why men are difficult to govern is because 'the nature of man is inclined to have its owne will'. Unlike beasts, therefore, since man is a 'rationall creature', he must be able to understand what is good for him in order to perform it; thus he must be *free* to attain this knowledge and behave accordingly.[2]

In practice, however, things do not work quite this way. For, even though the inclination for reaching the common good is 'so naturall in us, yet Nature is not able to make it perfect in most both persons and actions', because not everybody understands perfectly 'the nature of all things necessary to their owne private conditions'.[3] In order to supplement to this deficiency, however, by nature men are furnished with the inclination of making a free and rational choice to delegate the understanding of 'all things necessary to their owne private conditions' to few members of the community. In fact, White explains, the ideal model of government is one where every subject is aware of having made his decision freely and rationally for his own good:

---

[1] T. White, *The Grounds*, p. 2.
[2] Ibid., pp. 2–3.
[3] Ibid., pp. 9–10.

were it possible for a Governour to make every single person in his Dominion particularly understand, that what was ordered by the Government was his owne truest interest; such an one would be the most absolute and perfect Governour; and infallibly would find the charge of governing most easie and sweet, as well to himselfe as to his Subjects.[4]

Before examining what exactly White meant as the common good, or as one's 'owne truest interest', let us examine the foundation of White's notion of men as naturally free and rational creatures. The freedom of will that men enjoy as rational creatures is grounded upon a peculiar understanding of the virtue of obedience, which is the crucial argument of White's text. White writes that 'it is a fallacious principle, though maintained by many, that obedience is ... the greatest sacrifice we can offer to God, to renounce our own will, because our will is the chiefest good we have'.[5] By contrast, the kind of obedience by which, for White, 'Common-wealths and Communities subsist' is one that does not require men to renounce their will, because their freedom of will is a manifestation of their nature as rational beings, which is 'that by which we are the image of God'. Therefore, this specific virtue has to do less with 'being obedient' than with maintaining one's side of a bargain, or keeping one's side of a mutually beneficial contract:

> Wee use to say servingmen and waiting-maids ought to bee obedient to their masters and mistresses, whereas indeed, the vertue by which they serve is not that of obedience, but of fidelity and truth, which is manifest to him that looks into the nature of hirelings. For, none thinke a husbandman, who is hired to till or fence a piece of ground, obeyeth the hirer more then hee then selleth a piece of cloth or other merchandize obeyeth the buyer, because he taketh his moneys, but they are said to contract and performe their part of the bargaine faithfully and truly. So servants pay their duties, performe their bargains, and fidelity is their proper vertue, to doe it carefully and uprightly: not obedience.[6]

When it comes to governing men, White specifies, the 'good' that the people receive in exchange for their 'fidelity' is twofold. On the one hand, government allows men to live 'in quiet and content' by avoiding contention:

> And since reason is our nature, and every one's reason freer to see the truth in another's case then in his owne, and a wise and good man fitter then a fool or knave, the most naturall way for a multitude to live in peace is to have some man or men, accounted wise and good, chosen, to whose arbitrement all the rest ought to stand, the stronger part combining to force the weaker, in case of resistance, that is, the disinterested part, which is the multitude, to force the interested, which generally are but particulars if compared to the body of the people.[7]

---

[4] Ibid., p. 3
[5] Ibid., pp. 22–23.
[6] Ibid., pp. 27–28.
[7] Ibid., p. 45.

Secondly, just as it is natural for man to live in peace, at the same time 'many commodities are necessary to a multitude, which are to be furnished by common consent', and since 'these business cannot be carried on by the whole body of the community' men need to entrust somebody to take care of providing 'those accomodations of humane life, which they esteem necessary or conducing to their happinesse'.[8]

In other words, men, being rational creature, need to be loyal – not 'obedient' – to their governors not because they have renounced their will, but because they believe that doing what their governors tell them to do will result in *their own* good, which by themselves they could not achieve.

Let us pause a moment here. Perez Zagorin, in his survey on the English political thought during the Revolution, has briefly examined White's treatise, and judged it to be a secular piece of writing, without anything particularly Catholic in it.[9] By contrast, I argue that *The Grounds* is a distinctively interesting text in the history of political thought of its time precisely because it merged the language of natural law with that of Catholic theology.

The root of White's notion of 'fidelity', which is the theoretical key-point in White's reasoning, is theological, and Catholic at that: God governs men by granting them their freewill and rationality, which are not only the most important qualities of mankind, in that they make men similar to their creator, but also the necessary condition to create the consent by which men agree to be governed.

Theology and, in turn, Catholic theology, are not only the origin of government, but they also have a central role at the end of it, as it were. When discussing the question of slavery, White disagreed with Aristotle, who thought that 'some nations are naturally masters and commanders; others, slaves and subjects'[10]. By contrast, for White slavery, either of the individual or of the national kind, was 'extremely irrational and against nature'. Since what was 'natural and rational' was for men 'to be well, either in the next or in this present life', it followed that no man could rationally and naturally subject himself to slavery, 'which signifies a subjection to command in all things, and that meerely for the Master's profit', without any account of the subject's own happiness in either this or next life.[11] Pursuing this point, White considered the question of why a man should renounce his own life for the sake of the commonwealth. Some people, including Aristotle, spoke of the notion of a 'common good', but for White this was not enough: 'to cry "the common good" is a meere deceit and flattery of words, unlesse wee can shew that the common good is as great to us as wee make it sound'.[12] Even if we agree, White states, that what is good for the commonwealth is good for the subject – and we all should agree to that, since the good of the commonwealth

---

[8] Ibid., p. 46.
[9] P. Zagorin, *A History of Political Thought in the English Revolution*, Bristol 1997 (1954), pp. 90–91.
[10] T. White, *The Grounds*, p. 57.
[11] Ibid., pp. 55–56.
[12] Ibid., p. 71.

is the reason why Nature provided men with the rational ability to organize themselves in society, or, as the Ciceronian maxim, used as the epigraph to White's text, illustrates, 'Salus populi suprema lex' –, still a question remains. Namely, since the loss of one's life is the greatest loss that a man can incur, *pace* all the followers of Epicurus who teach 'that there is no harme in death, nor pain after it', 'upon what motive must he [a man] consent' to loosing his life?

All the reasons that are usually alleged in this case, White argued, are to be discarded as 'answers … for some hare-brained fool-hardy flashes or doating oratours', or in other words, baloney:

> *Fame* is a slender recompence, when the fruit of it (which chiefly consists in being respected in company, and having a power amongst his associates) is once passed. The good of his wife and children, that may rejoice a dying man, but if there rest nothing after death, it is a comfort which soon expires, being indeed nothing but a flash.[13]

White's conclusion is therefore 'that there is no good to bee expected here equivalent to the hazard of death, and consequently, none can bee rationally valiant, who sets not his hopes upon the next world'.[14] From the point of view of the government, since 'it is… evident that there is another life to bee expected', the consequence is:

> that it imports good government to plant deeply in the breast of the subjects a rationall apprehension of it. The cause therefore, and solid reason why men ought to bee valiant, is the hope of reward hereafter for doeing good to our neighbour here, and the commonwealth beeing our neerest and greatest neighbour, as including our friends, parents, acquaintance, and all of mankinde that our knowledge reacheth to, to perform service to it is certainly the greatest act of charity towards our neighbour, that is the highest externe act which God hath granted to us, and consequently to bee preferred before all others, and as such to expect a profit and recompence in the next life.[15]

In conclusion, the only solid reason for a subject to be willing to offer to the commonwealth the ultimate sacrifice of his own life is a religious one. Catholicism enters here not because White wanted the Catholic religion to be the one confession 'deeply planted in the breast of the subjects': the 'rational apprehension' of the existence of an afterlife was more than sufficient in this respect. Rather, the entirety of White's theory is built upon the Catholic notion of retributive justice, or that whatever we do or refuse to do in this life has an effect on the destiny of our soul after death.[16]

White is well aware that his political theory has to be considered against the background of existing Catholic political thought, and he is also well aware

---

[13] Ibid., pp. 72–73.
[14] Ibid., p. 75.
[15] Ibid., pp. 75–76.
[16] A.J. Brown analyzes White's statements on the impossibility for men to give up their lives unless they could hope for some reward on this or the next life as a 'statement in favour of some measure of religious toleration' ('Anglo-Irish Gallicanism', pp. 86–7).

of his own originality in this respect. When discussing other Catholic political theorists, White explicitly rejects those who support the view that authority is per se *jure divino*. Some of the Catholic divines, White writes, teach that 'God, by nature, is high Lord and Master of all; That whoever is in power receiveth his right from him; That Obedience consists in doing the will of his who commandeth'.[17] Those divines who hold the aforementioned notion of absolute authority, White says, 'imagine God commandeth it by expresse and direct words, and doeth it by an immediate position of the things said to be done; whereas in nature the commands are nothing but the naturall light God hath bestowed on mankinde'. Therefore God exercises his authority by giving things 'direction and motion...as truly as the wight of a Jack turns the meat upon the spit, and the spring of a Watch makes the clock of it strike'.[18]

It is important to notice at this point the influence of White's scientific theory on his political thought, starting with White's use of the metaphor of the clock, which both Digby and Descartes had used before him and which became a common *trope* during the scientific revolution[19]. Just as the physical world was composed of atoms, whose movements and compositions could be explained by a mechanical theory of nature precisely because God willed it this way, by the same token men can and ought to exercise their freewill in the realm of politics. In other words, to borrow one of White's formulations, God's government was as 'sweet' towards the atoms composing matter as towards men organizing themselves in society and choosing the ones in charge of ruling it.

The relevance of White's natural science for his political philosophy is also clearly visible for the other, minor, work that he wrote on government and governors. This is a part of chapter, remained manuscript, entitled 'The Supernumerary Chapter. That without Virtue Officers wil not bee Vigilant', which White probably wrote for Kenelm Digby's never-completed political treatise.[20] The general thesis of the chapter was supposed to be a demonstration that 'vigilancy in human action is not the least if not the greatest virtue, specially in offices of care and danger'.[21]

By 'vigilancy' White meant the ability of a governor to assiduously implement and sustain a certain 'moderate' action, such as curing one's expenses and avoiding prodigality, as opposed to the 'Heroick', one-time achievement, such as a military conquest. After giving a catalogue of examples of vigilant rulers,

---

[17] T. White, *The Grounds*, pp. 158–159.

[18] Ibid., pp. 161–162.

[19] Cf. K. Digby, *Two Treatises*, p. 227, and R. Descartes, *Principia Philosophiae*, in Id., *Oeuvres* (ed. Adam & Tannery), Paris 1897–1957, vol.ix p. 332. On the significance of the clock metaphor in seventeenth-century natural philosophy see L. Laudan, 'The clock metaphor and probabilism: the impact of Descartes on English methodological thought, 1650–65', *Annals of Science*, vol. 22 (1966), pp. 73–104. For an analysis of the 'mechanist' component of Harrington's *Oceana* see J. Scott, 'The rapture of motion: James Harrington's republicanism', in N. Phillipson-Q. Skinner (eds.), *Political Discourse in Early Modern Britain*, Cambridge 1993, pp. 139–163.

[20] The manuscript chapter can be found in BL, Additional Mss. 41846, ff. 180r–181v. The document is undated.

[21] Ibid., f. 180r.

the Catholic author explains that there is a scientifically demonstrable reason of the efficacy of being vigilant in peace and war. 'If we consider the nature of corporall and mortall things, wee shal finde their greatness to consist of a kinde of multitude of parts, the which in some are more in others less'.[22] Since matter is distinguished by different degrees of rarity and density, White continues, motion must be considered as a function of it, and the results of motion are in proportion to the density of the body moved: 'One hath a lent framer holding him by months and yeares another a sharp one who wil do him as much harme in 8 or fifteen dayes as the other in yeares'.[23] In other words, when we hit a dense body the motion produced is a 'sharp' one, while when we hit a rare body the motion propagates over the less dense substance, thus prompting a slower and less dramatic motion. But the different kind of motion in these two different kinds of bodies does not depend on the actual strength of the motion, but on the different composition of the bodies: in the first case the body appears to move faster and more violently only because it is dense. By contrast, in the second case the motion needs to be measured according to the time for which the body keeps moving, not the velocity or strength with which it moves, which depends on the composition of the body itself and has nothing to do with the strength of the force applied.

The conclusion of this explanation is:

> that it is as wel an Heroick action to maintaine a lesser Action long, as a greater for a short while. Nay if there bee a great proportion betwixt the quality and the degree of the two works the moderate work may exceed the greater by the recompense of the time which it endureth. My conclusion is, that a constant Vigilancy though it seemes but a moderate Action, yet by the length of it becomes a Heroick work.[24]

The fragment of the chapter ends with the beginning of a discussion on the tools that a governor has at his disposal to be vigilant. The first of those tools is his own conscience, which can provide the necessary barrier against 'the assaults of cupidity, whether pleasure, wealth, honour, or whatsoever'[25]. The document ends before White could continue with this list.

White's doctrine is, therefore, a version of consent theory steeped in Catholic theology and in White's own version of mechanical physics. One first important corollary of White's theory on the origin and aim of government is his elaboration of the right of the subjects to rebel against their Governor. The very nature of Government, White writes, implies the right of resistance.[26] But since governing by definition consists 'in the power of commanding, that is, of having no resistance', it is obvious that the clash between the Governor and his resisting subjects 'by consequence...draweth along the concussion of the whole state'. Therefore, White advises, the right of resistance should not be exercised

---

[22] Ibid., f. 180v.
[23] Ibid.
[24] Ibid.
[25] Ibid., ff. 180v–181r.
[26] T. White, *The Grounds*, pp. 109 and ff.

except for one single reason. Given that men choose to be governed in order to better attain the common good, whenever the governor appears to be fighting against the good of the people, instead of providing for it, then the Supreme Magistrate does not act as such anymore:

> Whence is it then that the people come to any such power? The answer is, As, when they first instituted Governement, they did it in the force of Nature; without having any other Power then the pure force of Rationality: so, if, by any circumstance they be devolved into the same state of Anarchy that they promise made bindes no more; then Rationality teacheth them and giveth them, by force of nature, to institute another Governement... the whole end and intention of their promise being, purely, to submit to Governement, that is, conduce to the common good & safety; which having failed, there is no more obligation in their oath or promise, then if they had never made them. This is, therefore, the ground of the peoples opposition, and onely circumstance to justifie their breaking their oath and promise: so that, in truth, the Magistrate, first, by his miscarriages, abdicateth himself from being a Magistrate, and proveth a Brigand and robber in stead of a Defender; and the people, in the way of naturall preservation of themselves, make resistance against him.[27]

To be sure, theories of resistance to an illegitimate king are by no means new in English Catholic political thought: from Nicholas Sanders and the Jesuit Robert Persons to Bellarmine, an important set of Catholic theologians had argued that since authority over souls was far more important than that over bodies, whenever a heretic governor jeopardized the salvation of the soul, Catholics had the right and the duty of rebelling against him and deposing him.[28] It was precisely the theory of *potestas papalis in temporalibus, directa* or *indirecta*, which these theologians endorsed.

For White, on the contrary, a governor is illegitimate not when he jeopardizes the souls of his subjects, but when he fails to provide for the people's *good on earth*.[29] And it is precisely for the sake of this earthly common good that a government should encourage 'a rationall apprehension' of the afterlife.

---

[27] Ibid., pp. 122–4.

[28] See N. Sanders, *De Visibili Monarchia Ecclesiae Libri Octo*, Louvain 1571, pp. 56–78; R. Doleman [*vere* Robert Persons], *A Conference about the next succession to the Crowne of England*, Antwerp 1594, pp. 72–74 and pp. 203–214; R. Bellarmino, *Controversia de Summo Pontifice*, in Id., *Controversiae*, Tomo II, pp. 486–902, Venetiis apud Societatem Minimam, 1603. On the significance of Bellarmine's doctrine of *potestas papalis in temporalibus* in the context of the debate over the Oath of Allegiance see J.V. Gifford, 'The controversy over the oath of allegiance of 1606', unpublished D.Phil. Thesis, University of Oxford 1971, and J.P. Sommerville, 'Jacobean political thought'; Id., 'From Suarez to Filmer: A reappraisal', *The Historical Journal*, vol. 25 n. 3 (1982), pp. 525–540. On the doctrine of the *potestas papalis in temporalibus* see H. Höpfl, *Jesuit Political Thought. The Society of Jesus and the State, c.1540–1630*, Cambridge 2004, pp. 339 and ff.

[29] White refuses to specify what exactly this means: he writes that damages to a private family or to a part of the commonwealth or a relatively light inconvenience, such as the imposition of a new tax, are not enough to justify resistance, and then he adds 'Nor doe I pretend, by these instances, to set any rule for enfranchising the subject; more then this, When *evidently* the tyranny of the Governour is greater than the mischiefe hazarded..for, this and this onely is the finall cause measuring all attempt, *What is best for the People*' (Ibid., pp. 110–115).

Resisting an illegitimate sovereign – in this latter sense – was possible because by failing to accomplish his task he nullified the 'contract' with his people, who agreed to obey him only insofar as obeying could grant them their good. In this respect, then, White's stances on the right of resistance appear to be an original variation of some of the arguments elaborated by the Jesuit Juan de Mariana at the end of the sixteenth century to argue for the legitimacy of regicide.[30]

Another extremely important consequence of White's doctrine is its application to the 1650s political situation in England. Although White had declared that he intended to 'deliver the abstract notions onely: leaving to the prudence of particulars, to draw such consequences, as every ones circumstances shall make necessary and evident unto him by the short hints I give',[31] it is manifest that the political 'consequence' of his 'abstract notions' is a *de facto* endorsement of Cromwell's regime.

For White, both in the case in which a governor has been rightly dispossessed, and in the case of an unlawful dispossession, 'it were better for the common good to stay as they are, then to venture the restoring of him, because of the publick hazard'.[32] There is a difference, in fact, between the good of the people, and the good of the dispossessed King and his family: the former has always to prevail over the latter. And if indeed the dispossessed King is truly a Supreme Governor, he will be the first one to renounce his right to the throne for the good of the people.

What about the new Governor, and when can he be said to be truly legitimate? As White writes, some 'have sought by terme of years to decide the difficulty'. For instance, Urban VIII 'an intelligent and generous Prince and well versed in politick Government', had established a rule according to which 'after five yeers quiet possession of an estate, the Church was not bound to take notice whether the title were lawfull or no'.[33] For White, on the contrary, it was necessary to 'proceed upon other principles, that is, the forelaid and main basis of our discourse, that the common good ought to bee the rule of the Magistrates title, and the subjects obedience'. According to this basis, then, 'when ever (considering all things) the common good is cleerly on the possessors side, then the dispossessed hath no claime'.[34]

Following this principle, White goes so far as to justify the murder of Charles I on 'quasi-Hobbesian' terms. In a passage devoted to the explication of the doctrine of resistance, White affirms that if the people seek reparation against a governor who has wronged them, they cannot act against him while he is still in Power. But once the governor is dispossessed, he is not a governor anymore,

---

[30] See Q. Skinner, *The foundations of modern political thought*, 2 vols, Cambridge 1983 (1978), vol. II, pp. 345–348; J.P. Sommerville, 'From Suarez to Filmer'; H. Höpfl, *Jesuit Political Thought*, pp. 239 and ff.
[31] T. White, *The Grounds*, Dedicatory Epistle to Sir Kenelm Digby, unfoliated.
[32] Ibid., p. 135.
[33] Ibid., pp. 151–2.
[34] Ibid., p. 152.

but a private man, 'the structure of the Common-wealth is dissolved', and in this scenario

> ...any who hath suffered wrong in the fore-declared manner may bee party against him and proceed as if there were no Common-wealth; by the Law, which, in a Wildernesse, warranteth us to kill a Tyger or a Robber that seeketh to kill us, not pretending Law for our action, but that it is manlike & rational. Neither ought it bee called punishment that is done against a dispossessed Magistrate, but rather revenge, or some other name that includeth no order to Law.[35]

It is evident, then, that in *The Grounds* White was declaring Oliver Cromwell as a legitimate new governor because he acted in the best interest of the people, which, according to the nature of mankind, is the essence of government. In this respect, White's contract-based political theory contains some rather interesting, and uniquely Catholic, elements of the secular *de facto*-ist arguments of thinkers such as Anthony Asham and Thomas Hobbes.[36]

4.2 The Context

White's political theory, deeply linked with his mechanist natural philosophy, is a theology-based Catholic consent theory. The link between White's political theory, theology, and natural philosophy and other theorists' – Hobbes *in primis* – has been recognized by a number of people, both in the seventeenth and in the twentieth century.[37]

After the Restoration, in fact, numerous pamphlets lumped together Hobbes's and White's works as two examples of the pernicious doctrines that in the previous years had brought about the destruction of both the Commonwealth and the Church. The first, hardly surprising, argument used to link Hobbes and White is based upon the interpretation of both as anti-monarchical, and, consequently, anti-Christian. A good example of this argument can be found in Roger Coke's *Justice Vindicated,* in which Thomas White, Thomas Hobbes and Hugo Grotius are linked together as Coke's polemical targets.[38] What do

---

[35] T. White, *The Grounds*, pp. 147–8. Cf. T. Hobbes, *Leviathan*, ed. by R. Tuck, Cambridge 1996, Chapter XXIX, pp. 221–230.

[36] See Q. Skinner, 'Conquest and Consent: Thomas Hobbes and the Engagement Controversy', in G.E. Aylmer (ed.), *The Interregnum: the Quest for Settlement, 1646–1660*, Hamden (Conn.) 1972, pp. 79–98.

[37] Q. Skinner, 'The ideological context of Hobbes's political thought', *The Historical Journal*, vol. IX n. 3 (1966), pp. 286–317; R. Tuck, *Philosophy and government, 1572–1651*, Cambridge 1993, pp. 320–322.

[38] R. Coke, *Justice Vindicated from the false fucus put upon it, by Thomas White Gent., Thomas Hobbs, and Hugo Grotius. As also elements of Power & Subjection; Wherein is demonstrated the Cause of all Humane, Christian, and Legal Society and as a previous Introduction to these, is shewed, The Method by which Men must necessarily attain Arts & Sciences*, London 1660. See also Coke's *A Survey of the Politicks of Mr. Thomas White, Mr. Thomas Hobbs and Hugo Grotius*, London 1662. Coke's arguments against White have been briefly analyzed by B.C. Southgate, in '"That Damned Booke"', pp. 247–8.

the three theorists have in common? Coke wrote: 'They all say, that by Nature all men are in a like equal condition, and out of society, until by voluntary pacts and acts of their will they shall have formed themselves into society. I say, that men are by Nature born into society and subordination'.[39] God, in other words, had 'made Adam a universal Monarch', therefore Monarchy was the only 'natural' and Christian form of government. Coke derives his principle from a modified version of Aristotelian epistemology: against the opinion of Aristotle, Coke maintains that no knowledge is possible by experience, but only by deduction from immutable Axioms.[40] In the case of government, the immutable principle on which it is based is 'the Law of Nature,' which is 'engraven in the minds of all men'. Because of this 'Law of Nature' men feel the need of living in society, and of organizing themselves into a hierarchical order. Since the Laws of Nature descend directly from God, Coke wrote:

> [they] are principles, necessary, and immutable by all the Men in the World; yet are they not principles, necessary, or immutable by God; but he might, if it had pleased him, made something else the Law of Nature, or otherwise revealed himself in the Scripture. So Humane Laws must be prime, necessary, and immutable by Subjects, or their conforming, or not confirming their actions to them, could not be just or unjust.[41]

This excludes any possible action on the part of mankind, whose rational character consists precisely in following this Axiom. In fact, as Coke added, 'all the Confusions which have lately hapned in Chrstendom, were not caused from any want of understanding of the Laws of God or Man, but from the perverse wills of Men, who would not be restrained from their wickedness, neither by the Laws of God or Man'.[42]

Coke's interpretation of the nature of mankind and its application to political theory constitute the bulk of his arguments against White's *Treatise*. White, for Coke, had misunderstood the notion of 'rational creature' applied to men: being 'rational' means abiding by the Laws of Nature. Consequently, the notion of obedience cannot be conditional; and it is immoral and pernicious to convince subjects otherwise. They do not need to know that what their governor does is good for them:

> for, Secrecy (the life of all actions and designs, a quality wherein Cardinal Richlieu was so eminent) cannot be, if the obeyer must be made to understand that it is for his good....it is sufficient for the obeyer to understand, that his Safety and Preservation depends upon his Obedience, and that his ruine follows his disobedience.[43]

Coke's conclusion is that government is 'natural', that is to say, 'proceed immediately from God...and therefore this Government is superior to the Wills

---

[39] R. Coke, *Justice Vindicated*, p. 53.
[40] Ibid., pp. 1–17 *passim*.
[41] Ibid., pp. 17–18.
[42] Ibid.
[43] Ibid., p. 3.

or Reason of the People, and cannot be by them dissolved; but the resisting of it is a violence upon Nature, and not only Irrational, and Immoral and unjust'.[44]

Given Coke's perspective, he was not interested in discussing White's *de facto*-ist arguments – or Hobbes's, for that matter –. In fact, Coke examined only the first fourteen grounds of White's treatise, leaving the rest for others to discuss. And others did discuss them. An interesting text that addresses the last part of White's treatise is a pamphlet entitled *Evangelium Armatum*, published anonymously in London in 1663, and reprinted in 1682. Its author was William Assheton, a Protestant divine and preacher, and chaplain to James Duke of Ormond.[45] Assheton starts by explaining that the great political disorder during the Civil Wars stemmed from the lack of a 'true Piety', which was substituted by 'the shew and pretence of Piety':

> A maxim, so veri[fi]ed by the late transactions among us, that the great Basis and groundwork of all the Villany that had been acted upon the stage of these miserable Kingdoms, has been to beget and fix in the People this Belief, that the great Design drove on by the Actors of it, was the advancement of the Purity of Religion, and the Power of godliness.[46]

And in order to provide his readers with examples of this kind of religious impiety that had caused the destruction of the political order, Assheton presented a 'short collection of the Sayings and Doctrines of the great Leaders and Abetters of the Presbyterian Reformation'. Among those, Assheton included Jenkins, Baxter, Mashall, and John Dury. No toleration, Assheton wrote, was possible with those people: 'their pleas or rather their Noise' could not be answered but by absolutely rejecting them.[47]

If these people were the first line, Assheton added, there was also a 'rear of this spiritual Brigade'.[48] This rear was constituted by the 'Papists and the Hobbians', and among the Papists Assheton chooses Thomas White, because, despite having the 'reputation of being moderate' and anti-Jesuit, he is nonetheless a 'pestilent asserter' of doctrines aimed at deposing legitimates sovereigns. But what are the characteristics that Assheton recognized as common between Hobbes 'the great Propagator of the Kingdom of Darkness' and Thomas White the 'most moderate' of the Papists? The one element that Assheton decided to underline is precisely the *de facto*-ist arguments we have already noted in examining *The Grounds*. The passages quoted in the *Evangelium Armatum* from *The Grounds*, *Leviathan* and *De Cive* are those that concern the necessity to obey a new governor, rather than attempt to restore the previous one.[49] Not only the content of White's and Hobbes's works, but also the 'circumstance of their writing & Publication', Assheton writes,

---

[44] Ibid., pp. 22–23.
[45] See *DNB sub voce Assheton, William*.
[46] *Evangelium Armatum*, London 1663, 'Preface to the Reader', sig. Ar-v.
[47] Ibid., unfol.
[48] Ibid., unfol.
[49] Ibid., pp. 53–59.

clarify their real aim, i.e. 'a publick disswasion of the People to endeavour the restauration of his Majesty'.[50]

Both Coke and Assheton, albeit with different arguments, accused Thomas White's and Thomas Hobbes's doctrines of being anti-monarchical and therefore anti-Christian. The same analogy between White and Hobbes was made in a positive sense, so to say. For instance John Austin, a supporter of the Blackloist cause, in 1651 and in 1653 published two pamphlets praising Cromwell and his allegedly friendly attitude towards the English Catholics: in those works Austin used (and misused) Hobbes's *Leviathan* as an example of a theory arguing for toleration towards the English Catholic Church with the same arguments that the Blackloists had used.[51]

But to what extent could the religious and theological dimension of White's text be used to link him with other theorists, rather than to single him out? And what role did his Catholic mixture of contractualism and *de facto*-ist arguments play within the context of English republicanism?

As far as religion is concerned, Richard Baxter, in his *Holy Commonwealth*, offered an interesting theory on how the religious element in White's doctrine distinguished it from not only Hobbes's, but also Harrington's. Roughly put, the commonwealth envisioned by Baxter was holy for two reasons: first, because its government could not and should not claim for itself an autonomous position with respect to the true religion. Secondly, it was holy because it was to be constituted by *holy* people. Among the enemies of such a commonwealth, Baxter included Hobbes and Harrington because they did not propose a 'holy' commonwealth in the first sense. That Hobbes's 'way of absolute Impious monarchy...tendeth not to secure us a Righteous Government', Baxter writes, 'is a point that needeth no proof with any reasonable man'; and Harrington's *Oceana* is a form of commonwealth 'most inconsistent with a Clergy: without which the Christian Religion never was maintained in any Nation upon earth'.[52] Catholics were enemies also, but in the second sense, because they were not 'holy' people, indeed they were the people of the Antichrist. Papists, Baxter wrote, are of three kinds.[53] The first are the 'bold' supporters of the theory of *directa potestas*. The second group, whose chief figure is Bellarmine, proposes the theory of *indirecta postestas,* although the two groups, Baxter wrote, are all the same. The third group, a 'more moderate' one, is the one constituted by the *politiques* and the French Gallicans, among whom William Barclay. Although they 'depose the Pope from his usurped Soveraignty over the Laity', they still 'leave him as the sole Judge of the Clergy'. Since the Clergy has a central role in Baxter's commonwealth, in reality they too introduce a form of Papal authority into the Commonwealth: in Baxter's words, 'Though it be about Clergy-men, surely it is a Civil Government'. For these reasons, no Papist should be tolerated in the Commonwealth. Where does White

---

[50] Ibid., p. 58.
[51] For an analysis of Austin's texts and of their treatment of Hobbes and White see J.R. Collins, 'Thomas Hobbes and the Blackloist conspiracy', pp. 329 and ff.
[52] R. Baxter, *A Holy Commonwealth*, London 1659, pp. 224 and ff.
[53] Ibid., pp. 311–2.

stand then? Baxter discussed White's opinion in the third chapter of his *Holy Commonwealth*, which addresses the question of 'the constitution of Gods Kingdome', and is, in Baxter's opinion, 'the foundation of all my following discourse'.[54] The reason why the doctrine of Thomas White is threatening to the constitution of Baxter's commonwealth is precisely the link between theology and mechanist physics, or, in Baxter's apt expression, the notion that 'God governeth as an Engeneer'.[55] Unlike Hobbes and Harrington, government for White has a theological origin – but in a mechanist context –. Unlike the other sorts of Papists, however, White's God does not meddle in civil affairs or even, in a sense, in religious matters: White's God, in fact, does not meddle with men, period. That is what makes White's doctrine different from either Hobbes and Harrington, and at the same time more threatening than both.

Baxter therefore identifies White's political theory as a *uniquely Catholic* consent theory: the Catholic's theology was for Baxter a rather strange kind of theology, and was so because White made use of theological arguments to speak the language of natural law in a 'mechanical' context.

Baxter, moreover, thought that White's theory was a *uniquely theological* consent theory, and the theological dimension differentiated, in Baxter's opinion, White from Hobbes and Harrington.

If the first of Baxter's stances highlighted an extremely important feature of the doctrine expressed in *The Grounds*, in the second one Baxter might have missed something important. And if Baxter is not willing to recognize any theological elements in Harrington and Hobbes, he is surely not alone.

The significance of the religious element in the historiography on English republican thought has been mainly ignored by those scholars who use the concept of classical republicanism as the only defining 'language' and 'programme' of English republicanism.[56] However, the importance of the language of religion in the history of English republicanism and indeed in the history of English political thought is currently being given much attention by contemporary scholarship.

First of all, much work has been done on the ecclesiological perspective in the theories of many republican thinkers. In particular, as far as Harrington is concerned, Jonathan Scott and Mark Goldie, among the others, have argued that far from simply being a work of republican opposition to Cromwell's regime, *Oceana* has to be read as a 'model' for an 'immortal commonwealth'. Within this project, the religious element has a crucial role, and it took the shape of a kind of national Church whose relationship with the secular government

---

[54] Ibid., pp. 18–49.
[55] Ibid., p. 21. The same concept of White's being aberrant – in this sense – with respect to the other Papists is expressed by Baxter in his *A Key for Catholics*, London 1659: see his dedicatory epistle 'To his Highness Richard Lord Protector of the Common-Wealth of England, Scotland and Ireland', unfoliated.
[56] See J.G.A. Pocock (ed.), *The political works of James Harrington*, Cambridge 1977, 'Historical introduction', p. 15. See also the discussion of Pocock's definition in J. Scott, 'What were Commonwealth Principles?', *The Historical Journal*, vol.47 n. 3 (2004), pp. 591–613, at pp. 593–595.

had to be based on an Erastian model that closely resembled the one that the Blackloists proposed for the English Catholic Church in 1647–8.[57] The same Erastianism, as Jeffrey Collins has argued, was at the core of Hobbes's model of relationship between Church and State, and that explained, in Collins's opinion, the close link between Hobbes and White.[58]

When it comes to Erastianism, however, there are theological and political distinctions that we should take into account. An Erastian position on the relationship between Church and State is not enough if we want to link White's formulations to other republican writings; in fact, it is not sufficient to understand the core of White's political theory either. While there are surely some Erastian elements in certain structural aspects of the Blackloist ecclesiology – as, for instance, the suggestion made by Holden and White that the Bishops in charge of the English Catholic Church should have been chosen by Parliament, rather than the Pope –, the role that Catholic theology played in White's political theory is much deeper than any version of Erastianism could ever even have dreamed of consenting to, since for White the very root of his natural-law arguments was a theological one. In other words, White would have welcomed the Parliament's role of authority in ecclesiological matters, especially because that would have meant to limit drastically the Pope's; for him, however, there was no doubt that the origin of government was of a theological nature.

If Harrington's Erastianism is helpful only to a certain extent if we want to understand the role of White in the English republican debate, Erastianism becomes a problematic notion also when it comes to overstating the similarity between White and Hobbes. As Anthony Brown has convincingly argued, if Erastianism correctly describes Hobbes's theory of the relation between Church and State, the same cannot be said for Thomas White. Hobbes's Erastianism, in fact, implied that the only thing that individuals could not hand over to the sovereign's control was the right to life itself. In other words, when push comes to shove, religion too is under the sovereign's control. For White, on the other hand, the governor did not control religion, but State and Church should have had separate jurisdictions: when one began, the other ended, in the dualistic tradition of Marsilius from Padua.[59] Once again, for Hobbes the origin of government was 'the foresight of their [i.e.men's] own preservation, and of a more contented life thereby; that is to say, of getting themselves out from that miserable condition of Warre, which is necessarily consequent (as hath been shewn) to the naturall Passions of men'[60]. For White, by contrast, what is 'so naturall in us' is the inclination to the common good, because God in his wisdom furnished men with both that inclination and the freewill

---

[57] M. Goldie, 'The Civil Religion of James Harrington', in A. Pagden (ed.), *The Languages of Political Theory in Early-Modern Europe*, Cambridge 1987, pp. 197–222. J. Scott, *Commonwealth Principles. Republican writing of the English Revolution*, Cambridge 2004, pp. 284–293.
[58] J.R. Collins, *The Allegiance of Thomas Hobbes*, pp. 114 and ff.
[59] A.J. Brown, 'Anglo-Irish Gallicanism', p. 85.
[60] T. Hobbes, *Leviathan*, chap. XVII, p. 117.

necessary for men to consent to choosing a governor who could lead them to that common good.

These ecclesiological and theological specifications, however, do not mean that Baxter was necessarily right, and that Hobbes, White and Harrington were creatures of completely different species. They rather point out to the fruitfulness of investigating the religious aspects of Hobbes's political thought, a necessary step to understand the historical and philosophical significance of his contact with Catholics thinkers in England and France. In this respect, Richard Tuck has provided an insightful explanation of both the theological issues in Hobbes's political theory and the role that Hobbes's collaboration with the Blackloists and with Thomas White in particular had in shaping them.[61]

At the same time, it means that we should also start investigating more profoundly the properly theological, and not just the ecclesiological dimension of English republican writing. And together with this, we need to take into account the role of natural law theories in the religious arguments. As far as natural law is concerned, it has been argued that 'natural law theory and republican theory may be considered as different genres and of different scope but they are not inherently incompatible'.[62] Through the inclusion of natural law into the conceptual definition of English republicanism, the religious and theological elements acquire a central role: as Jonathan Scott has insisted, 'far from being mutually exclusive, classical republicanism and natural law theory shared an appeal to the faculty of human reason which was Greek in origin, but frequently in the early modern period Christian in application'.[63] Thus, in this sense, the religio-theological dimension becomes a truly integral part of republican theories. As Scott has demonstrated, an element of rational theology was present in many important republican thinkers such as Harrington, Milton and Sidney. For these theorists, 'to replace kingship, and with it dependence upon the will of fallen man, by the self-government of God-given reason, was the nearest mankind could come to the government of God'.[64] If we consider that the theological dimension of natural law theories, that is to say the issue of what kind of government is connatural to man understood as God's only

---

[61] R.Tuck, 'The civil religion of Thomas Hobbes', in N. Phillipson-Q. Skinner, *Political Discourse in Early Modern Britain*, Cambridge 1993, pp. 120–138. On the religious elements in Thomas Hobbes's philosophy see also Q. Skinner, 'The Ideological Context'; S.A. State, 'Text and Context: Skinner, Hobbes and Theistic Natural Law', *The Historical Journal*, vol.28 n.1 (1985), pp. 27–50; A.P. Martinich, *The Two Gods of Leviathan: Thomas Hobbes on Religion and Politics*, Cambridge 1992.

[62] K. Haakonssen, 'Repulicanism', R.E. Goodin-P. Pettit (eds.), *A Companion to Contemporary Political Philosophy*, Oxford 1993, pp. 568–574, at p. 571. On the relationship between natural law theories and republicanism see also J. Scott, *England's Troubles. Seventeenth-century English political instability in European context*, Cambridge 2000, pp. 317 and ff; and Id., 'Classical Republicanism in Seventeenth-century England and the Netherlands', in M. van Genderen and Q. Skinner (eds.), *Republicanism. A shared European Heritage*, 2 voll., Cambridge 2002, vol. I, pp. 61–81.

[63] See J. Scott, 'What were Commonwealth Principles', p. 593.

[64] J. Scott, *Commonwealth principles*, pp. 58–60 at p. 60.

creature similar to his creator, is indeed important to understand English republican writings, then White does have a place in this story.

One extraordinarily interesting instance of this mix of natural law, republican theories and theology is the debate that opposed William Ball to Thomas White immediately after the publication of *The Grounds*. Ball's criticism of White came, as it has been written, 'from the left'.[65] According to Ball, White essentially gave too much power to the sovereign: his notion of obedience, Ball writes, which on paper should be the opposite of the 'blind' kind of obedience, in reality 'endeavoureth to enslave free men under the Bondage of Boundless Government'.[66] In particular, Ball takes issues with White's characterizing of the Magistrate as 'above the Law'. For Ball this meant to deprive the people of its essential right to resist, and to give to the Magistrate an unlimited authority too similar to tyranny.[67]

Ball's text has been analyzed by Steven Pincus as an example of a republican writing that, instead of arguing for agrarian society as the necessary condition for republicanism, emphasized the fundamentally positive role of the notion of interest. For Pincus, it was precisely this concept that could make 'possible – though not inevitable – a politics of popular participation and diversity'.[68] In other words, Ball substituted White's understanding of the notion of the 'common good' – which for Ball was not enough to secure the people from tyranny – with the notion of common interest as the basis for a truly *publica res*.

What I would like to draw attention to in Ball's criticism of White is its profoundly theological core. At the beginning of his text Ball writes that he intends to examine and discuss White's notion of obedience not only according 'to the rule of the Creature', i.e., on the basis of 'Politick Rules of Law', but first and foremost 'according to the Rule of the Creator'.[69] While White emphasized reason as the main characteristic which God has informed mankind with, for Ball the most distinctive feature of the 'reasonable man' that God created is the tendency to 'communicate good to others', just as God 'worketh to communicate his Goodness'. For Ball, White's text was incorrectly centered upon the issue of subjection, since White had started his treatise by comparing the task of governing beasts to the task of governing men. The truth, for Ball, was that God did not intend men to be subject to one another, just as Eve was not created to be Adam's subject:

> When God created Eve he said, "Let us make him an help; ut subjectum per quod"; he said not, "let us make him a subject to work upon, as subjectum quod"…therefore prudent Reason dictates also, that GOD is to be loved for his excellency, not for our own ends…and that man, or all

---
[65] B.C. Southgate, '"That Damned Booke"', p. 245.
[66] W. Ball, *State-Maxims*, London 1656, p. 1.
[67] Ibid., pp. 8–17.
[68] S. Pincus, 'Neither Machiavellian Moment nor Possessive Individualism: Commercial Society and the Defenders of the English Commonwealth', *The American Historical Review*, vol.103 n.3 (1998), pp. 705–736, at p. 730.
[69] W. Ball, *State-Maxims*, pp. 2–5.

mankind is to be loved for GOD's sake, because he hath dignified him with a Rational soul, and not meerly for the use one man hath of another: so that, according to prudent Reason, I should not onely have an *inclination* to do another man what good I can, without mine own prejudice, but even an *Actual Application* of what good I may prudently without my won wrong, if he will accept thereof.[70]

I think that Ball's use of this theological language cannot be reduced to a series of rhetorical tropes, but it has to be taken seriously in the context of his debate with Thomas White, whose notion of the implication of man's rationality was firmly grounded in theology. If Ball wanted, as he did, to attack the foundation of White's thought, he had to engage in theology. In this respect, I think that Ball's 'more extreme egalitarian standpoint' is not merely a political egalitarianism,[71] but also, and perhaps more interestingly, a theological one.

In conclusion, it appears clearly that the link between theology, natural law and English republicanism needs to be taken into greater account if we want to get a more refined and historically accurate perspective on the origin of certain crucial notions in early modern English and European political thought. White's text, in its richness and complexity, assumes a central importance in this intellectual operation. Undoubtedly, White does not belong to the group of classical republicans, and he might not even fit into the re-defined category of English republicanism seen as 'unity-in-variety', as has been proposed.[72] Nevertheless, his consent theory, based on both a 'rationalized' Catholic theology and a distinctive notion of mechanical science, represents an extremely interesting case-study showing how natural law bridged the complexity of the relationship between theological and secular arguments put forward in the debate around issues such as the nature and limit of government and the relationship between subjects and governors.

---

[70] Ibid., pp. 3–4.
[71] B.C. Southgate, '"That Damned Booke"', p. 246.
[72] See J. Scott, 'Classical Republicanism in Seventeenth-century England and the Netherlands', p. 81.

CHAPTER 5

The Blackloists and the Lord Protector

5.1 Thomas White

In the same year in which he published *The Grounds of Obedience and Government* White moved to London, where he enjoyed a rather busy 'retirement'. In the 1650s White was not directly involved in politics, but he was comfortable in the political climate of Cromwell's regime and he took advantage of the collaboration with many Protestant intellectuals, in particular the scientific circle that was formed during the 1650s at Oxford. Before making some considerations on the role and contribution of Thomas White to the Oxford circle, I would like to briefly summarize its origin and aims.

The leader of the group was John Wilkins, a Protestant theologian appointed as Warden of Wadham College, Oxford, in 1648, who had close ties with the Cromwell family – in 1656 he ended up marrying Robina French, Oliver's youngest sister –. Even if Wilkins's own scientific contribution to the mid-seventeenth century debate was not particularly original or remarkable, he had a crucial role in organizing and keeping together an important scientific community in Oxford, which counted among its members Robert Boyle (who decided to join Wilkins's group after his 1655 visit to Oxford), Seth Ward (the new Savilian Professor of Astronomy), Christopher Wren, John Wallis and Jonathan Goddard.[1]

From this (limited) list of names we can already discern a crucial feature of Wilkins's circle in Oxford, that is to say, the variety of political and religious backgrounds of its members, ranging from the Royalist Protestant Ward to John Wallis, who in 1644 had been appointed as secretary of the Westminster assembly of divines.

In order to explain the ideological background of the collaboration between scientists of such different religious and political opinion, a number of scholars, among them James Jacob and Barbara Shapiro, noting Wilkins's own latitudinarian theology, have proposed to extend it to the rest of the group as one of its main characteristics. In their interpretation, latitudinarianism, fostered by the need that the Oxford scientists and their leader saw of creating a sort of safe haven for intellectual communication in the midst of the turmoil caused by the Civil War, was based on two main pillars. First, a sort of religious, philosophical and political moderation; and secondly, the concept that a rational and natural theology, far from opposing natural philosophy, could be considered instead its best ally. In sum, borrowing Barbara Shapiro's definition, 'in their respective areas, both scientists and theologians sought a

---

[1] For the intellectual atmosphere of the Oxford circle and for Wilkins's role in it see B.J. Shapiro, *John Wilkins 1614–1672. An Intellectual Biography*, Berkeley 1969, pp. 118 and ff.

via media between skepticism and dogmatism'.[2] The extent to which Wilkins's latitudinarian theology was shared by every member of his group – we should remember that Seth Ward, for instance, was both a central member of Wilkins's group and anything but a latitudinarian – and indeed the significance of the very concept of 'latitudinarianism' as a homogeneous theological label used for something that was by no means theologically homogeneous, has been vivaciously questioned by current scholarship.[3] For now, however, I am interested in underlining that at Oxford men of different religious and political backgrounds had indeed collaborated fruitfully and peacefully despite, to a certain extent, their political and theological differences, and I would like to leave the question of the ideological and theological foundation of such a collaboration for later.

As for the more properly scientific interests of the Oxford circle, although we do not have an exact documentation of the themes and questions discussed at meetings, it seems certain that the group emphasized the importance of experiment, and also that the members were particularly interested in mathematics (in particular they were concerned with the relation between arithmetic and geometry and with questions such as the arithmetic indivisibles, to which we will go back in a moment) and astronomy (they were vigorous defenders of Copernicanism). The members of Wilkins's group were also interested in the areas of intersection between mathematics and astronomy: for instance, they discussed at length the problem of defining and refining mathematically the theory of elliptical orbits.[4]

In keeping with their spirit of a *via media* between dogmatism and skepticism in their approach to philosophy, the members of Wilkins's group were encouraged to discuss freely Aristotelianism. While Ward and Wilkins did not think that Aristotelianism could and should be thought as the only valid system of natural philosophy – neither one in fact fully subscribed to the Aristotelian principles of physics to the extent to which White and Digby did –, nevertheless they argued that at Oxford a serious and rigorous study of the

---

[2] B.J. Shapiro, *John Wilkins*, p. 228.

[3] Among the most representative voices in this debate over the use and definition of the concept of latitudinarianism see J.R. Jacob, *Robert Boyle and the English Revolution: A Study in Social and Intellectual Change*, New York 1977, pp. 152 and ff.; M.C. Jacob, *The Newtonians*; B.J. Shapiro, *John Wilkins*, pp. 153 and ff. *passim*; Id., *Probability and Certainty in Seventeenth-Century England*, pp. 104–116; J. Spurr, '"Latitudinarianism" and the Restoration Church', *The Historical Journal*, vol. 31 n. 1 (1988), pp. 61–88; Id., '"Rational Religion" in Restoration England', *Journal of the History of Ideas*, vol. 49 n. 4 (1988), pp. 536–585; M. Hunter, 'Latitudinarianism and the "Ideology" of the early Royal Society: Thomas Sprat's History of the Royal Society (1667) reconsidered', in Id., *Establishing the New Science. The Experience of the early Royal Society*, Woodbridge 1989, pp. 45–71; M. Boas Hall, *Promoting Experimental Learning. Experiment and the Royal Society 1660–1727*, Cambridge 1991, pp. 10–12. Among the historiographical reactions to the category of latitudinarianism as it was elaborated by Shapiro and Jacob see also the essays contained in R. Kroll, R. Ashcraft, P. Zagorin (eds.), *Philosophy, Science and Religion in England 1640–1700*, Cambridge 1992.

[4] B.J. Shapiro, *John Wilkins*, pp. 130–137.

new theories, 'Atomicall and Magneticall in Philosophy and Copernican in Astronomy, & c.' coexisted rather harmonically with Aristotelianism:

> And though we do very much honour Aristotle for his profound judgment and universall learning, yet are we so farre from being tyed up to his opinions, that persons of all conditions amongst us take liberty to discent from him, and to declare against him, according as any contrary evidence doth ingage them, being ready to follow the Banner of truth by whomsoever it shall be lifted up.[5]

The question of the role of Aristotle's doctrine within the curriculum of Oxford University is not only an important issue if we want to understand some of the main philosophical, scientific and theological features of Wilkins's group, but it also became one of the central questions in the debate that opposed Wilkins and Ward to the radicals Webster and Dell in the 1650s and that concerned the reform of the educational system and the role of science within it.[6]

But Aristotelianism, mathematics and astronomy were not the only natural sciences that Wilkins's associates were interested in. Oxford was also the privileged venue for discussing the implication of Harveian medicine, and for developing it further. Gabriel Harvey, as it is well known, was the man credited with the discovery of the circulation of the blood (his *De motu cordis*, in which he first presented and explained the main results obtained from the experiments he made, appeared in 1628). Harvey was also a great admirer of Aristotelianism and a staunch Royalist – he had been Physician Extraordinary to both James I and Charles I –. In 1642 Harvey arrived to Oxford with the entourage of the King, as Charles's senior physician-in-ordinary, a post to which he was appointed in 1639. Harvey left Oxford in 1646, after the city surrendered to the Parliament's army, but while he was there he managed to assemble around him a number of disciples and collaborators, who, like him, were interested in the discoveries that the practice of dissection was then making possible, and in their implications.[7]

Even if Harvey's closest collaborators, like him supporters of the Royalist cause, left Oxford after the victory of Parliament, just as Harvey himself had done, nevertheless his discoveries on the circulation of blood and his experiments on autopsies left an important mark. When, in the 1650s, Oxford academic community was re-organized under Wilkins's leadership, the study of anatomy and physiology picked up when Harvey had left. More specifically, the Oxford school of medicine, lead by men such as Thomas Clayton Jr., whose father had worked with Harvey, William Petty, and later Robert Boyle, applied

---

[5] S. Ward, *Vindiciae Academiarum*, Oxford 1654, p. 2.

[6] On the complex and manifold aspects of the debate that opposed Wilkins and Ward to Webster and Dell see, among the others, B.J. Shapiro, *John Wilkins*, pp. 98–110, and A.G. Debus, *Science and Education in the Seventeenth Century. The Webster-Ward Debate*, London and New York 1970.

[7] On Harvey and his Oxford disciples see R.G. Frank Jr., *Harvey and the Oxford Physiologists. Scientific Ideas and Social Interactions*, Berkeley 1980, pp. 21–30.

the newly refined atomic doctrine of Gassendi and Descartes to the circulation of the body, which Harvey still explained in Aristotelian terms. The result was a corpuscular and 'chemical' basis for biological phenomena, and the implications of the 'chemical' explanation led to a violent attack on Galenic medicine and Aristotelianism.[8]

Although virtually all of the existing scholarship on the Oxford circle utterly ignores the role of Thomas White, I think that the Catholic natural philosopher and theologian contributed actively to some of the main debates that were taken up among Wilkins's associates. Moreover, I want to suggest that understanding the extent of White's contribution will offer some insight into many of the features of the Oxford group, most notably the relationship between mechanical philosophy and theology, which is one of the fundamental questions in the historiographical debate over the scientific revolution.

In the 1650s, together with translating his *Institutionum Peripateticarum* in English, White wrote and published two major works on natural philosophy, *Euclides Physicus* in 1657 and *Euclides Metaphysicus* in 1658.[9] The extent of White's involvement in the Oxford circle already can be gathered by analyzing the dedicatory epistles of these works. *Euclides Physicus* is in fact dedicated to Ralph Bathurst, who was an important member of the Wilkins circle. Bathurst, together with being a minister in the Church of England and a supporter of the Royalist cause, was a medical doctor and participated in the experiments and studies that Nathaniel Highmore, a fellow Royalist, was making at Oxford in the 1640s. Unlike his colleague, however, Bathurst decided to remain in Oxford after Parliament's victory, thus abandoning his clerical career for the sake of science, and entered almost immediately into Wilkins's group. His main scientific contribution should be considered as part of the task, which he shared with many of his Oxford colleagues, to mix Harvey's medicine with the new atomic philosophy, and in that context Bathurst actively contributed to the development of chemistry – Robert Boyle discussed and much appreciated Bathurst's findings in explaining chemically the question of respiration.[10] Together with being involved in the scientific enterprise of Wilkins's circle, Bathurst had a pivotal role in coordinating its politics. Associated with Trinity College since 1634, Bathurst appeared to have acquired a considerable reputation: even if in the 1650s he did not have any official role in the government of the college, nevertheless he succeeded in having the Presbyterian Seth Ward appointed President of Trinity in 1659, a post that he himself would occupy in 1664. To this man, then, White dedicated his treatise, with the hope that it would be deemed worthy of the attention of

---

[8] For more details on the advancement of medical science in the seventeenth century and in Oxford in particular see A.G. Debus, *The chemical philosophy*, and R.G. Frank Jr., *Harvey and the Oxford Physiologists*, pp. 90 and ff.

[9] The complete titles are respectively *Euclides Physicus, sive de Principiis Naturae*, London 1657, and *Euclides Metaphysicus, sive de Principiis Sapientiae*, London 1658.

[10] On Bathurst's scientific interests and contribution to the history of medicine and chemistry see R.G. Frank Jr., *Harvey and the Oxford Physiologists*, pp. 106–113.

the Oxford men, who, as White put it, were the 'magnae aves' whose protection his 'quadrupes Euclides' needed.[11]

Euclides Metaphysicus is dedicated to another physician, Charles Scarburgh, whom White defines as 'Londini Ornamentum, Sanitatis publicae tutela, Mediciae Gloria, magni Magistri tui HARVAEI ingenii & indutriae heares'[12]. Charles Scarburgh was indeed Harvey's closest collaborator: he had worked with him in Oxford in the early 1640s, and when Harvey left Oxford he too moved to London, where he became a member of a scientific circle coordinated by the mathematician John Wallis. When Wallis joined Wilkins's group in Oxford, Scarburgh decided to remain in the capital, and in 1649 he was appointed lecturer on anatomy at Surgeons' Hall.[13]

Thus White dedicated his works to two physicians who had worked either with Harvey or on Harvey's theories, and therefore with two examples of natural philosophers engaged in both the experimental method, and the mixture of new science and Aristotelianism represented by Harveian medicine: as White wrote to Scarburgh, working on this kind of new medicine meant unifying experiments with theory, or exposing 'caelum Archimedaeum in Microcosmo'.[14] And White felt deeply committed to the task of making sense of experimental findings through a logical system of physics and metaphysics.

Also interesting are the paths of White's dedicatees: both of them were Royalists, and both of them had arrived in Oxford with the King. But one of them decided to remain there after the victory of Parliament, abandoned his clerical career for science, and was well-known in the Wilkins group for his 'dislike of religious controversy', as Barbara Shapiro puts it.[15] The other one, by contrast, left Oxford with the King, remained in London during the 1650s and re-entered the entourage of Charles II immediately after the Restoration. The King rewarded Scarburgh's loyalty by choosing him as his first physician, and by conferring upon him the title of knight in 1669.[16]

White's choice of dedicatees squares with his own attempts to elaborate a natural and rational theology that transcended the confessional perspective and also, to a certain extent, political allegiances. As we have seen in analyzing White's *Grounds* and the other Blackloists' political involvements, these Catholics, in different manners and with different agendas, all believed that Cromwell's regime could open up the possibility of coexistence among different political and religious factions. The common interest in natural philosophy could have provided a unifying factor for people who had found themselves on opposite sides during the Civil War, which was what White saw happening among Wilkins's associates.

---

[11] T. White, *Euclides Physicus*, sig.A3v–A4r.
[12] T. White, *Euclides Metaphysicus*, sig.A4r.
[13] On Scarburgh's role in Oxford see R.G. Frank Jr., *Harvey and the Oxford Physiologists*, pp. 27–30.
[14] T. White, *Euclides Metaphysicus*, sign.A4r–v.
[15] B.J. Shapiro, *John Wilkins*, p. 225.
[16] More details on Scarburgh's life can be found in *DNB sub voce Scarburgh, Charles*, and in F.G. Frank Jr., *Harvey and the Oxford Physiologists*, pp. 27 and ff. *passim*.

However, White's role in Wilkins's circle cannot be reduced to a generic endorsement of what White saw as its central features or to a social network and patronage-seeking. Rather, White in fact actively contributed to the properly scientific and philosophic debates in which the Oxford men found themselves involved. In particular, White was especially interested in two issues: the debate over the relationship between mathematics and physics, and, perhaps more importantly, the philosophical, theological and scientific implications of such a debate. As for the first, White discussed the relationship between mathematics and physics in his *Euclides Physicus,* in which he re-presented his atomic and Aristotelian theory of matter, this time partially reworked in mathematical language. In particular, White provided an explanation of how to combine fruitfully the mathematical concept of infinity with the physical world, in which matter is determined.

First of all, White strongly believed in the truth and usefulness of the concept of infinity in mathematics, and in the text he explained at length the logical consequences of applying such a concept to the study of superficies. As he put is, every surface can be measured with lines, 'but a very small line can be divided into as many parts as any other line can be divided'. The conclusion, therefore, is that 'there can be no end in adding one line to the other; and consequently there is no end to the parts of any minimal line, or of a body which can be measured by lines'.[17] In other words, assuming that every surface can be measured by measuring the lines it contains, since every line can be divided into infinitesimally small other lines, the consequence is that every surface contains an infinite sum of infinitely small components. If mathematically surface can be divided into an infinite number of parts, in physics the principle of infinitesimal needs to be corrected. In the physical world, since 'nothing can exist, which is not determined in itself', it means that for every body there must be a part that is determined and finite. But if we try to combine this with the mathematical principle of infinity, we might end up with an infinite entity resulting from the sum of finite and determinate parts, or, in other words, that 'an infinite length is included between a given point and the distance from it, which is infinite, that is to say…it is at the same time finite and infinite'.[18] However, since it is absurd to think that a sum of infinite parts can produce a finite result, White solves the question by recurring to the Aristotelian principle of the difference between *potentia* and *actus*. If potentially matter is both finite and infinite, *actu* matter cannot be infinite, but it must be determined in itself and must be conceived as 'quantitas', or quantity. And since the main characteristic of quantity is its being 'unitas & ratio uniendi partes suas', it follows that matter is composed of indivisible

---

[17] [linea autem brevissima divisi possit in tot partes in quot quaelibet alia secta est] [nullus autem possit esse finis addendi unam lineam ad aliam; consequens est nullum etiam esse finem partium cujuslibet lineae minimae, vel corporis a lineis mensurabilis] Ibid., pp. 19–20.

[18] [nihil existere possit quod non sit in semetipso determinatum] [infinita longitudo conclusa est inter punctum acceptum & palmum infinite distantem ab eo, hoc est…simul est finita & infinita] Ibid., pp. 20–21.

small particles.[19] Those particles, moreover, are assembled in different degrees of rarity and density, according to how densely 'packed' a certain number of particles are in a given space. And it is precisely the changing in density of matters, or the processes of condensation and rarefaction, that causes motion, since, as White had always maintained, following Aristotle, *vacuum* did not exist. By contrast, if 'principia naturae forent immutabilia', that is to say, if matter were homogeneous, like Epicurus's atoms, White argues, the result of the homogeneity would be a world 'as a rock, or something harder and more unalterable'.[20] When it comes to explaining in greater detail the issue of density and the quantitative nature of matter, White clarified that the Aristotelian four elements are not of a different nature, but rather represent the 'corpora simpliciora', or the sort of basic and extreme combination of rarity and density. The combinations of rarity and density, however, remain infinite and 'innumerabiles'.[21]

Now, if the main tenets of White's physical theory of matter are not particularly noteworthy here, for they are but a re-elaboration of his own and Digby's reflections dating back to the 1640s, the inclusion of the mathematical explanation of the concept of infinity is rather interesting. And it is so not because of its originality, but precisely because White was offering his atomical/Aristotelian theory as a contribution to a heated debate in which the members of the Oxford circle were profoundly involved. The main protagonists of the debate were Thomas Hobbes and John Wallis, one of the most prominent members of Wilkins's circle, who had helped Cromwell decoding documents and was appointed Savilian professor of geometry in 1649.[22]

The debate between Wallis and Hobbes was, to a certain extent, a part of the debate over the university curriculum – among other issues, it touched upon the question of what kind of mathematics should be taught in universities –, nevertheless it presents some peculiar characteristics, which it is useful to briefly sketch. The immediate origin of the clash was the publication of Hobbes's *De Corpore* in 1655, in which the English philosopher had explained the mathematical principles that allowed him to solve a number of central and open problems, first and foremost the squaring of the circle. Wallis replied almost immediately by challenging Hobbes's methods and findings, and the two continued to dispute bitterly until at least 1678.[23] The main point of contention between Wallis and Hobbes was the role of arithmetic in explaining geometry, and the ensuing consequences.

---

[19] Ibid., pp. 21–27.
[20] [veluti saxum, vel siquid durius & immutabilius] Ibid., pp. 27–28.
[21] Ibid., pp. 90–91.
[22] On the role of Wallis within the Oxford circle see A.R. Hall – M. Boas Hall, 'The Intellectual Origins of the Royal Society. London and Oxford', *Notes and Records of the Royal Society of London*, vol. 23 n. 2 (1968), pp. 157–168; B.J. Shapiro, *John Wilkins, passim.*
[23] On the dispute between Hobbes and Wallis see D.M. Jesseph, *Squaring the circle. The War between Hobbes and Wallis*, Chicago 1999, which contains an accurate bibliography for further reading on the specific point of the controversy.

More specifically, Hobbes started from the assumption that mathematical science's first task is to describe phenomena that we can experience in the physical world. Therefore he rejected the kind of mathematics that took into consideration abstract notions. Among the consequences of such a principle, particularly interesting is here the controversy between Wallis and Hobbes over the infinite and its mathematical and physical significance. John Wallis was a strong advocate of the theory of infinitesimal, and he maintained that continuous geometric magnitudes could be fruitfully described mathematically as being composed of infinitely divisible parts. He admitted that the content of the actual world was indeed different from mathematical abstractions, but that did not undermine, in Wallis's view, the results of those mathematical abstractions. Hobbes vigorously opposed Wallis on this point: since mathematics should only analyze what we can actually experience, and since we cannot experience the concept of infinite, but we can only think of 'infinite' as something inexhaustible and incomplete, it follows that the notion of a surface composed of infinite parts was mathematically untenable precisely because it was physically absurd. In other words, unlike Wallis, Hobbes saw mathematical reasoning as a function of physics: whenever a mathematical concept does not find any correspondence in what we can construct from the senses, it should be discarded.[24]

As for White, in describing the concept of infinitesimal and the difference (as he saw it) between the mathematical concept and the physical conclusions, he was offering his contribution precisely to the Wallis-Hobbes debate. More specifically, White shared Wallis's position on the legitimacy of mathematical concepts even if those could not be directly applied to the physical world, and offered his own modified Aristotelianism as an argument in support of Wallis's position.[25]

Beyond the specific mathematical controversy between Hobbes and Wallis, as well as beyond White's contribution to the debate, there is a much more important issue at stake. Hobbes's position on the mathematical infinitesimal is the direct consequence of his materialistic philosophy, on the basis of which Hobbes could not endorse any speculation on what he saw as truly 'metaphysical', as, for instance, the infinitesimal. By contrast, Wallis's insistence upon the epistemological and theoretical validity of the theory of infinitesimal is but a manifestation of the profound theological aspect of the natural science that Wallis (along with the members of the Wilkins group) was advocating. In other words, just as it was legitimate to study the infinitesimal even if there is no empirical evidence for it, by the same token it is legitimate to infer

---

[24] On this see P. Mancosu-E. Vailati, 'Torricelli's Infinitely Long Solid and Its Philosophical Reception in the Seventeenth Century', *Isis* vol. 82 (1991), pp. 50–70; and D.M. Jesseph, *Squaring the circle*, pp. 173 and ff.; P. Mancosu, *Philosophy of Mathematics and Mathematical Practice in the Seventeenth Century*, Oxford 1996, pp. 145 and ff.

[25] On the Aristotelian features of Wallis's mathematics see K. Hill, 'Neither ancient nor modern: Wallis and Barrow on the Composition of Continua. Part One: Mathematical Styles and the Composition of Continua', *Notes and Records of the Royal Society of London*, vol. 50 n. 2 (1996), pp. 165–178.

rationally the existence of a meta-physical being, i.e. God, even if no empirical evidence thereof can be found. And White was such an integral part of the debate that he contributed to this very issue of physics/metaphysics directly and originally.

Already in *Euclides Physicus* there is evidence that White realized that the battle in which the Oxford circle was engaged far surpassed the specific question of the relationship between mathematics and physics. In the dedicatory epistle to the reader, which is tellingly addressed 'ad paucos', White explained more specifically the role of the Oxford circle as he saw it by sketching a brief history of philosophy. After the 'Sophistae…lingua nitidi, mente inanes' corrupted ancient philosophy, White argued, Scholasticism opened up a way to 'free nature' from the idle discussions of the rhetoricians, with the help of the Christian faith. But 'mollities et vanitas' invaded Scholasticism, and therefore but a small 'Aeropagus' remained, constituted by 'those whom the mathematical practice and the most alluring aspect of the secrets of nature… allowed to rest'.[26] Thus, White saw the Wilkins group as the only venue in which mathematics and physics, that is to say, abstract concepts and natural philosophy, contributed to foster peace and unity, rather than division. In White's opinion the best system of 'abstract notions' was precisely Aristotelianism, which, once it was purged and improved with the findings of experiments, was the best bulwark against skepticism and materialism. And it is from this perspective that White saw the Oxford men as his allies.

If White's *Euclides Physicus* already was a step in this direction, his second major work of those years, *Euclides Metaphysicus,* represented an attempt to complete the unification of abstract notions and physical theories. As White wrote in the epistle to the reader, if his previous work was concerned with physics, this new one was the other side of the coin: metaphysics for White was not 'novam a materia abstractionem', as somebody – read: Hobbes – says, but both are parts of the same system, just as his *Euclides Metaphysicus* was nothing but the 'extensio' of his other *Euclides*.[27]

And indeed White's *Euclides Metaphysicus* is nothing but a version of the atomism that White explained in his previous treatise, only this time constructed in 'abstract', that is to say, metaphysical, terms. And since for White the best and only system in which both metaphysics and physics were explained was Aristotelianism, his *Euclides Metaphysicus* is a sort of translation of his theory of matter into Aristotelian terms. For instance, White separately defines the concepts of *substantia* and *quantitas*: while the latter is the matter, the former is the indivisible component of the matter, or, in other words, the atom. As for the atoms, or *substantia*, they are not an *ens*, that is to say, they are not distinguished qualitatively from one another, but only quantitatively.[28] *Spiritus*, on the other hand, being only pure *forma* without *materia,* cannot be reduced

---

[26] [quos mathematicarum usus & veritatum naturalium blandissimus aspectus…in quiete posuit] Ibid., T. White, *Euclides Physicus*, epistle 'ad paucos', unfol.
[27] T. White, *Euclides Metaphysicus*, epistle 'ad lectorem', unfol.
[28] Ibid., pp. 4–6.

to a quantity and is by consequence indivisible.[29] In White's synthesis there is also room for a lengthy discussion of the distinction between *materia* and *forma*, which for him do not exist separate from each other, but which both contribute to form the existing matter: 'therefore *forma* is a body insofar as it is distinct, or in that it is distinguished from the others, and on which basis it is what it is; *materia* is the same body insofar as it fits with others, or insofar it is what fits with others, and supports that which is distinguished by the others'.[30] Therefore, this matter in which *materia* and *forma* are inextricably combined is only quantitatively determined in its existence, given that the *substantia*, or essence of matter is the indivisible atom. And since no body differs from any other body except in a quantitative way, it follows that matter, deprived of every kind of internal qualitative difference, is passive, or, as White put it, 'it is clear, that the body and the species formed on the basis of their own differences with respect to it are not active'[31]. Therefore all motion depends on the quantitative nature of matter, or, in other words, all motion can be reduced to processes of rarefaction and condensation.

But what are the philosophical and theological implications of White's Aristotelian atomism? Since matter is mechanical and passive, because quantity is its defining character, it follows that it does not contain in itself the *existentia*, or to put it differently, it does not choose to exist, but a *vis causativa* needs to be applied to matter: therefore 'a being is given which exists by definition' and which communicates its existence to matter.[32] This *ens* is nothing but God, whose existence can be inferred precisely by describing in abstract notions the physical world.[33]

For White, therefore, mathematics and physics were not in conflict with each other, but rather two necessary parts of the same process of knowledge in which physics and metaphysics are necessarily linked. In fact, it is precisely through this link that we can avoid the danger of skepticism on the one hand, and materialism on the other; and that we can arrive at the 'rational apprehension' of God. Aristotelianism was the best weapon in this fight; so effective in fact that White translated his whole physical theories in Aristotelian terms. In his debate against Hobbes Wallis was fighting on the same side as White: for the Oxford mathematician Hobbes's materialism, not simply the solidity of his mathematical findings, was the target, and the single mathematical issues were but a manifestation of the real question. As Wallis had written in one of the many pamphlets he addressed against Hobbes:

---

[29] Ibid., pp. 132 and ff.

[30] [Est itaque Forma corpus, quatenus est distinctum, seu quo distingutur ab aliis, & de quo est hoc quod est; Materia vero est idem corpus, quatenus convenit cum aliis, seu quatenus est quo convenit cum aliis, & sustentat quod distinguitur ab aliis] Ibid., p. 12.

[31] [palam est, corpus & species natas per proprias differentias ipsius non esse activas] Ibid., pp. 37–38.

[32] [datur aliquod ens per definitionem existentem] Ibid., pp. 46–60.

[33] A large section of White's work is in fact dedicated to an exposition of Aristotelian proofs for the immortality of the soul and the existence of God, with the same arguments that he and Digby had used in the 1640s: see Ibid., pp. 73 and ff.

You deem ridiculous, and impossible to conceive with any imagination, that anything that is not a body could exist; and…you also think that all the "incorporeal substances" should be dismissed as "idle words of the Scholastics"; who does not see that you not only deny the Angels and immortal souls, but also God himself.[34]

While Wallis had used Aristotelianism as an argument to demonstrate Hobbes's atheism, White saw Aristotelianism as the best system in which a mechanist view of the world, perfectly in line with experimental findings, coexisted with natural theology. Or, as he put it in the final section of his *Euclides Metaphysicus*, 'Deus in gubernatione Mundi nihil immediate, & specialiter agit',[35] that is to say, God governs the world as a clockmaker.

If White's writings from the 1650s appear to be heavily influenced by the arguments and agenda of Wilkins's circle, it is important to note that the Oxford men recognized White as one of theirs, and appreciated his contribution to their philosophical and theological project. First of all, both Thomas White and Kenelm Digby had discussed at length with John Wallis on specific mathematical questions that Wallis was working on in the 1650s. In fact, Digby and White had a pivotal role in fostering Wallis's research. For instance, in 1657 Wallis sent a letter to Digby in which he thanked the Catholic, then in Paris, for having shared with him Fermat's findings on squaring parabolae and hyperbolae, which he did not know about: 'I gather from the letter that Fermat wrote to you (which you were so kind as to have D.White inform me of, for which I am obliged to you) that Fermat has asked and obtained an opinion on that issue'.[36]

The correspondence continued, and from it we can gather that Digby and White continued in their role of trait d'union between the English and the French mathematical community.[37] However, Wallis and the Blackloists did not talk only about Fermat's mathematical findings, but also about the various aspects of the controversy that opposed Thomas Hobbes to the members of Wilkins's circle. In august 1657 Digby wrote to Wallis:

---

[34] [Dum enim pro ridiculo habes, & quod nulla unquam imaginatione concipi possit, ut quicquam uspiam existat quod corpus non est; adeoque…. "Substantias incorporeas" omnes "ad inania Scholasticorum verba" amandandas velis; quis non videt te non modo Angelos, eotque immortales Animas, sed & Deum ipsum Optium Maximum…abnegare], J. Wallis, *Elenchus Geometriae Hobbianae*, Oxford 1655, p. 90. On this see also S. Probst, 'Infinity and creation: the origin of the controversy between Thomas Hobbes and the Savilian Professors Seth Ward and John Wallis', *The British Journal for the History of Science*, vol. 26 (1993), pp. 271–9; and D.M. Jessepth, *Squaring the Circle*, pp. 309 and ff.

[35] T. White, *Euclides Metaphysicus*, pp. 197–8.

[36] [persentio utique ex literis illis, a Nobilissimo D.Fermatio ad te scriptis, (quas pro summa tua humanitate, curaveris per D. White mihi communicandas, eoque me tibi obligatum devinxeris) tum Fermatii ea de re [i.e. de nostris lucubrationibus] sententiam rogasse tum & obtinuisse], Wallis to Digby, Oxford June 6 1657, in J. Wallis, *Commercium Epistolicum de Quaestionibus quisdan Mathematicis nuper habitum*, Oxford 1658, p. 7. On the controversy between Wallis and Fermat see D.M. Jesseph, *Squaring the Circle*, passim.

[37] The names of Digby and White recur very frequently in the letters contained in the *Commercium Epistolicum* as the persons in charge of connecting the Oxford circle with Fermat: see p. 19, p. 24, p. 74 and *passim*.

> I must not take leave of you, till I have spoken a word or two of your worthy Colleague Doctor Ward. It is some time since I have heard of his booke against M.Hobbes. and M.White had sent it over hither for me whiles I was in Languedoc; But I had not seene it till now, that I have greedily read it over with much content and pleasure...I will end this point concerning him, with beseeching you to present my most humble service to him (for I conceive, you see him often) with most harty and obliged thankes for his excessive civilities to me, together with his assurance that I esteeme and honour him with all my heart. It is a worthy Triumvirate that you two and Doctor Wilkins do exercise in literature and all that is worthy. Your names are famous abroad; and I heare of you from sundry hands; but from none more largely or more affectionately then from M.White; whom, your goodnesses have wonne to be entirely yours; and he amply expresseth it upon all occasions.[38]

If White had been 'entirely won over' to the Oxford circle, as we have seen, it is even more important to note that the Oxford men welcomed White's esteem and highly regarded his contribution. As Wallis replied to Digby,

> Those other two Gentlemen whom you are pleased to joyn mee with in your good opinion, D.Wilkins and D.Ward; I shall, upon their returns hither, acquaint how much they are obliged to you for that honour that you put upon them...and wee must all acknowledge ourselves deeply indebted to M.White, who is pleased not onely to judge so favourably of us, but to represent us to you in such a Character as hath gained us so advantagious a place in your opinion.[39]

Aside from Wallis's words of praise, even more interesting are the comments that Ward had made on Digby and White in his book *In Thomae Hobbii philosophiam exercitatio epistolica,* to which Kenelm Digby was referring to in the letter we have examined. In the session dedicated to the discussion of the concepts of identity and difference, Ward started by violently attacking Hobbes for his alleged ignorance of ancient and modern natural philosophy. In the seventeenth century, in fact, there were many natural philosophers 'either from our land, or from some neighboring lands, who can be rightly said either to have much enlarged the old Philosophy, or to have elaborated a new one'.[40] Among those, Ward wrote that there was no doubt but that the names of 'Gassendi, Digby, Albius and also many others..one day will be famous'. More specifically, if for Ward the merit of Gassendi was to have openly embraced Epicurus's philosophy and purged it 'from popular prejudices', the merit of Digby and White, whom Ward refers to as Digby's Achates, was to resurrect and re-elaborate Aristotelianism as an 'antidotum' to the elements

---

[38] Digby to Wallis, Paris, 1 August 1657, in J. Wallis, *Commercium Epistolicum*, pp. 11–12.
[39] Wallis to Digby, Oxford 3 September 1657, in Ibid., p. 13.
[40] [vel ex gente nostra vel ex vicinis aliquibus, qui Philosophiam vel veterem auxisse plurimum; vel novam condidisse... non immerito dicantur], S. Ward, *In Thomae Hobbii Philosophiam exercitatio epistolica*, Oxford 1656, p. 92.

of Epicureanism which 'seem to charge rather ruthlessly against religion.[41] Concerning the Blackloists in particular, Ward wrote that:

> Those very famous men, worthy of immortal honor, indeed destined undoubtedly to immortality, eagerly strived to offend nobody, and to promote piety, and to avoid contention in any sense, but in fact they advanced all their positions with modesty and with accuracy (as far as possible) and in a demonstrative manner.[42]

In other words, for Ward, Wallis and the rest of the Oxford people, White and Digby had two main functions. First, they corrected the materialistic consequences of atomism, which was re-proposed and defended by Descartes and Gassendi, by reviving also the 'other leg' of ancient philosophy, i.e. Aristotelianism. The union between those two lines strands of 'ancient' philosophy, properly 'modernized', was the bulk of the new natural philosophy as it was construed in Oxford. Secondly, and concerning the 'modernizing' aspect, what Ward valued in the Blackloists' revival of Aristotelianism was its logical rigor. Ward insists a great deal on the 'legitimate demonstrations' that Digby and White endorsed: for instance he insisted that Digby's arguments for the immortality of the soul were presented 'legitima demonstratione'.[43] And that is what he laments about Hobbes, who, being ignorant of this new way of combining atomism and Aristotelianism, in Ward's opinion is neither a true and solid Aristotelian, nor a true and solid atomist.[44]

From the perspective of this research, to a certain extent it seems obvious that White's and Digby's natural philosophy as it developed in the 1640s was perfectly fitting the philosophical and scientific agenda of the Wilkins circle. It might also seem obvious that Wilkins and his associates realized precisely how compatible White and Digby were with the Oxford project, and how useful their Aristotelianism could be in the polemical struggle with Hobbes's materialism. Once the target becomes demonstrating that natural science was not inherently contradictory with theology, but rather the two could fruitfully work together in a mutual kind of relationship, then White and Digby become very useful indeed. Another obvious consideration concerns the political aspect of the relationship between the Oxford group and the Blackloists: Wilkins's emphasis on political latitudinarianism was perfectly compatible with White's and Digby's own political involvement and White's political thought.

What might be less obvious, then, is why the contribution of White and Digby to the Oxford circle has been so far overlooked by current scholarship.

---

[41] [Gassendi, Digbaei, Albii, aliorumque etiam multorum...futura sint olim Illustria] [in religionem importunius ruere videatur], Ibid., p. 93.

[42] [At hi quidem viri praeclarissimi atque immortali honore digni, imo immortalitati indubiae consignati, illud impensius studuerunt neminem laedere, pietatem vel promovere, vel nullo modo destruere, quin sua omnia modeste, at (quantum fieri potuit) accurate demonstrative proferre], Ibid., p. 93.

[43] Ibid.

[44] In Ward's sarcastic expression: '[Malmesburiensis] neque Peripateticus est, cui insanit ubique Aristoteles, neque in Horto Epicuri versatus esse videatur, cui (inanis licet sit omnis oratio) nihil tamen inane esse decernitur', Ibid., p. 94.

An explanation of this can be that although much work has been done to problematize the history of science in seventeenth century as a story of ancients vs. moderns, with the happy ending of the triumph of the latter over the former,[45] there is more work to be done. The problem here is just how much 'antiquity' we are willing to allow. While we have come to terms with the existence of some 'old' Aristotelian remains in Wilkins and his associates' position, it remains true that they turned out to be 'modern' in other aspects of their thought. In other words, in the complicated area between past and present the Oxford men had a complicated role of trait d'union, and therefore they must necessarily present a little bit of both past and present. White and Digby did not share the same good fortune: in the complicated area between past and present they have been irredeemably left behind, and there is nothing in their thought that the 'moderns' and the 'more-moderns' could make use of. I think that despite such unfortunate outcome, Digby and White's contributions to the Oxford circle could be further analyzed and much insight into the politics of science in the 1650s could be gained by studying the Blackloists' science.

Also, the other area in which it might be useful to think about the Blackloists' role in mid-century England concerns their religious view. In the debate over the religious character of the Oxford group, and more specifically over the extent and significance of the category of latitudinarianism as a viable way to describe the religious affiliation of Wilkins's associates, I think that new insight can be gained if we think about the role of Catholicism in the picture. White's combination of Aristotelianism and atomism was supported not by a generic notion of rational theology, but by a specifically *Catholic* version of a voluntarist rational theology. As he wrote in the conclusion of his *Euclides Metaphysicus,* what he thought we gained in combining physics and metaphysics was not only a validation of the mechanical science on the basis of a rational theology, or the assurance that God who, being absolutely free, could impose on the physical world any rule he pleases, decided to govern it 'like and engineer', but also a guarantee of man's free will:

> Since God through creation and conservation bestows upon intelligences both the understanding of what needs to be done to govern the world rightly, and the will to do it, and since the intelligences, once they instill the first movement into bodies establish the universal course of nature, and when need be, they change this order for the necessity of spiritual animals, and that nothing else is required to govern the world rightly, it is clear that God did not leave anything besides creation and conservation, which is to say, nothing concerning the government of the world, but that this is entirely entrusted to the creatures, so that they may not err from the divine laws that have been introduced at the moment of creation.[46]

---

[45] Concerning the specific question of the mid-seventeenth century debates between Hobbes and the Wilkins circle, already in 1970 A.G. Debus reminded scholars that 'a quick glance at recent literature relating to this debate [i.e. the debate on the reform of universities] clearly points out the difficulty in trying to define just what was modern in the middle decades of the seventeenth century', *Science and Education*, p. 1.

[46] [Cum enim Deus per creationem, & conservationem infundat intelligentiis, & cognitionem quid sit agendum ad rectam mundi gubernationem, & volitionem id perficiendi: Et intelligentiae

Taking into account White's voluntarist Catholic theology, which, as we have seen before, was deeply influenced by Gassendi's, in combination with his Aristotelian mechanism, could greatly benefit the historiographical debate over the question of the theological character of Wilkins's group in a context in which current scholarship is more and more aware of the shortcomings of the category of latitudinarianism as a rather simplistic tool to understand the complexity of the theological spectrum of the 1650s English natural philosophers. In this respect, analyzing specific sets of theological and philosophical tenets such as the voluntarist theology on both sides of the Channel can be one of the solutions to investigating the question. As Margaret Osler has recently demonstrated, Boyle's theological positions and the relationship between those and his mechanical science can be best understood if we consider 'the importance of voluntarist theology as the foundations for all its views'. And it was Gassendi's version of voluntarist theology that Boyle was influenced by.[47] The Blackloists, whom Boyle held in great esteem, were one of the most important links between French atomism and theology and English mechanical philosophy. As in the case of Boyle, I believe that the question of 'latitudinarianism', or the theological foundations of seventeenth-century English natural philosophy could become much more nuanced and historically accurate if we keep the Blackloists in the picture.

If Thomas White found a congenial environment in the Protectorate, and actively contributed to the philosophical and theological agenda of the Oxford men, the 1650s saw the strengthening of his authority and prestige within the English Catholic Church and within the Roman hierarchy as well. During this decade, in fact, White published the majority of his most famous and controversial theological works. His *Villicationis suae de medio statu animarum,* in which he wrote on the doctrine of Purgatory, came out in 1653, the *Sonus Buccinae* and *Tabulae suffragiales,* in which he denied that the doctrine of Papal Infallibility was to be believed *de fide* were published respectively in 1654 and 1655, and in 1654 he also published the *Apology for Rushworth's dialogue.* Moreover, the opposition that White had to face within the English Chapter was growing stronger: the faction opposite to the Blackloists, whose leader was George Leyburn, was actively and vocally denouncing White's political manoeuvres, as well as his dangerous theology. However, in the 1650s the Catholic hierarchy, both in England and in Rome, was not willing to let Leyburn complain too loudly. As for the internal affairs of the English Catholic Church, Richard Smith, Bishop of Chalcedon, had

---

immisso motu primo in corpora universalem cursum naturae faciant, & quando opus est ad necessitatem Animalium virtute spiritualium eundem ordinem immutent, & nihil praeterea requiratur ad rectam gubernatione Mundi, palam est, Deo nihil reliquum esse praeter creationem & conservationem, hoc est nihil omnino de gubernatione, sed eam integer commissam esse creatures non erraturi a legibus divinis in creatione ipsis inditis] T. White, *Euclides Metaphysicus,* pp. 197–8.

[47]   M.J. Osler, 'The intellectual sources of Robert Boyle's philosophy of nature: Gassendi's voluntarism and Boyle's physico-theological project', in *Philosophy, science, and religion,* pp. 178–191, at p. 190.

urged repeatedly Leyburn to cease to discredit White and his doctrine, and this in a rather brusque tone:

> Deare Sir, have diverse times written to you for to suppress all clamors against Mr.Blacloes Noveltyes, and as you have written to mee, you have so done but still divers write to mee that do the contrary, and have lately written all my chiefe officers very eagerly against them, which I am very sorry to heare, for so you will cause the inconvenience and schisme which will bee woorse then the Bookes are, whose esteem will fall of it self if you cry less against them.[48]

Smith's disapproval of Leyburn's actions against White is not motivated by the fact that the Bishop of Chalcedon actually agreed with the Blackloists' position, which in fact he vigorously opposed. As he wrote to Leyburn, 'for myne owne part I desire nothing more then that the See Apostolicke would iudge of his opinions, and if it approved them I should straight submit my iudgement thereunto, but really as they are I can not like them'.[49] The problem was, as Smith wrote to Leyburn, that White was powerful, and he had threatened him by saying that if the Bishop had not intervened on his behalf, then White 'will frame an accusation iuridically against me.' Smith realized White's prestige and authority, and did not want to risk a public war against somebody who might have proved too strong an enemy: 'I feare that the prosequution in iuridicall manner will bee offensive to the publicke, and not followed with that clarity and modesty as should bee, and hath beene hearetofore'.[50]

Leyburn was not the only enemy that White had: in the 1650s Walter Montagu, the man who, together with Kenelm Digby was in charge of collecting money for the Queen from the English Catholics in the 1640s, had turned against White, presumably for both theological and political reasons. In a letter he wrote to White in 1654, he complained about the Catholic's arrogance and polemical virulence which did not spare even the Bishop of Chalcedon: 'you could have not branded, Montagu wrote, any position of Luther and Calvin with fouler markes of your censure'[51]. Montagu concluded by saying that

> For my own part, I am sorry a person I have so much esteemed, should oblidge mee to retract that opinion; & truely, if I ever in place of questioning your works, I should thinke my selfe oblidged to doe it in regard of those outrages you offer to so many worthy authors of your own Religion I represent unto you my understanding of the Matter, wich all the ingenuity I can, & shall never lessen the charity I owe you, in praying that you may

---

[48] Smith to Leyburn, 6 July 1652, in Westminster Diocesan Archives Mss., vol. XXX, document n. 150, f. 503v.
[49] Ibid.
[50] Ibid.
[51] Montagu to White, 30 March 1654, in Westminster Diocesan Archives Mss., vol. XXX, document n. 177, f. 622

be as usefull to Gods church as your abilities well managed would make you .[52]

White's reply shows clearly how safe and confident he felt in his position. On Montagu's remark on Luther and Calvin White commented:

> You add, I could not have branded any position of Luther or Calvin with fouler markes. I confess it: neither do I thinke any position in them either more prejudicious to the faith & church of Christ, nor (abstracting from accidentall circumstances) to deserve a great Censure.[53]

As for his own doctrine, White believed that it was perfectly orthodox according to the doctrine of the Church of Rome. By contrast, the 'Court of Rome' was responsible for denying the conciliarist aspect of the ecclesiology of the *primitiva Ecclesia,* and thus he felt compelled to actually defend the Catholic orthodoxy against the attack:

> For my own part, had not the position been of men of so great valew, & the practise so present to make it pass for an Article of Faith, & verely breake the very sinews of Christian faith, wich are to be Catholicke & Apostolick; I should not have held my selfe obliged to speake so plainely of it.[54]

Evidently, White's arrogance had some grounds, for in the first half of the 1650s the English Chapter refused to side with Leyburn, and suggested moderation and unity, and that even after White's *Sonus Buccinae* was censured by the Inquisition.[55] In a very interesting move the English Chapter noted how detrimental the division between Leyburn's and White's faction was for the government of the whole Chapter, and therefore it sent to both Leyburn and White a letter in which it asked them to cease fighting. Also, they sent the letter addressed to White to Leyburn and viceversa, so as to mark the Chapter's role as *super partes*. In the letter to Leyburn, the Chapter underscored the need of avoid any 'common pretext of all rebellion against authority',[56] and reminded Leyburn that even if he thought that White's doctrine was unsound, nevertheless he was not the one in charge of establishing doctrinal matters:

> But the Catholike Church (God bee thanked) hath her legall & authoritive meanes, both subalternall & supreme, to examine & condemnde what soever may bee amisse either in his or in any other man's writings whatsoever. Particular men can only informe those, whose office it belong's unto, of what they judge to bee erroneous or dangerous. Though as friends

---

[52] Ibid.
[53] White to Montagu, 6 April 1654, in Westminster Diocesan Archives Mss., vol. XXX, document n. 177, f. 623.
[54] Ibid.
[55] The censure can be found in ACDF, Decreta Sancti Officii, Decretum 12 May 1655, ff. 53v–58v.
[56] The Chapter to Leyburn, in Westminster Diocesan Archive Mss., vol. XXXI, ff. 378–9. The catalogue dates the document to 1657, but the letters were definitely sent before May, when White submitted his writings to the Holy See as the Chapter requested him to.

& breathren wee may cover & defende what wee thinke wee are not necessarily obliged to complaine of.[57]

In other words, Leyburn had no business in meddling with White's supposed errors, which were not to be judged as such unless the Catholic Church decided against them. Therefore Leyburn should comply with Rome's decision.

When it came to writing to White, the Chapter acknowledged that his doctrine were somewhat 'exoticke', but not certainly heretic.[58] However, in order to 'preserve our body (whereof you are a principal member)' they suggested that White proceeded with moderation. In particular, in order to clear the way from any suspicion of doctrinal unsoundness, the Chapter urged White first to 'give your breathen & the world some publicke & convenient testimony of your submitting your writings to the censure of the Catholick Church, & see of Rome'.[59] Secondly, they advised White to circulate his future writings before publication among the member of the Chapters, following a well-established practice followed by 'the learned D.rs of Divinity of the famous faculty of this towne'.[60]

Once again, this correspondence is a testimony of White's reputation and authority within the Chapter: even though from 1652 Leyburn had been appointed President of Douai College, and even though his side had the sympathy, if not the open support, of Bishop Smith while he was alive, nevertheless both Smith himself and the Chapter realized that White was at least as powerful as his adversary. Indeed, among the members of the Chapter were many supporters and pupils of White's: John Sergeant, for instance, was appointed secretary of the Chapter in 1655.[61]

White decided to comply with the Chapter's requests, and in May 1657 he submitted his writings to the Holy See.[62] The Chapter was satisfied with White's formal submission, and in a meeting immediately after 1657 the members, discussing White's doctrine and the continuing opposition on the side of Leyburn, formally confirmed that 'all the chaptermen did awow to condemne and allow all doctrines and customes as they are condemned and allowed by the Sea Apostolike'.[63]

The question now is, did a strong and final condemnation of the Holy See ever arrive? As I have argued elsewhere, Rome did not take a strong disciplinary action against White and his doctrine until after the Restoration: in a confused and uncertain moment, the Papacy did not want to risk severing all relations with Cromwell, unless the return of the King was certain.[64] The political

---

[57] Ibid.
[58] The Chapter to White, ca. 1657, in Ibid., f. 379.
[59] Ibid.
[60] Ibid.
[61] On Sergeant and his role in the Chapter see D. Krook, *John Sergeant and his circle*.
[62] A copy of White's declaration, dated on May 18th 1657, can be found in Westminster Diocesan Archives Mss., vol. XXXI, document n.73, f. 341.
[63] The minutes of the Chapter's meeting can be found in Westminster Diocesan Archives Mss., vol. XXXI, document n. 85, f. 411r.
[64] S. Tutino, 'The Catholic Church and the English Civil War'.

sagacity of the Roman Catholic hierarchy can also explain the reaction of the English Chapter: if in Rome people thought that White was a useful link with Cromwell (as long as Cromwell was in power), all the more reason for the English Catholic hierarchy to protect White's 'exotike' doctrine as much as it was possible. And for much of the 1650s it looked as if it was indeed possible.

5.2 Kenelm Digby

During the 1650s Thomas White enjoyed an intellectually active and fruitful life thanks to his advantageous political position, while being able to count both on the support of many of the members of the Chapter and on the protection, if not the esteem and admiration, of the Catholic Church in Rome. However, he kept clear of direct political involvement. With Digby, things went differently.

The first element to note is the high esteem in which Ward, Wallis and his colleagues seemed to hold Kenelm Digby, as is evident from the correspondence between Wallis and the Catholic author. Also, in the passage of Ward's book on the contribution of White and Digby that we have analyzed above, it is interesting to notice how the relationship between the master (White) and the disciple (Digby) is almost reversed, as Ward calls White Digby's 'Achates': it is Digby, then, who is the Aeneas of the pair. What were, then, the grounds for the Oxford men's esteem towards Digby?

To answer this question, we should first note that Kenelm Digby did not directly contribute to the more properly scientific issues that concerned Wilkins's associates. More specifically, Digby was not interested in mathematics, and the fullest formulation of his philosophy of nature, that mixture of Aristotelianism and atomism that Ward identified as the main contribution of the Blackloists, remained the 1644 *Two Treatise*. As for the other element of Digby's philosophy mentioned by Ward, that is to say, the Catholic's 'legitimate demonstration' of the immortality of the soul, he returned to it in the only major treatise he wrote in the 1650s, i.e. *A Discourse concerning Infallibility in Religion* dedicated to George Digby.[65] The text needs to be read in the context of the (posthumous) debate between White and Falkland: White's reply to Cary's *Infallibility* was published in 1651, and an entire chapter of Digby's work is devoted to a confutation of 'the Socinians and the Independents'.[66] As to the content of the text, Digby's *Discourse* is a re-proposition of two of the intellectual questions that the Catholic philosopher had always been concerned with, namely, the immortality of the soul and the notion of tradition. As for the former, Digby's first ten chapters work are a kind of summary of the arguments and conclusions already expressed in the *Two Treatises*. As the Catholic wrote:

---

[65] K. Digby, *A Discourse concerning Infallibility*.
[66] Ibid., pp. 199–209.

> I conceive I have fully performed this in a former treatise...but I may reasonably apprehend that the length of that, and the heape of various arguments cumulated there one upon another, may not obtain...that discussion which belongeth to every one of them in particular... And therefore I will here select some few of the chiefe ofthose which that treatise abundeth with.[67]

The second part of Digby's text is a re-working of the Blackloists' notion of tradition, and in this case Digby too is aware of the lack of originality of his conclusions, which he acknowledges are indebted to Thomas White.[68] Indeed, as evidence of the fact that Digby's treatise needs to be considered as one of the version of the Blackloists' 'official party line' on tradition, at the end of the book we find the approbation by the Doctors of Divinity in Paris, signed also by Henry Holden. Digby's text, in the Parisians' opinion, 'doth clearely shew how Grace is engrafted upon Nature, that is, how the Divine & revealed tenets of our Catholike Church, are framed to heighten, as most connaturall to, the light of reason'.[69]

Thus Digby did not win the esteem of Wilkins's associates for his direct participation in the scientific debates of the 1650s, but for his earlier work. And this is a testimony to the long-lasting influence of Digby's atomism and theology, fully expressed in the 1640s. As in the case of White, evidently Digby's philosophy of nature and rational theology, far from being a negligible relic of the Aristotelian past, was being taken extremely seriously in those debates.

Also, in order to understand Ward's praise of Digby we need to take into account that he, unlike Thomas White, had a direct and significant involvement at many levels in the politics of the period. First, Digby had a pivotal role in coordinating the 'politics of science' across the Channel. His knowledge of French academic, scientific and social milieu allowed him contact with the leading theories and theorists of the period. As a further evidence of the intellectual and scientific prestige that Digby enjoyed across the Channel, the Catholic was invited to give a lecture in Montpellier on how to cure wounds through the sympathetic powder.[70] In a sense, Digby had gained prestige in Wilkins's circle because of his role of trait d'union and of 'facilitator' of scientific communications between the English and the French, cashing in, as it were, on the work on natural philosophy and theology done a decade earlier and in collaboration with White.

Secondly, Digby also concerned himself with politics in the proper sense of the term. In 1654 he returned to England after the exile to which he was

---

[67] Ibid., pp. 11–12.

[68] In particular, Digby refers his dedicatee to 'Maister Whites Dialogues (under the name of Rushworth)... and to the same author's sacred Institutions': Ibid., pp. 164–5.

[69] The approbation can be found at the last, unnumbered, page, and is dated 28 November 1652.

[70] Digby's lecture was printed in England as *A late discourse made in a solemne assembly of Nobles and Learned Men at Montpellier in France by Sr. Kenelme Digby*, London 1658. On the significance of Digby's theories for the history of medicine see B.J. Dobbs, 'Studies in the natural philosophy of Sir Kenelm Digby', *Ambix*, vol. XVIII n. 1 (1971), pp. 1–25.

condemned in 1649, and there he collaborated with Hartlib and his laboratory. In 1655 he set out again for France, but this time with the approval of the English government. In a letter sent to John Thurloe from Paris, Joseph Bampsfield, one of his informers, while reporting on the military and political maneuvers in France, wrote: 'I am informed both out of England and here, sir Kenelme Digby is employed by you to discover secrets of…'.[71] But what kind of secrets was Kenelm Digby supposed to discover, and what were his intentions? The question is further complicated by rumors that were spreading in England of the Catholic's double allegiance. For instance, Joseph Bampsfield, in the same letter to Thurloe, warned the Secretary that if even if Digby was working for him, Thurloe should not completely trust him: 'his interest seems, and I believe, is diametrically opposite to what he undertakes, he and mr. Montaguef [sic] are the principall instruments for the pope…They will all cozen you, if they can, and have but too many agents amongst you'.[72] Also, one Robert Walsh or Welsh had contributed to slandering Digby,[73] who, for his part, wrote to Thurloe claiming his innocence against the accusation of Welsh, 'an Irish Papist (whose whole tribe, have an implacable animosity against me)' and magniloquently attesting his allegiance to the Lord Protector:

> My obligations to his Highnesse are so great, that it would be a crime in me to behave myselfe so negligently as to give cause for any shadow of the least suspition, or to do any thing that might require an excuse or Apology. I make it my businesse every where, to have all the world take notice how highly I estime myselfe obliged to his H; and how passionate I am for his service and for his honor and interests; even to the exposing of my life for them. If y. Ho: can not readily find out the bottom of this villany plotted against me, upon notice of so much; I will take post the next day to returne into England (though it may be much to the preiudice of my domestike affaires, in my broken estate; because my debts are not yet quieted) and I doubt not but I shall soone make discovery of some wicked treachery intended against me.[74]

There is no evidence of Digby's alleged treacheries against the Lord Protector, with whom Digby maintained a friendly relationship; indeed, too much so for Clarendon, for instance, who in 1656 accused Cromwell of enjoying the

---

[71] Bampsfield to Thurloe, Paris 24 November 1655, in *A Collection of the state papers of John Thurloe*, ed. by T. Birch, 7 vols, London 1742, vol. IV, pp. 194–196 at p. 195. The name of the person appears in ciphers in the text as '847'.

[72] Bampsfield to Thurloe, p. 195

[73] Not much is known about Robert Welsh or Walsh, and he does not appear in the *DNB*. In March 1655 Walsh wrote to Thurloe to 'beg the grace to be admitted to the honour of waiting upon your highnes': see Walsh to Thurloe, 3 March 1655, in *A Collection*, vol. IV, p. 574. We also know that Walsh did become a spy for the Protectorate: he lived in Flanders with the king and reported to Lord Broghill until he was arrested in Brussels in 1658 (see P. Little, *Lord Broghill and the Cromwellian union with Ireland and Scotland*, Woodbridge 2004, p. 170).

[74] Digby to Thurloe, Paris, 18 March 1656. There are many copies of this letter: the one I quote from can be found in BodL, Rawlinson Mss. A 36, f. 299r. A second manuscript copy can be found in BL, Additional Mss. 4106, ff. 254r–v, and the letter can be found also in *A Collection*, vol. IV, pp. 591–2.

support of the Catholics, and in particular Kenelm Digby, whom he identified as the Lord Protector's 'favourite', to whom White's *Grounds,* an obviously philo-Cromwellian work, was dedicated.[75] William Prynne also complained of the esteem that Cromwell showed Digby.[76]

Once we assume that Digby was in fact working for Cromwell, it remains to be seen what kind of mission he was in charge of. A letter written by Sir Edward Nicholas, secretary of state for Charles II during his exile, to Joseph Jane, one of his informants in the Netherlands, may explain what exactly he was doing: 'I heare that Sir Kenelm Digby is become a great pensioner of Cromwell's, & that his business in France is principally to hinder any agreement betweene Spain & France: wich he will not find very difficult to effect, for long as the Cardinall Mazarin rules soe absolutely in France: for warre & not peace is his interest'.[77]

From Digby's own correspondence with the English government it seems that the Catholic author was indeed working to smooth the relationship between England and France. In December 1655, soon after his arrival to Paris, he wrote to Thurloe informing him of the discontentment felt by 'the merchants of Calais' regarding a problem with taxation of English goods. More specifically, the merchants complained that the governors of Boulogne and Monstreuil, the towns through which English merchandise shipped to Calais had to go on its way to Paris, imposed a tax 'upon every cart of English goods, that goeth through their towne'.[78] Digby's role in this business was that of a mediator, and as such reported the merchants' request to Cromwell to lobby with the French ambassador so 'that so…violent a taxe may no longer be exacted, but that trade may have its free course'.[79]

Although in 1649 Digby seemed to have enjoyed the protection of Queen Anne, regent of France, whom he claimed helped him to obtain a passport to England,[80] there is no evidence of Digby's dealing directly with Mazarin at this date, and I would be inclined to argue against a actual form of agreement between the English Catholic and the French Cardinal, for two main reasons. First, Digby never had a relevant role in French political circles; rather, his influence and prestige were always of an intellectual and academic nature. Secondly, Mazarin had strongly opposed the Blackloists' action in 1648–9: even if he needed Cromwell's alliance, it seems unlikely that Digby would have been Mazarin's only option to obtain it.[81] Yet, it is true that Cromwell was anxious to maintain a good relationship with France and to foment division between France and Spain, and Digby's intellectual, of not political, prestige could only foster the Lord Protector's goals.

---

[75] See his *A letter from a true and lawfull member of Parliament*, s.l. 1656, pp. 64–5.
[76] *A true and perfect narrative*, London 1659, pp. 43, 57.
[77] Nichols to Jane, Cologne 4 March 1656, State Papers 18/125, document no. 4.
[78] Digby to Thurloe, 4 December 1655, in *A collection*, vol. IV, pp. 244–245 at p. 245.
[79] Ibid.
[80] See J.R. Collins, 'Thomas Hobbes and the Blackloist conspiracy', p. 320
[81] For a different view see R.T. Petersson, *Sir Kenelm Digby*, p. 254.

Also, another important factor to consider in explaining the relation between Cromwell and Digby is the Irish question. As we have seen, Digby had worked actively to oppose Rinuccini's mission and the Pope's attempt to foster the Confederates' rebellion in the 1640s. In the 1650s the tension continued between the Blackloist faction and the pro-Confederation faction of Irish Catholics – many of whom had gone into exile and were working for Charles II –, at a moment in which in Rome the Catholic hierarchy was unwilling to openly oppose White and his associates.

The controversy between the Blackloists and this faction of the Irish Catholics is extremely interesting in its complexity. Beyond the question of the political allegiance, some of the pro-Confederation Catholics and the Blackloists held different religious and theological views. For instance, in 1658 the Irish Franciscan John Ponce, who had been an agent for the Catholic Confederates in Rome in the 1640s, wrote an aggressive letter to Digby attacking his treatise on infallibility.[82] For Ponce, a leader in the seventeenth-century revival of Scotism and author of a textbook on Scotus's theology, Digby's fault was his attempt to prove rationally the immortality of the soul:

> God be pleased we have noe neede of such a demonstration, the light of faith is sufficient enough for to persuade that truth as it is to cause us beleave the mysteres of the holie Trinitie Incarnation, Eucharist & c. And who is not disposed to beleave the souls immortalitie without a demonstration of it, though it might be demonstrated, certainelie is noe good Christian, but must be dealt with ...as with heathens, Turks and Jews.[83]

Ponce's extensive comments on Digby's book are really a pretext to attack the philosophy of Thomas White and to defend the 'Philosophie of the Schooles': in Ponce's opinion White had been 'presumptuous' in his criticism of dogmatic philosophy, which he willfully distorted to his own purposes, making 'the poore vulgar ones beleeve, black to be white, and white black. May be it is therefore Mr. White tooke the name of Blacklow'.[84]

I do not mean to imply that Cromwell, in supporting Digby, was trying to foster the controversy within the Catholic group, but he could have certainly taken advantage of if through Digby's role of cultural and religious reference point across the Channel. After all, Cromwell maintained friendly relations with Digby in London and Paris while employing Robert Walsh in Flanders.

Let us now briefly look at the other side of the coin, that is to say, Digby's interest in pursuing Cromwell's favor. Petersson and Gabrieli both argue that Digby's intention was to take advantage of the Protector's alleged religious moderation in order to obtain some form of toleration for the English Catholics.[85] While I do not disagree with these scholars' opinion, I think that

---

[82] Ponce to Digby, undated but post-1658 (the Franciscan quotes from the 1658 edition of Digby's treatise), in BL, Additional Mss. 41846, ff. 67r–73v.
[83] Ibid., f. 67v.
[84] Ibid., ff. 70v–71r.
[85] Cf. R.T. Petersson, *Sir Kenelm Digby*, pp. 254–6; and V. Gabrieli, *Sir Kenelm Digby*, pp. 228–9.

Digby's efforts to secure tolerance for the Catholics cannot be isolated from other factors. As we have seen when examining the Catholic's political activities in the 1640s, for Digby working for the Catholic cause did not exclude the possibility of working for his own career: it was thanks to Cromwell that in 1656 Digby won restitution of some of the properties that had been confiscated after 1649.[86] Also his Blackloist-style Catholicism was an integral part of English and European scientific and theological debates, in which many of Cromwell's supporters were engaged, as we have seen in examining White's contribution to the Oxford circle.

In conclusion, Digby's role during the Protectorate was a relevant one not so much because of his political status. Rather, Digby's own good fortune during the Protectorate depended on his being a link between issues of different natures, such as theology, natural philosophy and politics; as well as a link between Rome, Paris and London. In this respect, Kenelm Digby becomes an interesting figure to argue for the importance of the Catholic community in the English and European political landscape. In other words, Digby, like any Catholic on any side of the political and theological debate, could count on a double status: he was an Englishman and he was a member of the *catholic,* that is to say, universal, community. This double status is on the one hand the reason for a part of the English establishment's questioning of Digby's real agenda (as Bampsfield wrote to Thurloe, Digby's interest was 'diametrically opposite' to that of the Protectorate). On the other hand, broad possibilities could be opened if one were to take advantage of this double status, as Cromwell had done in Digby's case. If we agree that the European dimension is indeed important in order to understand England's religious and political history, then the English Catholic community appears to be a good place from where to start.

5.3 Henry Holden

In the 1650s Henry Holden remained outside of England, and concentrated his efforts in systematizing the main tenets of the Blackloist ecclesiology in what would become his major work of the decade, the treatise *Analysis Divinae Fidei,* whose first edition, in Latin, was printed in Paris in 1652. An English translation, with important modifications, came out in 1658.[87]

The weighty and complex text is divided in two parts. In the first, identical in both the Latin and English edition, Holden expressed the more properly ecclesiological and theological part of the Blackloist doctrine. In the dedicatory epistle to the reader, reprinted in the English edition, Holden wrote that he had decided to write his text after realizing that there was 'much contention and debate even amongst us Catholics' on the true doctrine of the Church of Rome. In this perspective, Holden proposed to eliminate all the doctrines that should

---

[86] See V. Gabrieli, *Sir Kenelm Digby*, pp. 229–230.
[87] H. Holden, *Analysis Divinae Fidei*, Paris 1652; and Id., *The Analysis of Divine Faith*, Paris 1658. I will quote from the Latin edition only when it differs from the English one.

not be believed *de fide,* and to concentrate on the core of Catholic belief, and on the reasons why the Catholic Church is the true and only continuator of the *primitiva Ecclesia* And the outcome that Holden hoped to obtain from such a process was 'to find out any means how to conjoyne and unite the disagreeing thoughts and minds of all Christians'.[88] The arguments are the by-now familiar ones: in order to establish the infallibility of the Catholic faith, neither Scripture alone nor individual reason is sufficient. By contrast, the only sure way to prove the truth of Catholicism is tradition. Since 'by how much any tradition is more universal, by so much it is the more strong and certain', and since the Catholic tradition is truly universal, therefore the tradition of the Catholic Church is the one true mark of its truth.[89]

Having established this principle, Holden continues by scrutinizing some of the most controversial Catholic doctrines in order to prove what descends directly from Scripture and tradition, and as such has to be believed *de fide,* and what is merely at the level of 'opinion'. For instance, when dealing with the prerogatives of the Pope, Holden wants to defend the Catholics from the Protestants' accusation, that 'we make the Pope a God'.[90] Therefore, Holden opposes the notion of Papal infallibility, since just as the General Council can err, 'the Pope can also err'.[91] The Pope does have a special authority over the rest of the Church, but despite this authority, 'it is most true, that every Bishop in his own Diocesse is superior overall the inhabitants of it, and hath both the whole Clergy and the whole Body of the people so truly subject unto him, both by *Divine and natural right,* as that it is not lawful for any authority upon earth, to violate this sacred order'.[92]

We have already analyzed the implication of Holden's conciliarism and its link with Gallicanism, and from this perspective the *Analysis* adds nothing new. One element is worth underlying however, that is, the confessional perspective that informs the Catholic's work and, once again, suggests that this text was not an 'ecumenical' treatise. The notion of tradition is defended precisely because it proves the truth of the Catholic religion with respect to the Protestants. Therefore, when Holden in the dedicatory epistle spoke of hoping to 'conjoyne and unite' the Christians, he was not seeking to establish a new latitudinarian blend of Christianity, but rather to establish the Blackloist model of Catholicism as the only true faith, to which everybody should have converted. I will return to this point when examining the English translation, where this appears more clearly, but for now I would like to point out that in this perspective it is significant that both the Latin and the English edition of the *Analysis* contain an 'appendix of Schisme', in which Holden argues against the Protestants that they, and not the Catholics, are the ones who broke from the primitive Church.[93]

---

[88] H. Holden, *The Analysis*, 1658, letter to the Reader, unfol.
[89] Ibid., p. 89 and pp. 1–181 *passim.*
[90] Ibid., pp. 229–230.
[91] Ibid., p. 224.
[92] Ibid., p. 226.
[93] H. Holden, *Analysis* 1652, pp. 477–536; Id., *Analysis,* 1658, pp. 318–471.

The second part of Holden's work, however, is more controversial, and it will be dramatically changed in the second edition. Its theme is politics, and in particular the origin and scope of government.[94] Holden's text starts by highlighting the centrality of pacts in the formation of government:

> …man is obliged by the law of nature common to every reasonable and humane creature by such a bond, as cannot be dissolved by any created authority whatsoever, to keep and observe his promise given, and his covenant made. This is the ground of all Kingdomes, Common-wealths, Societies and Communities whatsoever.[95]

Following the classic neo-Thomist explanation, Holden continues that since the stipulations of a pact depends on the law of God, it follows that the pacts stipulated with heathen kings are also valid:

> Hence we may certainly conclude, that such mens doctrine, as doe affirm that a promise freely and rightly given to Infideles and Hereticks, may be lawfully violated and broken, is most wicked, contrary to the law of reasonable nature, and destructive to the whole fabrick of nature, in relation to humane society.[96]

After this defense of the authority of kings, Holden changes gear, and mixes Vitoria with Thomas White. There are three foundations to a commonwealth: 'that the common good….is to be preferred before a particular good'; 'that man hath a natural inclination and propension to enter into society, and to live in mutual peace with one another'; and lastly, 'that men are obliged to keep all the lawes, conditions and covenants, whereunto they do freely, lawfully and mutually engage themselves'.[97] Since 'men are naturally free and rational', the consent by which men agree to be governed has to be voluntary: 'wherefore every Society ought to take its beginning from the free consent of all those who will enter into it'.[98]

The consequence is that although obedience to a 'superior authority lawfully constituted and justly governing' is a divine precept, and one, Holden specifies, that Catholics are not less willing to follow than Protestants, despite all the unjust accusations against the alleged treachery of the English Catholics,[99] nevertheless there may be a case in which such an authority is not 'lawfully constituted and justly governing', and in this case resistance is indeed possible.[100]

What are the cases in which this authority is not legitimate? As for religion, the case is relatively simple, for a government should be resisted if it seeks to

---

[94] Holden, *Analysis* 1658, pp. 325 and ff.
[95] Ibid., p. 339.
[96] Ibid., p. 342. See also pp. 344–379 *passim* on the question of promises made to heretic kings and binding in conscience.
[97] Ibid., p. 345.
[98] Ibid., p. 348.
[99] Ibid., pp. 351–7.
[100] Ibid., pp. 356 and ff.

'extinguish this Belief and Religion, and would bring in its place, and establish the law of the Jewes or Turks, or of any other prophane worship or Idolatry'.[101] More complex is the secular issue, or the conditions in which a government can be said to have failed to respect the pact with its people, which is the origin and foundation of its authority. In this case, Holden writes, since the underlying principle of government is 'That the safety of the people, is the Supreme law', there are three corollaries to this principle, the neglect of which jeopardizes 'the very essence of such a society':

> 1) The temporal good of the whole Community. 2) The natural liberty of the subject. And 3) The peculiar propriety which every particular member of the Commonwealth hath over such things as are not to others, nor doe belong unto any but himself.[102]

But how does one know when exactly one or more or those conditions arise, and therefore how does one know that it is time to act? The answer to this question is the conclusion of the second section of the Latin edition of Holden's work:

> Since the subjects' obedience to the higher power is evidently and indissolubly owed jure divino, naturali & humano, with equal evidence and without any exception, the reason for removing and abandoning authority has to appear most just to the rest of the people who should be free from partial zeal. The sole judge of this is the common reason of men who are free from perturbation of the soul and interests.[103]

In analyzing the political part of Holden's treatise two elements should be taken into account. First, Holden's political reflections represent, to a certain extent, the implications of the Blackloists' emphasis on reason in the realm of political theory. If in Holden's *Analysis* those political implications remain for the most part unexamined, Thomas White will systematize them and work them into an organic political theory three years later in the *Grounds*.

Secondly, Holden's reflections are extremely interesting because of their current-day political edge. In other words, in the second part of his work Holden wanted to provide a rationale for the endorsement of the Independents and of Cromwell that the Blackloists and a sector of the English Catholics had expressed. In order to achieve his aim, he moves in two directions. First, by re-proposing the neo-Thomist point that the origin of government resides in God's law rather than God's grace, Holden wanted to free the English Catholic community from the stigma of treason. Consequently, Holden sought to assure the English Catholics a proper and legitimate political space within

---

[101] Ibid., p. 359.
[102] Ibid., p. 360.
[103] [Cum enim subditorum obedientia potestatibus sublimioribus sit iure divino, naturali, & humano, evidenter & indissolubiliter debita, aequali saltem evidentia atque ab omni exceptione immuni, debet cunctis partium studio non laborantibus, apparere, imperij detractionis, & defectionis causam esse iustissimam. Cuius, hominum omni perturbatione animi liberorum, vel quorum minime interest, communis ratio solus est iudex] H. Holden, *Analysis* 1652, pp. 474–5.

English politics. And if Holden's ecclesiological model is heavily indebted to the Gallican one, this political part constitutes a uniquely English addition to that French model. Secondly, by appealing to the 'ratio communis' as the sole judge of the question of legitimate resistance to a sovereign, he presented the English Civil War and the Catholics' intervention in it in a non-confessional framework. In this context, the action of the Blackloists is justified insofar as it was a decision made for the good of the commonwealth, not of the Pope.

Holden's political reflections posit a scenario that in 1652 was not completely unlikely, with Cromwell gaining power and the main lines of his religious policy still in formation. And in this situation the Blackloists, as the only link between Cromwell's regime and the See of Rome, could count on the protection of the Catholic Church as well. Moreover, the treatise came out in Latin, and was printed in Paris, which means that the text was tailored to the French academic milieu, which could, to a certain extent, read Holden's statements regarding the origin of commonwealth and the obvious link with the recent events in England *sine ira et studio*.

As Holden prepared his text for an English translation, he decided to explain and modify the final statement made in the political section of his Latin *Analysis*. In the English version, in fact, the political portion does not end with the dangerously general endorsement of the 'common reason' as the sole judge in the controversy between king and people, but with a clarification of what Holden meant in his interpretation of the Civil War and the Catholics' role.[104] It is absurd, Holden wrote, to think that the English Catholics, despite their respect for political authorities, 'could think, that subjects were obliged to obey such commandements as we supposed to be against the laws of God, of nature, of justice, of reason'[105]. Indeed, every English man, be he Protestant or Catholic, should recognize this basic principle, which, Holden insists, can work and should work across the political spectrum. When Charles I was in power, in fact, he did his best to:

> …protest in publick Parliament, & divulge in words and writing, that he would never go obout [sic] to innovate any thing against the Divine law, or Religion then established, nor against the fundamental lawes of the Kingdome, nor against the true liberty, or propriety of the subject; nor in fine, against the antient rights and priviledges of Parliament. But his adversaries on the contrary cryed lowder then he, and their votes prevailed.[106]

By the same token, Cromwell too had to deal with the same kind of problems:

> This all people discontented with the present government have ever pretended, as the chief cause of their revolt; which, when once they can instil it into the peoples ears with rumors, though never so false, And then

---

[104] H. Holden, *Analysis* 1658, pp. 366 and ff.
[105] Ibid., p. 366.
[106] Ibid., pp. 366–7.

with tumultuous clamors make it sound all the Kingdome over, it is no smal argument of eminent danger to the supream power.[107]

In other words, in Holden's opinion, just as his political reflections had to be interpreted in a cross-confessional perspective – Holden's argument in the neo-Thomist part of his treatise was precisely that the Catholics must not and should not do anything differently than the Protestants –, at the same time they cannot be labeled as pro-king or pro-Parliament: 'I wondred therefore that our English Schismaticks, who are on the Kings party, could take amisse what I proposed in common suppositions, with a sincere intention, looking only upon the truth in general'.[108] Moreover, Holden added, if the Protestants wanted to search for truly seditious doctrines, they needed to look no further than 'Luther, Melanchton, Bucerus, Osiander, Calvin, Zwinglus, Beza, Knox, Buchanan and others of the same stamp'.[109]

Thus, against those who thought that the passage on common reason was indeed dangerously general, Holden insisted that his treatise did not deal with politics, but with the principles underpinning politics: giving practical political advice 'was …neither my purpose, nor is it my profession'.[110] Also, his treatise was not an endorsement of one particular regime over the other, but rather dealt with the institution of covenant as a way to legitimizing the supreme authority 'whether it be in one, or in many', and that 'this truth ought to be common to all men of what profession in Religion soever they be'.[111]

But who is the intended audience for Holden's modification? Whose opposition was Holden trying to avoid? On the surface, he seems to be concerned with his Protestant opponents, who thought that the Blackloists' siding with Cromwell was yet one more instance of the intrinsically seditious character of the Church of Rome. However, we should remember that in 1658, the year in which the English *Analysis* was published, in England there was still no King whose favor Holden could wish to acquire. In fact, if we read the text attentively, we realize that Holden had an important message to convey not to the English Protestants, but rather to the English Catholic community, to which he, after all, dedicated the treatise in the first place. As we read in the dedicatory epistle Holden's aim was 'to conjoyne and unite' the Christians by eliminating the controversies within the Catholic community, and as the 1650s progressed, the controversy between the Blackloists and their Catholic opponents was growing more and more violent.

Even if Thomas White and his associates enjoyed the protection of the Chapter, Holden did not think it was a good idea to keep pushing, but realized that moderation on White's part was the best strategy. In 1657 he had vigorously sought to convince White to submit his writing to the Holy See, and when he did, Holden printed White's letter of submission, accompanied

---

[107] Ibid.
[108] Ibid., p. 367.
[109] Ibid.
[110] Ibid., p. 370.
[111] Ibid., pp. 369–372 *passim*.

by his own 'letter to a friend of his'[112]. In the text, he maintained that although White 'useth expressions & manners of speach not common in our schooles, & hee hath severall exotick & peculiar opinions', nevertheless his doctrine is 'solide, sound, & substantiall'.[113] Despite the soundness of White's doctrine, however, Holden decided to encourage his old mentor to submit his work and to publish his letter of submission because he thought that such an act would 'reduce & undeceive such as have erred in their judgments to his prejudice' so as to avoid an internal controversy, all the more vicious because it was directed 'against a brother'.[114]

It was in the Blackloists' interest, Holden thought, to foster peace and conciliation, because peace and conciliation could contribute to affirm the overall solidity of the Blackloists' ecclesiology and theology, which, far from being an element of dissent, should by contrast unify the Catholic community. And unifying the Catholic community was what Holden wanted to do in his *Analysis*.

Now, if in 1657 Holden thought that White's submission to the Holy See could achieve peace in the theological debates, his addition to the 1658 *Analysis* should have contributed to pacify the souls of the English Catholics in the political realm as well, for he insisted that his theory could be valuable also for the fellow Catholics who opposed the Protector, and sided with the exiled King.

But there was another issue on which the anti-Blackloists needed to be reassured, namely, the role of the Pope. And to this aim, Holden added another small part to his 1658 edition, in which he briefly commented on Du Perron's 1615 address to the Third Estate, and, more specifically, on the passages in which the Cardinal defended the right of the Pope to depose a king.[115] Holden affirmed that even the Cardinal endorsed the position of those who maintain 'that this obedience [to the king] is due by divine right', as Holden had done, since for Du Perron this position did not in any way jeopardize the duty of a Catholic to both be obedient in conscience to his sovereign, and to God's commandments.[116] In other words, Holden used Du Perron's arguments to defend himself against those who could accuse him of demonstrating a much deeper respect for supreme political authority rather than religious authority, thus showing that his and the Blackloists' position was not detrimental to the Pope's authority. In the same commentary, Holden insisted that his reflections on Papal infallibility were not meant to diminish the supreme authority of the Pope within the Church, which he fully supported. Rather, his was an attempt to discuss 'the Doctrine of our famous School of Paris, "That the Pope out of a Councel is not infallible in his definitions and decisions of questions; especially

---

[112] *Doctor Holden's letter to a friend of his, upon the occasion of Mr. Blacklow's submitting his writings to the See of Rome, together with a Copie of the said Mr. Blacklow's submission*, s.l. s.d. but after 1657.
[113] Ibid., unfol.
[114] Ibid.
[115] H. Holden, *Analysis* 1658, pp. 373–379.
[116] Ibid., pp. 374–5.

if they be speculative, not even decreeing out of his chaire, as they call it"', which Holden proposed as an 'opinion'.[117] Surely if Holden wanted to appeal to the English Protestants of either political side, he would not have quoted those passages from Du Perron's 1615 address as supporting evidence.

Up until this point, then, the analysis of Holden's addition reveals, in my view, that the Catholic author's goal was to reassure his Royalist and Papalist coreligionists that the Blackloist doctrine was not politically and theologically controversial enough to justify a dangerous division among Catholics. However, this is not the only aim of Holden's English translation. In fact, once the English Catholic community found itself unified, nothing prevented the English Catholics from proselytizing among the Protestants, and especially those who had vehemently and unsuccessfully opposed the Presbyterians and the Puritans: what better choice could they make rather than converting to the Catholic Church, especially if the model of Catholicism was the Blackloists' one?

This is the context in which we should interpret the last of the additions of Holden's text, namely, a commentary on Henry Hammond's *Treatise of Schism*, in which Holden made clear that the English Protestants, and not the Catholics, were to be properly called 'schismatics', for the Church of Rome was and remained the only true and infallible Church, thus reinforcing the points that he had made in the earlier part of the work.[118] Hammond's moderation and his will to seek a 'union' were certainly commendable, but such a union could not be achieved if the English Protestants continued to oppose the true Catholic Church: 'I must confesse I know not how he [i.e. Hammond] intends to make the whole Christian and Catholick Church one; if neither in one head, nor in the same substantial articles of Christian belief; nor in the same essential acts of Religion'.[119] At best, Hammond's strategy could achieve 'a civil commerce amongst Christians, as moral honest men', certainly not any form of theological and religious unification.[120]

The last piece of the puzzle is the dedicatory letter written by the author of the *Analysis*' English translation: the same William Grant who we saw had collaborated with the Blackloists in the late 1640s, when they tried to strike an agreement with the Independents on the basis of their anti-Papalist ecclesiological model. In his epistle, addressed to 'my Christian Countrymen the meer English Reader, especially those who call themselves of the Church of England', Grant specified that Holden's book was not written for 'these men who will have God Almighty to have let only an immediate, miraculous, and Enthusiastical way of informing their soules abstract from all principles of common sense and reason'.[121]

Rather, Holden's treatise

---

[117] Ibid., p. 376.
[118] Ibid., pp. 417–471
[119] Ibid., p. 427.
[120] Ibid.
[121] Ibid., Epistle to the reader, unfoliated.

> to my understanding laid a way open for an Union between the Church of England and the Roman; a Union I must confess I had long desired, but could not apprehend the meanes, not onely in respect of several temporal interests, but also for that I was perswaded that Church imposed many things of necessity to be believed and practised…from which the reading of this ingenuous and moderate Doctor hath freed me.[122]

Except, what Grant (and also Holden, as we have seen) wanted was not so much a 'Union' between the Church of Rome and a defunct Church of England, but what can me more properly called an 'annexation' of the latter into the former:

> I say I shall not doubt to conclude, that there is nothing so essential as should hinder any one that was really and truly of the late English Church, and well understood what She taught from entring into the Communion of the Roman: the onely Church that I know in the World, which seems to fulfill those glorious Prophecies so often mentioned in Scripture.[123]

In the case of Grant there is some ground to believe that the 'annexation' did indeed take place: in 1661, the year before Holden's death, a pamphlet entitled *A Letter written by Dr.Holden to Mr.Graunt* came out.[124] In the text Holden wanted to reassure one 'Mr. Graunt' that Thomas White's opinion on the Purgatory were sound and orthodox. Holden acknowledged some faults in White's argument. Yet White could not be considered a heretic, for he did not question any fundamental points of the Catholic doctrine, but only those 'opinions' open to discussion. Therefore, both White's and his opponents' considerations did not concern the core of Catholic beliefs:

> I am confident there is nothing so infallibly resolved upon these points, and so be universally received by the Church, as that either side ought to be acknowledged for an Article of our Catholick faith. I will not say but that a truly-learned Divine, profoundly grounded and knowing in the Principles of natural Philosophy, may demonstrate the truth of these questions. And I am perswaded it is no harder to know their true and certain resolution, than to evidence by natural reason, the pure spirituality and immortality of the Soul of man. But this I will not meddle with, as being unnecessary to the satisfying of your demand: *However I dare assure you that as a Roman Catholick, you are not obliged to believe any thing in these points, as being determined, and universally received by the Church, for an Article of our Faith.*[125]

Now, if we assume that 'Mr. Graunt' was indeed William Grant, we can infer that after 1658 Grant had considerably moved towards the Church of Rome, and possibly he had already become a 'Roman Catholick' concerned with the theological basis of his confession. Aside from the question of Grant's

---

[122] Ibid.
[123] Ibid.
[124] The complete title is *A Letter written by Dr. Holden to Mr. Graunt concerning Mr. White's Treatise de Medio Animarum Statu*, printed in Paris in 1661.
[125] Ibid., p. 7. My italics.

identity and confessional decisions, on which there is no solid proof – after all George Leyburn's *alias* in the 1640s was Winter Grant –, I want to point out that even after the Restoration Holden did not seem to abandon the belief that the Catholic Church was the only true one, and that the Blackloist model of Catholicism, which was theologically founded on 'natural reason' and on the 'Principles of natural Philosophy', and politically grounded on the notion of contract à la Thomas White, was still theoretically valuable.

The Restoration, however, put an end to the period in which the actual realization of the Blackloist project did not seem out of reach. After the Restoration, in fact, many things changed, and it is now time to explore and analyze those changes.

CHAPTER 6

'To Little Purpose': The End of the Blackloist Group

6.1 Thomas White

As the 1650s ended, so did Thomas White's influence, on two fronts. First, the Restoration deprived White of the support of his political patrons; secondly, it hastened and completed his condemnation by the Catholic Church. In this section I would like to analyze more specifically the reasons and the significance of White's change of fortune, and will start by examining the relationship between the Blackloist leader and the Church of Rome in the late 1650s and 1660s.

As I have explained before, White had always been a controversial and polarizing figure for the English Catholic Church, for doctrinal, ecclesiological and political reasons. Indeed, many attempts had been made in the 1640s and 1650s by White's religious opponents to have his doctrines condemned by the Church of Rome. In particular, George Leyburn repeatedly tried to have White's doctrine censured in England, but as long as White had the support of the English Chapter, and Rome issued no censure, as Smith had written to Leyburn, it was necessary to 'suppress all clamors against Mr.Blacloes Noveltyes'.[1]

But when exactly did Rome begin to 'speak of Mr.Blackloes Noveltyes'? And what did it say?

In 1655 the Inquisition condemned White's *Sonus Buccinae* (Paris 1654),[2] in which White had defended the value of tradition over the Protestant notion of *sola Scriptura*, but had also taken issue with the doctrine of Papal infallibility. This was a first step taken by the Roman Church against White's and the Blackloists' theology at a moment in which White's political and theological influence was extremely high. White's circle immediately recognized that if the Blackloist group was to survive the fracture would have to be mended. Henry Holden, who was the member of the group most concerned with questions of theology and ecclesiology, urged White to submit his writings to the Holy See, which White did in the summer of 1657, as a sign of the Blackloists' peaceful intention towards Leyburn and the Holy See. As White wrote in his letter of submission, his decision to comply with Holden's request was not to be read as an admission of guilt. Rather, White sought to clear up any misunderstanding

---

[1] Letter from William Smith to George Leyburn, 6 July 1652, Westminster Diocesan Archives Mss., vol. XXX, document n.150, f. 503v.
[2] ACDF, Decreta Sancti Officii, Decretum 12 May 1655, ff. 53v–58v.

over his obedience to the Pope 'upon a motion of peace made by some worthy friends'.[3] White communicated also personally with Holden, to clarify his intentions to his collaborator:

> Nothing shall bee demanded of mee which can stand with peace which I will not assent unto, and so though I understand that what the Dr. [i.e. Leyburn] demands is a disgrace to mee, as making the world thincke I was contrary hitherto to the Popes authority, and that hee will ingratiate himselfe as having reduced mee to submission: yet neglecting all that concerns my person, I will and doe with those send you what the Dr. desires'.[4]

Holden printed White's letter in a pamphlet entitled *Doctor Holden's letter to a friend of his*, and added his own defense of the Blackloists' leader:

> I can assure you, to satisfy your demande in this point, that I have ever clearely found his doctrine to bee throughly solide, sound, & substantiall. I confesse that, omitting voluminous citations of skeptike phansies, & endeavouring to incite Divins to seek for reall science, & to shew how connaturall true Divinity is to the better portion of man, hee useth divers expressions & manners of speach not common in our schooles, & hee hath severall exotick & peculiar opinions which, (be it spoken with due respect, though in opposition to so great a schollar & so learned a man) are much different from my sentiments. But I never saw, nor ever heard as yet, any one of his tenets inconsistent with the essentiall & perfect integrity of our Cartholick faith.[5]

In 1657 and after the first condemnation Holden thought that the Roman action against White was taken, so to say, out of some personal antipathy. White's 'exotick and peculiar opinion', Holden writes, should not have been considered representative of the Blackloist doctrine, which was only concerned with advancing the 'true Divinity' by showing it perfectly compatible with the 'reall science', and by eradicating the ghost of skepticism. As such, Holden showed some confidence that White's submission, which the English theologian regarded as a good public-relation move to improve the Blackloist leader's image, would have been enough to silence the matter for good. Also, the English Chapter seemed perfectly satisfied by White's submission, out of confidence that a peaceful resolution of the conflict between the Blackloist leader and the Holy See could be reached.[6]

No such resolution was to be reached, however. For in the fall of 1657, immediately after White's submission, Rome condemned White's *Tabulae Suffragiales* (London 1655)[7] a text written in response to the criticism received

---

[3] The text of White's letter of submission was printed in a pamphlet written by Holden and entitled *Doctor Holden's letter to a friend of his*, unfol.

[4] White to Holden, 18 May 1657, in Westminster Diocesan Archives Mss., vol. XXXI, document n.73, f. 342. The same document contains a draft of White's letter of submission (f. 341).

[5] *Doctor Holden's letter*, unfol.

[6] See *supra*, chapter V, pp. 99–101.

[7] ACDF, Decreta Sancti Officii, Decretum 6 September 1657.

for the previous text. Also between 1657 and 1658 the Congregation of the Index attentively examined White's *Institutionum Peripateticarum*, in which he had synthesised his own distinctive mixture of new science and Aristotelianism. Its conclusion was that 'opus hoc prohibere censeo donec corrigat'.[8] On the 10th of June 1658 the Congregation of the Index decided to prohibit the book.[9]

This second condemnation raised more clamor: evidently it was not White's personality that caused a problem, but White's very doctrine. Holden wrote another pamphlet in defense of his master, but with different arguments this time. In this work, Holden begins by questioning the validity of the prohibitions issued against White, for prohibitions 'are only acts of a particular Court or Congregation in Rome, though put out in the Pope's name, as all other acts of the several Courts of that City usually are. And therefore do not oblige, nor are commonly held to be of any force out of the Pope's territories'.[10] The reference to the limited jurisdiction of the Pope is reinforced again in the text, when Holden mentions specifically the case of France, in which Inquisitorial prohibitions are 'often rejected by the Parliament of this town [i.e. Paris], the most famous and learned Seat of Judicary in the Christian world'.[11] This argument squares with Holden and White's ecclesiological stances, and we should remember that the English translation of Holden's *Analysis Divinae Fidei* came out around the time in which this pamphlet was published.

After doubting the territorial validity of the prohibition of the Holy See, Holden goes on to explore the significance of prohibitions. In Holden's opinion the Pope and the Inquisition do not always censure the doctrine of the books they prohibit, which might well be fully orthodox. Rather, they sometimes act simply to avoid to 'expose many thousands of infirm and unlearned men to the danger of being disedified'. White's doctrine fits in that category, for while its orthodoxy cannot be disputed, it 'being both profound and obscure, is beyond the reach of every common reader'.[12] In other words, the 'obscurity' and peculiar character of White's doctrine, which in the previous pamphlet was considered by Holden as a negative personal quality, becomes now a quasi-positive attribute of the theologian's work, as opposed to the unlearned and unintellectual attitude of the Court of Rome. White's case, Holden continues, is analogous to that of Arnauld, some of whose works were also censured by the Roman See. The Jansenist's main purpose, according to Holden, was 'to shew that his opinion, concerning efficacious Grace, is nothing different from the doctrine of the antient Fathers...and sure it would be a scandal to have it thought that the doctrine of those Fathers...should now come to be censured and condemned'.[13] White sought to prove that 'our Catholike faith is to be resolved into universal tradition' and 'that the Pope is not unerrable

---

[8] ACDF, I I (ii) 32, Decreta Congregationis Indicis, ff. 365r–376r.
[9] See J.M. De Bujanda, *Index Librorum prohibitorum*, sub voce White, Thomas.
[10] H. Holden, *A Letter written by Mr. Henry Holden touching the prohibition at Rome of Mr. Blacklow's book, intituled Tabulae Suffragiales*, s.l.s.d., p. 4.
[11] Ibid., pp. 4–5.
[12] Ibid., pp. 7–9.
[13] Ibid., p. 11.

and infallible in his own singular person', tenets that are both 'that great truth and essential rule of Christianity', and 'the antient opinion of our faculty at Paris'.[14]

If Holden sees a parallel between White's and Arnauld's doctrine, both condemned notwithstanding their overall soundness, there is a difference in the geo-political context in which these condemnations took place. In France, Holden writes, where Catholics are 'living in the open profession of our Catholick Religion', they 'take no notice' of the Inquisition's decrees. In England, by contrast, where Catholics are 'living under the yoke of persecution', the Inquisition's decrees are given more weight than they deserve.[15] Behind this formulation lies a precise and important accusation of the Court of Rome, which Holden sees as benefiting from the condition of minority, and persecuted minority at that, in which the English Catholics were obliged to live. For it was precisely this condition of minority that allowed the Roman decrees to be followed more closely than they would have been if Catholicism were not persecuted.

The question of context is extremely important for the entire Blackloist ecclesiology, and particularly so in this polemic, and Thomas White himself, in a 1659 pamphlet written to defend his doctrine and attack the Inquisition procedure, refers to it with two arguments. On the one hand, he insists on the global, or rather European-wide scope that doctrines like his own and the Jansenists' have. As the case of Jansenism demonstrates, 'whatsoever falls once under one press, it little imports whether it first sees light here, or any adjacent Catholick Country: Take for proofs the French Provincial Letters; not only vulgarly known, but render'd also into our vulgar tongue'.[16] On the other hand, regarding the distinctive status of minority of the English Catholics, White affirms that it is especially necessary for them to discard 'superfluous controversies' in order to concentrate only on 'necessary Doctrines', as this is the only means that can prevent divisions.[17]

In these passages Holden and White are affirming what they saw as the fundamental characteristic of the Blackloist doctrine with respect to the Church of Rome. In other words, the Blackloists rejected the Jesuitical and Papalist stances precisely because they sustained a sectarian vision of the Catholic Church. The Blackloist doctrine, on the contrary, was the only kind of theology that could fit the context of seventeenth-century Europe, in which the superiority of the Catholic Church could not be affirmed through religious uniformity. As White explained, the Holy See accused him of following 'the very same method' that the Heretics followed. However, it would be false to conclude that 'what both Catholics and Hereticks indifferently do, should be ill because Hereticks do it'. Far from being a philo-Protestant doctrine, Blackloism represented instead the true triumph of a 'rationalized' Catholicism,

---

[14] Ibid., p. 13.
[15] Ibid., pp. 14–15.
[16] T. White, *A letter to a person of honour written by Mr. Thomas White*, s.l. 1659, unfol.
[17] Ibid., unfol.

in that it could offer a generalized theology 'concerning all points of Faith' inserted within a coherent and innovative 'body, or course of Philosophy and Divinity'.[18] The Catholic Church, for its part, by the initial condemnations showed its disapproval of such a theological project, especially because of its implications on the issue of the Papal authority. Theology by itself, however, was not the only reason for White's fall.

As we have analyzed in the previous chapters, one of the most important corollaries of the Blackloist view of the Church of Rome with respect to the Protestant Churches and to the European political and religious context is White's political theory. This theory was based on the assumption that the Roman Church à la Blacklo in principle supported no political regime, since it also threatened none. An important consequence of these theoretical premises in properly political terms was the endorsement on the part of the Blackloists of Cromwell's regime. It is important to note at this point that until 1660 the only books by White that had received an official condemnation or were closely scrutinized were the theological ones, in which Papal infallibility was denied. There is no mention of *The Grounds of Obedience and Government* even if the text was rather well-known in Rome.[19] As I have argued elsewhere, this evidence shows while Cromwell was in power the Catholic Church did not want to sever its only political connection with the Lord Protector. It was in November1661, after the Restoration and when the Holy See needed to give a strong signal of its support to the King, that the Inquisition condemned White's *opera omnia*.[20]

Indeed, Holden and the Blackloist sympathizers in the English Chapter seemed to have understood that defending White's doctrine only was not going to help, and that the political issues needed to be addressed. In fact, in an extreme attempt to save the Blackloist project and its sympathizers in the Chapter, in September 1661 –two months before the condemnation of White's *opera omnia*- Holden and the philo-White members of the Chapter signed a letter addressed to the Holy See, in which they denounced Leyburn's manoeuvres against them and declared their obedience to the Pope. More specifically, they showed themselves willing to comply with the Inquisition's prohibition of White's book, adding that

> we have ordered to every clergyman and layman everywhere in England to declare and make public that nobody should and must read those aforementioned books [i.e. White's books expressly condemned by Rome], unless they had permission to read prohibited books. Moreover from the bottom of our heart we affirm that we despise, condemn and reject completely any thing in the book entitled 'On the grounds of obedience and government' by the same author, that in any way could either displease

---

[18] Ibid., unfol.
[19] The Vatican Library holds a manuscript of a translation of White's text in Italian, very faithful to the original, entitled 'I fondamenti d'ubidienza e Governo da Tomaso White Gentilhuomo', Barb. Lat. 5406, ff. 1r–50r.
[20] ACDF, Decreta Sancti Offici, Decretum 17 November 1661, ff. 187v–189v. For more details on this issue see S. Tutino, 'The Catholic Church and the English Civil War'.

even minimally our Serene Highness by God's grace Charles II (on whose kingdom may God grant a long duration on earth, and eternity in heaven), or with harmful principles jeopardize the peace and tranquillity of this Kingdom in any way.[21]

As even Holden at this date had understood, with the Restoration the political leverage that Thomas White could count on disappeared. Indeed it was politics that sealed the theological fate of the Blackloists' leader, and, to a certain extent, that of the Blackloist program, as it can be seen from the documents sent to Rome concerning Thomas White.

For instance, on August 28 1660 the Nuncio in Brussels sent to Rome a detailed report on the situation of the English Clergy, in which he explained in depth the existence of the two factions, and listed the names of the supporters of either side. The Nuncio wrote a lengthy passage on White, starting with a biographical summary and a report on his latest movements:

> He left London about two years ago, and moved to Frankfurt. Now I hear he is in Rotterdam, in Holland. He is considered a man of wit, of scholarship and of great memory: he speaks, besides Latin, Greek and Hebrew, also Italian, Spanish, French and Flemish. He must be around 65 years old. I am not going to write on his erroneous doctrine on the Purgatory, the Indulgences, the Pope's Authority, and other matters, for they are already fairly well-known, and some of his books are here prohibited. Since in his books he wrote in favour of the Commonwealth of England and of Cromwell, he will not dare come back to that Realm, knowing how much the King is displeased.[22]

This letter suggests that the Nuncio did not think it necessary or appropriate to take a strong action against White: aside from his doctrinal errors –which had been already censured by the Roman Inquisition–, he is described as a man of wit and an able scholar, fluent in many ancient and modern languages. His political support of Cromwell is mentioned only to justify his escape from

---

[21] […duximus universis Fratribus nostris Laicisque per totam Angliam ubilibet sparsis declarare ac publicare, praefatos Libros a nemine legi oportere vel debere, qui legendi libros prohibitos facultate non gaudeat. Ulterius ex imo corde profitemur nos reprobare, damnare, ac renunciare penitus quicquid in praedicti Authoris libro *De Obedientiae ac Regiminis fundamentis* inscripto, quovis modo Serenissimo Regi nostro CAROLO Dei gratia Secundo (cujus imperium diuturnitate in terris, aeternitate in coelis coronet Deus) vel in minimo displicere poterit, vel principiis niti paci et tranquillitati hujus Regni quomodocunque noxiis]. The letter, dated 17 september 1661, was included in a folder sent by the Nuncius in Paris to Mons. Varese, the Cardinal of the Holy Office in charge of the English affairs, from Paris on December 9th 1661. It is found in ACDF, St. St. SS 2–b, ff. 23r and ff. The Chapter's letter can be found at ff. 29r–34v (quot. at ff. 30v–31r)

[22] [Parti' circa due ani sono da londra verso Francfort, ora dicesi trovarsi in Roterdam, in Olanda. Vien stimato huomo d'Ingegno, di studio e gran Memoria, versato oltre le tre' lingue Latina, Greca et ebraica, nell'Italiana, Spagnuola francese, e fiammenga. Puo' haver circa 65 anni d'eta'. Non parlo degl'errori suoi circa il Purgatorio, le Indulgenze, l'Autorita' del Sommo Pontefice, et altre materie, essendo a' bastanza noti, e costa' gia' proibiti alcuni suoi libri; nei quali come egli servisse in favore della Repubblica d'Inghilterra e del Cromuello, non ardirebbe ora ritornare in quel Regno sapendo quanto il Re' gli sia sdegnato], ACDF, St.St. SS 2-a, Bruxelles 28 August 1660, ff. 285r–288r, at ff. 287v–288r.

England, and to suggest that he probably would not be returning any time soon.

The 8th of January 1661 the same Nuncio of Brussels sent to Rome another letter addressed to the Holy Office. This time the attitude towards White was different. It was the right time to take a side, Leyburn's and the King's side, and thus a stronger action against White needed to be taken:

> In order to repair the damage of Albio's doctrine, and to avoid it being spread further in England, I think ... that maybe it would be appropriate if your Excellency wrote a letter to the Chapter, telling them with disgust that Albio, instead of recognizing his mistakes, sinks into worse and worse errors, and prints new books filled with pernicious dogma. In order for English Catholics not to be infected by them, and until we think of more effective remedies, Your Excellency judges timely that they communicate to the members of the Chapter, with circular letters, to admonish everyone in those Provinces not to listen to his doctrine nor to read his books nor to have any relationship with him. And in order for the members of the Chapter to give an example, they should exclude him as a rotten member from the Chapter (in which he was appointed as Canon). It has to be considered that His Majesty will be grateful when he happens to remember that Albio dared writing in favour of Cromwell, with such displeasure on His Majesty's part, and that Your Excellency should take occasion to remind the members of the Chapter to behave, as far as loyal service towards His Majesty is concerned, in such a way that they can be taken as example for every other subject of the same Crown. Besides, they could be speedily informed of Your Excellency's opinions by me.[23]

This letter was written in January 1661. As the year progressed, the situation looked worse and worse for White. In another anonymous report on English affairs sent to Rome in May 1661, the author is asked to comment on the dangers faced by the English Catholic Church. He sees two main sources of danger: the first is the possibility of Jansenism infiltrating into England. As far as this was concerned, Rome could be reassured: 'Two Fathers of the Society of Jesus, friends...of mine, told me that, thank God, little or nothing of

---

[23] [Per rimediar fratanto alli danni della Dottrina dell'Albio et impedirne l'ulteriore propagatione in Inghilterra mi viene in mente....che forsi potrebbe esser bene che V.E. scrivesse una lettera a' detto Capitolo significandoli d'intendere con disgusto che l'Albio in luogo di mostrar resipiscenza d'immerga sempre in peggiori errori e dia alle stampe nuovi libri pirni di dogmi perniciosi, da quali afine che non venissero infettati i Cattolici di quel Regno mentre si pensa ad altri piu' efficacii rimedii stima l'E.V. opportuno che loro per lettere circolari scritte per tutte quelle Provincie ammonissero ciascuno a' non dar orecchio alla di lui dottrina ne' leggere i suoi libri o' tener seco commercio alcuno, e per dar essi Capitolari in cio' esempio agl'altri lo dichiarassero absciso dal loro Capitolo (in cui gia' fu assunto per Canonico) come membro putrido considerando anco che tal risoluzione sara' grata a S.M.ta' quando per caso la risappia per haver l'Albio osato di scrivere in favor del Cromuel con tanto disgusto della M.ta' Sua e che V.E. con tal occasione li ricorda a' continuar di portarsi in modo verso il fedel servitio della M.ta' Sua da poter esser additati in cio' per esempio a' tutte l'altre sorti di persone soggette alla medesima Corona, e che nel resto potrenno sentir da me alla giornata i sentimenti dell'E.V.], ACDF, St.St. SS 2-a, Bruxelles, 8 January 1661, ff. 411r–412v, at ff. 411v–412r.

Jansenius's malicious seed had infected the people, and that after the censure from Rome, they did not hear about that doctrine anymore'.[24]

The second source of danger was White's doctrine: even in this case, however, there was nothing to worry about any more, since White's influence seemed to have faded:

> As for Albio's doctrine, there is no risk that it could provoke great damage, because he is considered such an extravagant man, and peculiar in his opinions, that if one wants to follow him, one must have a twisted brain, like his own. Chancellor Digby, who is his patron, is already so discredited in religious matters that nobody wants to take a lead from him on such an important issue. Moreover, the superior of the English Clergy told me that in the whole Mission there was no doubt that there were only two or three who followed Albio, and that they were waiting for the Inquisition's censure against his books any day, which could cut off any future communication with him, and so he hoped everybody would have abandoned him.[25]

After 1661, from the point of view of the Roman Church White ceased to be a problem. White, however, did not accept the condemnation from Rome without a fight: in 1661, in fact, he published a pamphlet entitled *Apologia pro Doctrina Sua adversus calumniatores*, written as an epistle dedicated to the Pope. In this text White addressed to the Pope the same complaints that he voiced in the 1659 English pamphlet. His doctrine did not contradict any authority 'constanter in Ecclesia Catholica pro infallibili receptae'.[26] Moreover, the censure of the Roman Church was really a censure against an intellectually free debate on matters of theology, a necessary procedure to fix mistakes and to move forward.[27] Finally, if the true Church wanted to triumph over the heretics it should not forbid intellectual and theological debates, but it should get rid of 'futile quarrels' and it should concentrate on the essential doctrines.[28]

Also, White's complaints and his aggressive defence of his own doctrine reached the Roman Inquisition. Among the documents in the Inquisition file regarding Thomas White there is an anonymous report, written in support of the Blackloist leader after 1661. In the report, White's doctrine is defended on

---

[24] [Duoi Padri Giesuiti miei amici... mi dissero che per gratia di Dio fra il popolo era passato poco, o' niente di quella cattiva semenza di Giansenio, e che doppo la censura venuta da Roma di quella dottrina, non se ne sentiva parlare più], ACDF, St.St. SS 2-a, 'Relatione Breve dello Stato presente d'Inghilterra, 1661', ff. 609r–618v, at f. 616r. The anonymous relation was inserted in a dossier sent to Rome from Paris the 20th of May 1661.

[25] [In quanto alla dottrina dell'Albio, non ci era pericolo che faccia gran male, perche passava per un huomo cosi' esottico, e singolare nelle sue opinioni che per seguitarlo bisognava haver il cervello atraverso come lui. Il Cancelliere poi Digby ch'e' il suo mecenate, e' huomo gia' tanto screditato in materia di Religione che nissuno lo vuole per conduttiere in cosa di tanta importanza. Di piu' il superiore medesimo del clero mi disse che in tutta la Missione non ci era se non duoi o' tre ch'adherivano al suddetto Albio e che aspettava di giorno in giorno la censura della S.Congregatione contro i suoi libri per levare ogni communicatione con lui per l'avvenire, e cosi' sperava di darlo abandonare da tutti], Ibid., f. 616r.

[26] T. White, *Apologia pro doctrina sua*, London 1661, p. 12.

[27] Ibid., p. 20.

[28] Ibid., pp. 26–7.

two main grounds. In the first place, White is accredited with having build a coherent theory, 'always aiming at the rigorous reasonableness of philosophical and theological truths'.[29] From the point of view of Catholic theology, by concentrating on the necessary truths and discarding the unnecessary opinions, White sought to make it 'not only defensible, but infallibly victorious' among the heretics.[30]

Secondly, the author questions the political and religious value of the prohibition from the Inquisition, an expression, according to the report, of the hostility that the Jesuitical faction showed towards White and the Blackloists. The Jesuits in England wanted to keep the conflict between the Pope and the English government alive, and by doing this they neglected the interest of the English Catholics:

> The recently passed laws of our Catholics strictly prohibit the exaltation of the authority of the Bishop of Rome, that is to say, they deny their extraordinary authority: these men, and their followers go fast ahead, and they intend not only to raise beyond measure the Pope's authority as Head of the Church, but also the authority of the Roman Inquisition, which they seek to make dominant over English subjects without the magistrate's permission. This intrusion is insinuating itself little by little, by invading the legitimate rights of the civil power, in order to reach that arrogant, and scandalous doctrine that the Court of Rome has too much legitimated with its decrees. And this is the principal aim of the Jesuits, to keep this principle alive, even though they see that today it is not expedient to come to its application. But they meet more honest and better learned adversaries, that is the loyal English Clergy, the ancient order of St. Benedict, and other regulars, whose voluntary and perfect submission to the English laws that do not pertain to matters of faith makes them incapable of any slight stain....[31]

Moreover, the author insists, the Inquisitorial prohibition will help to foster division within the English Catholic camp, because it will provoke the formation of two factions. The one, composed of 'the more zealous and credulous, who would take any trifle for a matter of faith', will attack violently the Blackloists

---

[29] [mirando sempre alla rigorosa razionalita' di filosofiche e theologiche verita'] The anonymous report, undated but datable to 1661 circa, can be found in ACDF, St St SS 2-b, ff. 45r–69v. Quotation at ff. 45v–46r.

[30] [non solo difensibile, ma infallibilmente vittoriosa] Ibid., f. 46r.

[31] [Le Leggi delli nostri Cattolici ante passati, strettamente prohibiscono l'esaltatione della potesta' del Vescovo di Roma, cioe' impediscono la Sua autorita' straordinaria: Questi Huomini, e Loro seguaci passano gia' inanzi, e presumono non solamente d'estollere sopra misura l'autorita' del Papa, come Capo della Chiesa, ma' anco quella della Romana Inquisitione, e di farla dominare sopra Li Sudditi Inglesi senza Licenza del Magistrato. Questa intrusione si va'a' poco a' poco insinuando con invadere i dritti legittimi della potesta' civile per avanzarsi fino a quella superba, e scandalosa dottrina La Corte di Roma in questi ultimi tempi ha' troppo accreditata con Li Suoi Decreti. E questa e' la principal mira de Gesuiti di preservar vivo questo principio, benche veggono che non e' hoggi di' opportuno di venire alla conclusione. Ma' incontrano con Avversarii piu' honesti, e meglio instrutti cioe' col Clero Leale Cattolico d'Inghilterra, con l'antico ordine religioso di S.Benedetto, e con altri Regolari, La volontaria, e perfetta sommissione de quali alle Leggi Inglesi non spettanti alla fede, Li rende incapaci di qualsivoglia minima macchia....] Ibid., ff. 50r–v.

and their leader. The other, 'the more solid and intelligent persons, who know how to distinguish things, will behave as before, both toward the book, and toward its author'.[32]

The author of this complaint could have been White himself, or maybe Henry Holden. However, in either case the game with the Roman See was already lost. For, in 1662, shortly after this complaint arrived, the Inquisition received a letter from Leyburn, which officially closed White's case for Rome. The letter was indeed important for the members of the Holy Office, as it was copied twice. A summary was also made, in which the most interesting points of the letter were isolated.[33]

First of all, Leyburn had reassured the Fathers of the Inquisition that the decree against White 'is sufficient to eliminate the novelties and heresies that he brought to life, even though it probably will not be sufficient to bend his obstinacy, but it was better to lose one sheep than infect the whole flock'.[34] As for White, Lyeburn did not know his whereabouts, but he guessed that he was now hidden at the home of Digby, and continuing there to write against the decree of the Holy See and against the Papal authority. Should Rome be worried about that? In Leyburn's mind, there was nothing to worry about, for 'until now they did gain nothing but dishonour, and [Leyburn] believed that it will be the same in the future, unless they emendate themselves, for neither the King nor the Catholics like White's doctrine'.[35]

Together with losing their political supports and the support of the English Catholic Church, Leyburn reported that a crucial fracture had erupted within the Blackloist factions: 'Holden, the Parisian Doctor and together with Digby a follower of White, during an illness had acquired wisdom, because he declared that he wanted to emendate his own mistakes, and if he does that, that will be the cause of the extinguishing of that faction'.[36] We do not have any evidence of Holden's abjuring the Blackloist positions, and he died in 1662, only months after Leyburn's letter. Holden's last published work before his death is the 1661 letter to one Mr. Grant, which indeed serves as evidence that even after the Restoration Holden did not loose his faith in the possibility of creating a philosophically sound and rational version of Catholicism, of which White's doctrine of Purgatory constituted an example.[37] However, if Holden's belief

---

[32] [li piu' zelanti, e Credili, che pigliano ogni bagattella per cosa di fede] [le piu' solide, giudiziose, et intelligenti persone, che sanno distinguere le cose si portaranno come prima, e verso il libro, e verso l'autore] Ibid., f. 54r.

[33] The copies of the letter, sent by Leyburn to Rome on the 8th of January 1662, can be found in ACDF, St.St. SS 2-b, ff. 63r–66v. The summary is at f. 62r.

[34] [e' bastante a togller le novita', et heresie da lui messe in luce, benche forsi non bastara' a' piegar la sua pertinacia, ma e' stato meglio perdere una pecora, accio' non infettasse tutto il Grege'], Ibid., f. 62r.

[35] [..sin qui non hanno guadagnato altro che dishonore, e tanto crede sara' per l'avvenire, se non si emendano, perche ne' al re, ne' a' Cattolici piace la Dottrina dell'Albii], Ibid.

[36] [..L'Holdeno, Dott. Parigino dopo il Digbeo seguace dell'Albii in una malatia ha acquistato Intelletto, perche' ha protestato di voler lasciare li suoi errori, il che facendo sara' cagione, che s'estinguara' quella fattione], Ibid.

[37] See *supra*, chapter V, pp. 114–15.

in a rational Catholicism had not faltered, he had some doubts on the actual possibility of carrying out the Blackloist program.

Let us see the beginning of Holden's pamphlet: 'Sir, for your private satisfaction I am willing to let you know my opinion concerning the book and controversie you mention [i.e. White's *The middle state of souls*]; though otherwise I conceive it is to little purpose. Besides that, my long absence from England hath made me almost a stranger to all particulars of your proceedings there'.[38] Holden's assessment of the debate is that 'it is to little purpose', for evidently Holden was aware that White's days had passed, and with them any hope of carrying out the Blackloist program. Holden does admit his disagreement with White's 'too many exotick and uncouth opinions' and with his 'very style and manner of speech', which Holden deems 'offensive to the Reader, though even his friend'.[39] However, he does not deny his old master's tenets: White, Holden writes, 'is my antient friend, and shall ever be so, as long as I conceive him to be a faithfull servant to Christ Jesus, and his Church'.[40] And there was nothing in White's doctrine of Purgatory, Holden maintains, that was contrary to the Catholic Church, because the issues touched by the Blackloist leader were not an article of faith, but free to be discussed.

By 1661, then, Holden had lost faith in the possibility of realizing White's program. Apparently the Catholic Church also saw it unfeasible, for in the Inquisition records Leyburn's letter is the last document concerning directly Thomas White. That does not mean that White's name disappeared within the English Catholic community. We need to remember that John Sergeant, White's disciple, remained secretary of the Chapter until late 1667, and as such contributed to keeping alive the faction of Blackloist sympathizers in the Chapter. As George Leyburn wrote to Abbot Montagu in July 1667, it was not easy 'to keepe Mr. Blacklows spirit out of the house'.[41] Moreover, White's 'spirit' and the division within the English Chapter in the early 1660s coincided with a particularly troublesome time for the Catholic Church, engaged in managing the delicate situation in Ireland, where a group of Irish Franciscans were rumoured to be working on a draft of agreement with King and Parliament.[42] Indeed, according to Thomas Courtney and to Robert Pugh, White's archenemy, the Irish Franciscans and the Blackloist sympathizers in the Chapter had formed a dangerous alliance. In a folder sent by Courtney to the Congregation of the Inquisition, the Jesuit reported to Rome Pugh's opinion that:

> that part of the English clergy who usurps the title and jurisdiction of the Dean and Chapter, completely supporting the said Albio, has formed a new oath or protestation worse than the Irish one…the same Dean and Chapter, in order to strengthen their faction, illegally and sacrilegiously

---

[38] H. Holen, *A letter… to Mr. Graunt*, p. 1.
[39] Ibid., p. 2.
[40] Ibid.
[41] Leyburn to Montagu, 29 July 1667, in *Blacklo's Cabal*, pp. 110–112-, at p. 111.
[42] The records of the Holy Office concerning the Irish Franciscans can be found in ACDF, St. St. SS 2-b, ff. 74r and ff.

gives to the Irish friars and priests faculty of confessing, preaching and administering the sacraments, with great danger for the souls, and disdain for the Apostolic See.[43]

The Catholic hierarchy in Rome did not seem to take Pugh's and Courtney's concern seriously, as it did not follow up on the supposed link between the Irish Church and White's faction. Indeed, after 1661 the Blackloist question remained an internal problem in the intricate story of the English Catholic Church: it ceased to be a Roman, and therefore European, affair. The point that I would like to underscore in conclusion is that there is an obvious and crucial link between the case of Thomas White and the English political situation. With the Restoration White lost his political patron, and with him he also lost his influence and protection in Rome. So what did White do after the King's return?

Thus, after the Restoration White, fully aware of the dangers that he would have incurred for having supported Cromwell, fled to the Netherlands. In 1661 he published another defence of his doctrine, prefaced by a letter addressed to Leyburn and written from The Hague at the end of 1660.[44] In January 1661 the Nuncio in Brussels reported him in Rotterdam. Also, White's post-Restoration visit to the Netherlands must not have been his first, since the Nuncio in Brussels in the same 1661 letter reported White as 'fluent in Flemish'. Indeed, the connection between Thomas White and the Netherlands is rather interesting, and worth some considerations.

In the first place, it seems that White's connections in the Netherlands were not political. White did not appear to have had any official role, and no record concerning Thomas White can be found in the Nationaal Archief. Moreover, while in the Netherlands White kept a low profile: during his sojourns in The Hague, for instance, he did not rent property, nor did he sign contracts of any kind. It seems that White kept bases in the Catholic Low Countries, and that the arrangements for his travels must have been made and paid for by Digby, for in the British Library there is a note in Digby's handwriting commenting on White's lodging. In Antwerp, Digby wrote, White 'tient pension et chambre… en la maison qui estoit de l'advocat Rubens'. Digby was satisfied with the

---

[43] [che quella parte del Clero Inglese, ch'usurpa il titolo e giurisditione di Decano e Capitolo, totalmente aderente al sudetto Albio, habbia formato un nuovo giuramento, o Protesto peggiore di quello dell'Ibernesi… S'avvisa, ch'il medesimo Decano, e Capitolo per fortificare la lorofattione, conceda facolta' di confessare, predicare, et amministrare sacramenti, benche nullamente, e sacrilegamente a frati, o sacerdoti Hibernesi con gran preiudicio dell'anime, scandalo, e disprezzo della Sede Apostolica] The folder sent to the Congregation of the Inquisition, undated and unsigned but in Courtney's handwriting, summarized and translated in Italian the content of a letter sent by Pugh on November 17th 1622: see ACDF, St. St. SS2-b, unfol. The original letter by Pugh, in Latin, is included at the end (Ibid., unfol.).

[44] T. White, *Muscarium ad Immissos a Jona Thamone Calumniarum Crabrones et Sophismatum Scarabeos Censurae Duacenae Vindices Abigendos*, London 1661. The accompanying letter, written from The Hague, is dated December 1660.

arrangement he provided for his master: 'good treatment there, he commented, and the best company of Italian and other nobility'.[45]

However, White seemed to be part of a very interesting intellectual and philosophical network that connected the Low Countries with France. The first link between White and the Low Countries is Constantijn Huygens, an amateur poet and connoisseur of art, who served as the secretary of Frederik Hendrik, Holland's Stadholder from 1625 to 1647. Huygens was also the father of Christiaan, one of the most important natural philosophers of his time.[46] In 1642 Constantijn sent to Descartes, who was then in Leiden, a copy of White's treatise *De Mundo*, which was given to him by 'Monsieur Spanhemius, personage de grand sçavoir' and was recommended by Mersenne. Huygens noted that White was 'assez hardi pour vous avoir osé' contredire', and asked Descartes for his judgment.[47]

Descartes did not keep Huygens waiting, and a few days after receiving White's book wrote back to Huygens, expressing a not unfavorable judgment on White's *De Mundo*: 'I find many very good things in his third dialogue, however in the second, where he wanted to imitate Galileo, I think that all that this contains is too subtle for being true, as nature uses means which are very simple'. As for the relation between White's theory and his own, Descartes did not find in *De Mundo* any major source of contention, for even though White expressed some criticism on Descartes' calculations, 'there he speaks so well of me that I would have to be of an evil spirit if I took this badly'.[48]

Huygens's role as a liaison between White and Descartes has to be put in the context of the circle of Mersenne, with whom Constantijn Huygens was acquainted through his numerous French diplomatic contact, and who in mid-1640s was corresponding also with Constantijn's son, Christiaan, on mathematical problems, such as the squaring of the circle and the calculations of the oscillations of a pendulum.[49] Also interesting is Huygens's mention of Friedrick Spanheim the Elder as the man who brought him the copy of White's treatise to send to Descartes. Spanheim (1600–1649) was a Calvinist theologian, from 1642 professor of theology at the University of Leiden. Spanheim is interesting in this context because of his direct engagement with the religious strife in England in the mid-1640s. The Leiden professor in fact

---

[45] Digby's note, undated, can be found in BL, Add. Mss. 41846, document n.4, f. 58.

[46] Not much work has been done in English on either Constantijn or Christiaan. The only biography of Christiaan written in English is C.D. Andriesse, *Huygens. The Man behind the Principle*, Cambridge 2005. On Constantijn see J. Israel, *The Dutch Republic. Its Rise, Greatness, and Fall 1477–1806*, Oxford 1995, pp. 486 and ff. *passim*.

[47] Constantijn Huygens to Descartes, The Hague 7 October 1642, in *Correspondence of Descartes and Constantijn Huygens 1634–1647*, ed. by L. Roth, Oxford 1926, pp. 179–180.

[48] [Ie trouve plusieurs choses fort bonnes en son troisiesme dialogue, mais pour le second, où il a voulu imiter Galilèe, ie iudge que tout ce qu'il continent est trop subtil pour estre vray, car la nature ne se sert que de moyens qui sont fort simple] [il y parle si avantageusement de moy que ie serois de mauuaise humeur si ie le prenois en mauuraise part] Descartes to Constantijn Huygens, from Endegeest, 10 October 1642, in Ibid., pp. 180–183.

[49] On the relation between Constantijn, Christiaan and Mersenne see C.D. Andriesse, *Huygens*, pp. 75–79.

wrote a treatise in 1645 in reply to David Buchanan, a sort of spokesman for the position of the Scottish commissioners against the Independents and against the possibility of granting a form of religious toleration.[50] Spanheim's treatise, published with the imprimatur of the theologians at the University of Leiden, examined a set of ecclesiological questions raised by the Scottish Presbyterians, and it presented an interesting mixture of philo-Presbyterian theology and a call for religious and political moderation. The author's main goal, as he wrote in the dedicatory epistle addressed to Buchanan himself, was to contribute to eradicating dissention within the Church of England and within the English state:

> As we pray to God both privately and publicly that those deadly wars which will not be victorious for either side could be ended for the dignity of your Majesty and for the illustrious Parliament of the Kingdom, and that a cicatrix could cover this internal wound: So we wish with all our heart that those controversies that upset and divide your Churches could be timely sedated by holy advices.[51]

As to the specific content of the text, Spanheim starts by examining the question of whether the true Church should be inclusive, or admit only those who gave 'evident and certain proofs of true faith and sanctity'. In such a question, Spanheim writes, one can either sin 'in excessu' or 'in defectu'. As for the former, one can go to the extreme side of the spectrum by believing that 'infideles adulti', 'haeretici', 'athei, epicurei, libertini' should be admitted in the true Church. On the opposite side of the spectrum, there are those who think that 'no sacred agreement can or should be made with the open enemies God'.[52] While Spanheim affirms that extremities must be avoided, he thinks that if one has to sin, it is better to sin 'in excessu' than 'in defectu'.[53] That does not mean that Spanheim thinks that infidels should be welcomed in the Church, but that sometimes it is simply impossible for a Church which, according to the Scripture, was indeed supposed to be composed of both weeds and wheat, to distinguish clearly between the two and to eradicate the former.[54] In other words, one must distinguish between 'the evil ones in the forum of their own conscience…and the evil ones in the forum of other people's conscience, or in that of the Church. The latter we say should be kept away from the Church, the former should not'.[55]

---

[50] Spanheim's treatise, entitled *Friderici Spanhemii Epistola ad nobilissimum virum, Davidem Buchananum*, was published in London in 1645.
[51] [ut vero Deum quotidie in vota publica privataque vocamus, ut bella illa internecina nullos habitura utrinque triumphos, ex dignitate Serenissimi Regis vestri, Illustrissimorumque Regni Ordinum componantur, & cicatrix tandem obducatur domestico isti vulneri: Sic toto animo optamus, ut eae, quae Ecclesias vestras turbant & scindunt Controversiae, mature sanctis sopiantur consiliis] Ibid., p. 10.
[52] [nulla societas sacra iniri potest vel debet cum apertis Dei hostibus] Ibid., pp. 13–4.
[53] Ibid., p. 15.
[54] Ibid., pp. 18–19.
[55] [mali in foro conscientiae propriae..cum malis in foro conscientiae alienae, vel Ecclesiae. Istos arcendos ab Ecclesia fatemur, illos non item] Ibid., p. 26.

At the same time, however, Spanheim showed himself sympathetic to some of the Presbyterians' ecclesiological stances. For instance, he insisted that 'potestas Ecclesiastica' what is commonly called 'potestas clavium', did not reside in the whole Church, but in the Presbytery composed of the pastors and the elders.[56] For Spanheim, Presbytery was an 'Ecclesia repraesentativa' not in the sense that

> it should represent the entire body of the Church, as…the delegate represents that which delegates, in that its authority depends entirely on that which delegates it: but rather in that sense, as since the whole multitude cannot congregate…the jurisdiction of the Church, or the power of the keys, is entrusted by God to the people nominated and elected by the Church, and these people should represent the whole Church.[57]

In other words, the Presbytery did not receive its authority only from the Church, but from God himself. On the same line, he also vigorously denied that the authority in the Church resides in the single independent Churches, but that it should be placed instead in a general Synod.[58] The text, however, ends with the same note of moderation with which it had begun. Although of the two dangers looming over the Church of England, tyranny and anarchy, the anarchy brought about by independent Churches is worse than tyranny, yet Spanheim ends by wishing 'that, preserving the truth of doctrines, we might rather concede some part of our right, if we had some, than hinder either the peace of the Church or the increase of the Kingdom of God'.[59]

Now, what are we to make of the relation between Spanheim and Thomas White? It would be incorrect to postulate an interest on the part of Spanheim towards White because of a common Protestant-Catholic interest in a latitudinarian model of Church. Spanheim was a staunch Calvinist, and even though he supported a form of moderate toleration, he never advocated, either explicitly or implicitly, any form of toleration towards the Catholics. Besides, even in the relatively liberal atmosphere created during Frederik Hendrik's tenure as Stadholder anti-Catholicism was deeply rooted in the Netherlands.[60] The key to understand the relation between White and Spanheim is natural science. During the 1630s and 1640s, in fact, the Netherlands was stirred by a large and important intellectual debate that concerned the implications of Cartesianism in the realm of theology. The Dutch academia split between those who accepted Cartesianism and the mechanist world-view that it introduced, and those who rejected it, defending Aristotelian natural science. Possibly the most influential member of the latter faction was Gisbertus Voetius, a

---

[56] Ibid., pp. 42 and ff.
[57] [repraesentaret totum corpus Ecclesiae, prout …delegatus delegantem, utpote cuijus auctoritas tota pendet a delegante: verum eo duntaxat sensu, quatenus, quia tota multitudo nec adiri potest…jurisdictio Ecclesiastica siva potestas clavium electis vel nominates ab Ecclesia personis committitur a Deo, quae repraesentent velut totam Ecclesiam] Ibid., p. 49.
[58] Ibid., pp. 54 and ff.
[59] [ut, dogmatum veritate salva, de jure etiam nostro, si quod esset, cedamus potius, quam ut intercedamus sive paci Ecclesiasticae, sive incremento Regni Dei] Ibid., pp. 91–92.
[60] On Dutch anti-Catholicism see J. Israel, *The Dutch Republic*, pp. 637–645.

professor of theology in Utrecht and a staunch opponent of Arminianism, referred to by Spanheim as 'Celeberimus [sic] Theologus', who had engaged some of theological issues that Spanheim and Buchanan were discussing.[61]

It is not my intention here to examine in any detail the philosophical and theological debates in the Low Countries in the seventeenth century. I merely want to point out that Thomas White needs to be inserted into a wide European intellectual movement whose main preoccupation was to elaborate the relationship between natural philosophy and theology in a way that could respond to the challenges presented by the new science. In a sense, the philosophy of Thomas White represented a via media between the extremities of the mechanist world-view which excluded, at least potentially and logically, the role of God in the functioning of the universe, and a conservative Aristotelianism which, even if safeguarded the centrality of the divine action, could not make sense of the discoveries that Galileo the 'new scientists' were making. In this respect, the interest of Spanheim for White's *De Mundo* is a testimony of the English Catholic's role in this debate. Also, and more generally, inserting Thomas White in this context allows us to realize that while in mid-seventeenth century Europe theologians and philosophers were still engaged in the confessional battle between the true Church and its adversaries, they were also engaged on another front, on which nothing less was at stake than the very theological foundations of the framework with which the world was understood. While this new front did not erase the old confessional battle, it surely contributed in posing it in a different manner.

While in the 1640s White's name was associated with one of the most important intellectual debate in seventeenth-century Netherlands, in 1660, when White returned there after the return of the King, he did not seem to play any role in the heated ideological conflict that erupted in early 1660s over republicanism and heightened by the deteriorating relationship between the Dutch and the English king. Rather, White tried to defend his political theory, hoping to be able to go back to England. From his exile in fact he wrote an *Apology for the Treatise of Obedience and Government,* which remained unpublished. In the text White clarified that *The Grounds* was concerned with 'the question ... of supreme Goverour; this name I doe use that it may eschew it selfe to all sorts of Goverments for I never restrained my selfe from this latitude in my former writing, as beeing a Philosophicall piece, and abstracting from all particularities'.[62] White's treatise, therefore, was not meant to support either the republican or the monarchical form of government, but only to illustrate the ground upon which any commonwealth was founded. This was the Ciceronian idea of the *salus populi*, or 'common good', defined as 'the substantiall, and radicall Unitie, and the steadfastnesse of the Commonwealth, without which it is rather a chaine of slaves, and an Argier's prison, then a conspiring multitude

---

[61] On the theological and philosophical issues at the core of the Voetius-Descartes controversy see J.A. van Ruler, *The crisis of causality. Voetius and Descartes on God, Nature and Change*, Leiden 1995. On the larger social and intellectual context in which the debate has to be put see J. Israel, *The Dutch Republic*, pp. 581 and ff.

[62] T. White, *Apology*, f. 532

and free nation'.[63] It was for the common good, in White's opinion, that when a governor is dispossessed, if restoring him presented more hazard for the good of the people than endorsing the new one, the dispossessed governor himself would have had to resign, because it is 'the horridst calumny that can bee fained against a lawful Magistrate...that his people are for him, and not hee for his people'.[64]

Thus, in the *Apology* White re-enforces the *de facto*-ist and consensual arguments that he had put forward in the *Grounds*: given that the common good is the only solid ground for obedience, in times of uncertainty and changing, being obedient to the new governor was preferable than risking a war to restore the old one to the throne, provided that the new governor abides by the same principle of the good of the people. If this doctrine, White wrote, is mistakenly interpreted as an endorsement of the right of rebelling, then 'nay that Cromwell himself (who then was in power) by the doctrine of that booke, might bee killed by any private man; soe that, if his sillie vote be accepted of, my writing was neither out of flatterie, to the then extent Government, nor contained any spetiall aversinesse from his maiestie'.[65]. White's text, then, should not have been read as an anti- or pro-Royalist manifesto. Rather, the true meaning of the *Grounds* was 'that his maiesties right and service would and ought to bee rooted in the hearts of his people, as long as this motive keeps its force, that his Maiestyes Returne was Good for the people'.[66] Unfortunately for White, only 'some fewe Intelligent persons' understood his text in its proper significance, and the 'vulgar sort', able to 'penetrate not farr into questions', slandered him. Having lost his Majesty's favor, White had to leave England for fear of not being able to defend his opinion in a fair trial. Were this trial to be held, White concludes, 'could the iudge pronounce any other sentence, then 'Nullam Causam in hoc homine invenio'; and that 'per invidiam eum tradiderunt'.[67]

The King ultimately decided to pardon White – possibly because of the intercession of Digby, who had managed in the meanwhile to get back on the King's good side –, and White returned to London in 1662. The opposition against White's political theory did not end however, as can be proved by the publication of Assheton's *Evangelium Armatum* in 1663.[68] White, however, maintained his line of defense, that is to say, his mixture of consent theory and *de facto*-ist arguments. As he wrote in a letter to Kenelm Digby on the accusations waged against him in Assheton's text, *The Grounds* was not meant to support a particular form of government, but rather 'the whole discourse is grounded upon the Principle that as long as a Governors restitution stands

---
[63] Ibid., f. 538.
[64] Ibid., f. 541.
[65] Ibid., ff. 539–540.
[66] Ibid., f. 549.
[67] Ibid., ff. 549–551.
[68] On this text see *supra*, chapter IV, pp. 75–76.

with the good of the commonwealth so long hee loses not his right…A principle that distinguishes betwixt Governours and Tyrants'.[69]

After this, White did not seem to have engaged himself with politics any longer, but that does not mean that he abandoned his intellectual activities altogether. In fact, he continued to publish on two of the themes that had always been intellectually central to him, namely, the relationship between reason and faith, and the question of skepticism. As for the first, White addressed the question of a rational Catholicism in the context of a fierce polemic stirred by the publication of the English translation of his *Villicationis suae de medio statu animarum,* which came out as *The middle state of souls* in 1659. The controversy begun when John Sergeant, White's pupil and secretary of the English Chapter, published anonymously a treatise in which he took issues with some of his master's theses.[70] White replied with his 1660 *Religion and reason*. Also, White defended his doctrine of Purgatory in a text published the following year, entitled *Devotion and Reason,* written specifically in reply of a book entitled *Remembrance for the Living to pray for the Dead,* written by an English Jesuit named James Mumford in 1641, reprinted and translated several times over the course of the seventeenth century.[71]

Both of White's lengthy treatises are articulated as a complex defense of his own doctrine and life, and as an attack of the Roman Court and of the Inquisition; in this respect White rehearses many of the same arguments that we have already analyzed. In particular, White decided to treat the doctrine of Purgatory as a manifestation of a larger question, that is to say, the relation between theology and philosophy. As he wrote in *Religion and Reason,* behind the debate over his denial of the corporeal nature of punishment in Purgatory there is a much more important issue at stake, namely, the role of reason in establishing theological truths: 'Philosophy is the wax unto which the seal of Divinity is printed…for, if Definitions be the Principles of Science, and Philosophy defines the words Divinity uses, it must needs have a materiall priority to it'.[72] And if producing 'demonstrations of the Articles of Faith' can be considered 'Paganism', as Sergeant contended, so be it, for 'Faith is not desirable for its Obscurity, but for its Certainty. We govern out lives by *knowing* the objects, not by the *defect* in the knowledge'.[73]

If the previous text was discussing a text by a fellow scholar, the target of *Devotion and Reason* was a very popular text dealing with the liturgical consequences of the Catholic traditional doctrine of Purgatory, such as the doctrine of indulgencies. In this context, White built his text as a defense of

---

[69] The letter from White to Digby is dated 29 April but without the year. The *terminus post quem*, however, is the publication of the *Evangelium Armatum* in 1663. The text of the letter can be found in BL Add. Mss. 41846, ff. 84t–86r, at f. 85r.

[70] The title of Sergeant's book is *Vindication of the Doctrine contained in Pope Benedict xii his Bull*, Paris 1659.

[71] On Mumford see *DNB, sub voce* Mumford, James.

[72] T. White, *Religion and reason mutually corresponding and assisting each other*, Paris 1660, p. 25.

[73] Ibid., p. 190.

his rational Catholicism against the practices of the common people, so that a large part of the text is devoted to denouncing the superstitious character of many of the proofs adduced by Mumford to argue for the corporeality of the soul in Purgatory, such as apparitions, revelations, miracles, etc.[74] As the foundations for such a superstitious religion are false, for they do not spring from reason, so are their applications, as indulgencies, or the celebration of masses for the dead:

> Before Christ, Miracles belonged to the ordinary Government of the Church by God Almighty; since Christ and his Apostles time, these are become parts of Extraordinary Providence....now...we have order to govern our selves by Reason, and Faith is given us to help and strengthen our Reason, that it may reach the motives propounded to us out of the state of the next World, and to expect rewards and punishments there which spring out of our lives here.[75]

To a certain extent, these two works on Purgatory constitute a summary of the main concerns of White's theology, that is, a faith that does not contradict, but 'strengthen our Reason'. In this respect, the controversy over White's doctrine of Purgatory became a controversy over this fundamental tenet of his whole theology. The Roman Church noticed this, and the Congregation of the Index decided to condemn *De medio statu animarum* in November 1662, after the Inquisition had condemned White's *opera omnia*.[76] It is also significant to note that the English regime also decided to condemn White's doctrine of Purgatory: in October 1666 *The middle state of souls* was censured by the Parliament, together with Hobbes's *Leviathan*, for 'atheism and profaneness'.[77] This final condemnation on the part of the English state represents the definitive end not only of White's intellectual influence, but also of his political standing. When the English monarchy wanted to take a stand against Thomas White, it did not even bother mentioning his *Grounds of Obedience and Government*.

From White's two contributions to the controversy over the doctrine of Purgatory we also find the second intellectual concern that accompanied White to the end of his life, that is to say, his belief that such a rational and un-superstitious religion is also infallibly certain. In his *Devotion and Reason* there is a chapter dedicated to confute Mumford's argument that even if we granted the character of 'probable opinion' to the traditional doctrine of Purgatory,

---

[74] T. White, *Devotion and reason. Wherein modern devotion for the dead is brought to solid principles and made rational*, Paris 1661, pp. 61 and ff.

[75] Ibid., pp. 252–3.

[76] J.M. De Bujanda, *Index Librorum prohibitorum*, sub voce, White, Thomas.

[77] In the *Journals of the House of Commons* it is reported that on October 17th 1666 it was 'Ordered, that the Committee to which the Bill against Atheism and Profaneness is committed, be impowered to receive Information touching such Books as tend to Atheism, Blasphemy, or Profaneness, or against the Essence or Attributes of God; and, in particular, the Book published in the name of one White; and the Book of Mr. Hobbs, called 'The Leviathan'; and to report the Matter, with their Opinion, to the House' (vol. VIII p. 6360). A.à Wood identifies White's book with the one on Purgatory: see *Athenae Oxonienses*, ed. by P. Bliss, 4 vols., London 1813–1821, vol. III p. 1121.

the fact that many theologians and divines have supported such a probability makes it 'rational to follow'.[78] To this argument White replies:

> In Metaphysical rigour of truth, no multitude of men can be so vast, no gravity and wisdom of them so high and great, as to oblige any ingenious man to believe that which themselves profess *they do not know whether it be true or no*. For all Belief is grounded upon the *knowledg* of another. If I be secured he does not know the thing I should beleeve upon his credit, I have no ground of belief.[79]

The absolute certainty of the Catholic doctrine, or better, the possibility of the absolute certainty of any form of knowledge, was questioned by different strands of theological and epistemological skepticism, against which White had already written and would continue to write in his post-Restoration life. More specifically, all through the 1660s White was engaged in a significant debate provoked by Joseph Glanvill's 1661 *Vanity of Dogmatizing*.[80]

Thomas White ended his life at the political margins, but did not abandon his intellectual debates and concerns. The elderly White liked to converse especially with Thomas Hobbes, one of his life-long intellectual partners. In Anthony à Wood's narrative:

> Hobbes of Malmsbury had a great respect for him [i.e. Thomas White], and when he lived in Westminster, he would often visit him, and he Hobbes, but seldom parted in cool blood: for they would wrangle, squabble and scold about philosophical matters like young sophisters, though either of them was eighty years of age; yet Hobbes being obstinate, and not able to endure contradiction, (tho' well he might, seeing White, was his senior) yet those scholars, who were sometimes present at their wrangling disputes, held that the laurel was carried away by White.[81]

This image of the octogenarian Thomas White debating philosophical theories with Thomas Hobbes like a 'young sophister' is very fitting to conclude the narrative of a man who had made reason the central concern of his intellectual life. The laurels that the Blackloist won then can be taken as a somewhat sad irony of all the laurels he was not able to carry away earlier. In this still engaging intellectual environment, almost completely beyond the care and the interest of the world, White died in 1676.

6.2 Kenelm Digby

After the Restoration the life of Kenelm Digby, White's pupil, patron, intellectual partner and friend, took a different turn than his master's. When the King

---

[78] T. White, *Devotion and Reason*, pp. 112 and ff.
[79] Ibid., p. 113.
[80] The implications of White's anti-skeptical positions in seventeenth-century England have been treated at large by Beverley Southgate in '*Covetous of truth*', pp. 66 and ff., and Dorothea Krook in *John Sergeant and his circle*, pp. 41 and ff.
[81] A.à Wood, *Athenae Oxonienses*, ed. London 1813–1820 (4 vols.), vol. III, pp. 1247–8.

returned to the throne, unlike Thomas White, Digby managed to be reinstated at court as Henrietta Maria's Chancellor, a post that he maintained until the end of his life.[82] Although Kenelm Digby participated to the political life of the Stuart Court – for instance, he was directly involved in the struggle between his cousin, George Digby second earl of Bristol, and the earl of Clarendon, over the King's marriage, and was briefly banned from the court in 1664[83] – his role at court remained rather marginal, as was Henrietta's. Among the reasons for Digby's marginality was certainly his staunch defense of Catholicism, to which he remained committed even after the Restoration. Indeed, religion seemed to be the most important political priority of the last years of Digby's life, as can be inferred from the petition that the Catholic courtier wrote immediately after the Restoration, asking Charles II to abolish the penal laws against the English Catholics.[84]

The petition is really a short historical essay on the persecutions and unjust legislations of which the English Catholics had been victims since Henry VIII's time. It is also to be noted that while Digby briefly addressed his father's participation to the Gunpowder Plot, a mistake that Kenelm ascribed to Sir Everard's 'tender and unexperienced youth, his unaffected zeal that exposed him to be seduced to those mischievous hypocrites',[85] he did not make any reference to Cromwell's regime, nor to his own relationship with the late Lord Protector. Rather, he simply remarked that now that 'God through his infinite mercy sent your Majesty to our desolate Nation, to repair those breaches that those unhappy distempers have made in the state and in the lawes' it was a right time to look at the Catholic question with a more moderate attitude.[86]

Digby's analysis of the English Catholic question is centered upon the distinction between Jesuitical Catholicism, which Digby himself repudiated, and the Blackloists' Catholicism, to which the King should not hesitate to grant toleration. The kind of Catholicism that Digby believed in, he explained to Charles, did not question the authority of the sovereign in temporal matters: 'wee believe that no power on earth can absolve us from our duty and Allegiance to our sovereign'.[87] The anti-Papalist tone of this position is later reaffirmed by Digby, who explained to the King that the Catholic religion was warranted by 'the word of God, the Tradition of the Church, the consent and practise of the fathers, the acts of Generall Councils, the resolutions of the learnedest men, the practise of the piousest persons of both sexes, and

---

[82] For a detailed account of the financial and logistic details of Digby's return to England see R.T. Petersson, *Sir Kenelm Digby*, pp. 288 and ff.

[83] A letter by Thomas Clifford written on the 6th of January 1664 reports that Digby was exiled from the court; Digby appeared to have re-gained the King's favor a couple of weeks later: see Clifford to Williamson, 6 January 1664, in *Calendar of State Papers Domestic*, vol. XC doc. N.36; and Salisbury to the early of Huntingdon, 20th January 1664, *Historical Manuscripts Commission, Hastings Papers*, 3 vols, London 1928–1934, vol. II, pp. 143–5). Further details on Digby's involvement in this affair can be found in R.T. Petersson, *Sir Kenelm Digby*, p. 292.

[84] Digby's petition can be found in BL, Add. Mss. 41846, ff. 76r–79v.

[85] Ibid., f. 77r.

[86] Ibid., f. 77v.

[87] Ibid.

the whole course of Christianity in all times, throughout the whole world, without any interruption in the universality and succession of it'.[88] The Pope is a conspicuous, if by now unsurprising, absentee in this list.

Thus, it is the Blackloists' Catholicism-without-the-Pope that Digby hoped Charles could come to see as an ally, rather than an enemy, of the monarchy. In this respect, it is also interesting that in the previously quoted letter from White to Digby on the criticism by William Assheton of *The Grounds of Obedience and Government*, the defense of the Blackloists' political theory is accompanied by a defense of the Blackloist Catholicism as something separate from the Pope's, and, unlike the latter, not unfavorable to monarchical regimes in general, and to the English monarchy in particular. Assheton, White wrote, 'seems to mee when it would speak against Papists to play the Prevaricatour. For whereas hee pretends to shew Catholicks fomenters of Rebellions hee brings upon the state one whome himself professes to bee the most moderate amongst them'.[89] Indeed, when writing to Digby, White did not defend every Catholic theorist from the stigma of treason, but he set his own text apart: Assheton's fault, among others, was that while he sought 'to shew Antimonarchicall principles out of Catholick Authours hee accuses a book which is wholy and strongly written for Monarchy…I challenge the greatest Monarchist to shew any book that makes the subiection to Princes either a greater vertue or of greater necessity and that it bindes to greater sufferings'.[90]

It is clear, then, that Digby tried once more to use his political role in order to push for a form of toleration for the 'moderate' Catholicism that the Blackloists represented.[91] This effort was of little significance for actual political dynamics, since after 1660 Digby had less political power than ever, and if the possibility of granting toleration to the Catholics in 1647–8 was remote, in 1661–2 was unimaginable, even if the Blackloist-style Gallican ecclesiology might have been an important element in the context of the toleration fights during the reign of Charles II.[92]

Aside from politics and from the Catholic question, in the last years of his life Digby returned to and continued his works on natural philosophy. As a token of the fame acquired by Digby in the scientific community of his time, he was elected as Fellow of the Royal Society on December 1660, and in 1662–3 he joined the Royal Society Council.[93] Digby's scientific activities during his last years centered upon the study of alchemy and chemistry, which he had begun in his Oxford years with Thomas Allen, and he had continued in the

---

[88] Ibid., ff. 78r–v.
[89] White to Digby, 29 April, BL Add. Mss. 41846, f. 84r.
[90] Ibid.
[91] It seems that Kenelm Digby was not the only Catholic member of his family: in September 1663 Digby's son John was indicted for recusancy together with the Early of Bristol. On the 4th of April 1664 a pass was issued for John Digby, his wife and his servants to go to France: see *Calendar of State Papers Domestic*, vol. LXXX doc. n.9, and *Calendar State Papers Domestic* vol. XCVI doc. n.53
[92] I owe this point to Jeffrey Collins, whom I thank.
[93] See the catalogue of the Fellows in M. Hunter, *The Royal Society and its Fellows 1660–1700. The Morphology of an early scientific institution*, Chalfont St. Giles 1982, p. 161.

1650s in collaboration with Samuel Hartlib. The main works Digby produced after 1660 are a treatise on the vegetation of plants, born out of a lecture delivered at Gresham College in 1660, which arose the interest of many of Digby's colleagues, including Henry Oldenburg,[94] and his *Chymical Secrets*, a collection of alchemical recipes published posthumously.[95]

Historians of science, and in particular Betty Jo Dobbs, have already provided a fine analysis of Digby's late alchemical works, and have shown their importance in the history of pharmaceutics and chemistry.[96] In this context, it is interesting to note that there is evidence that Digby was not only interested in 'high' alchemy and natural philosophy, but also in the 'lower' side of the topic, that is to say, the making of 'natural' remedies for every day's life. In the hugely successful treatise entitled *The Queens closet opened*, which contained a collection of Henrietta Maria's recipes, Digby participated by adding his own version of *Aqua mirabilis*, a concoction of, among the others, cloves, mace, ginger, cinnamon and rose water that, among the many benefits, 'preserveth the Lungs without grievances…it suffereth not the bloud to putrefie…conserveth Youth, and procureth Memory'.[97]

For the purpose of the present research, however, I would like to highlight three features of Digby's reflections on alchemy as a part of natural philosophy. First of all, even at the end of his life Digby did not abandon his role as scientific 'facilitator', but he continued to serve as a trait d'union between scientists of different background, from Robert Boyle to Athanasius Kircher, whom Digby mentioned for an experiment aimed at showing the possibility of revivification of plants ('Kircher at Rome assured me he had done it'), an experiment he himself would have liked to perform.[98]

Secondly, and regarding the nature of the scientific enterprise that Digby was invested in, throughout his career Digby remained committed to one of the pillars of Blackloist science: the mechanical world-view of nature which does not deny, but rather proves God's role in the Universe. When touching upon this subject in his book on plants Digby commented:

---

[94] On Digby's role in the early 1660s scientific circles in England see B.J. Dobbs, 'Digby and alchemy', at pp. 159 and ff., and M.Boas Hall, *Henry Oldenburg. Shaping the Royal Society*, Oxford 2002, p. 61.

[95] K. Digby, *A discourse concerning the vegetation of plants*, and Id., *A choice collection of rare chymical secrets and experiments in philosophy*, London 1682.

[96] See in particular B.J. Dobbs, 'Digby and alchemy', and Id., 'Digby's experimental alchemy: the book of *Secrets*', *Ambix*, vol. XXI n.1 (1974), pp. 1–28.

[97] The first edition of *The Queens closet opened. Incomparable secrets in Physick, Chirurgery, Preserving, Candying, and Cookery* was published in London 1655 (Digby's recipe can be found at pp. 290–1). The anonymous editor in the epistle to the reader explained that the decision to publish Henrietta's private collection of recipes was a means to prevent those from spreading unofficially, given the instability caused by 'my Soveraign mistress her banishment, as also this continued change' (unfol.). The treatise was reprinted in 1656, 1658, 1659, 1661, 1662, and again in the 1670s and 1680s. Starting from the 1659 edition, however, the treatise was accompanied by a different dedicatory epistle, that highlighted the success of the first edition and 'the benefit which so many have receiv'd from these, which we shall now rather call Experiments then Receipts' (*The Queens closet opened*, London 1659, dedicatory epistle, unfol.)

[98] K. Digby, *Vegetation*, p. 75.

> ...he that should look barely upon the two extreme terms, the beginning and the completing of a plant, might think there were a perpetuall miracle in the production of vegetables, and might be excused for having recourse to a *vis formativa*, and such other insignificant terms. But another that considereth the whole course of nature set on foot by God Almighty for this admirable work; and fixeth his foot at every particular joynt, not stirring it from thence till he have fully examined and discussed what must necessarily follow out of such or such matter, in such or such circumstances, so and so tempered, and so and so wrought upon; will evidently discern that it is throughout impossible, any thing should happen in it otherwise then just what and how it doth. And it is want of consideration and judgement, which maketh men fly to occult and imaginary qualities, to shroud their ignorance under inconceavable termes: Whereas nature in her self is pervious and open to human discovery, if a due course be taken to dissect and survay her.[99]

This passage should not be taken as an endorsement on Digby's part of experimental science as we know it: while Digby rejected the 'occult of imaginary qualities', he did not have any problems in writing about a 'Universall Spirit... homogeneall to all things, being in effect the Spirit of Life'.[100] The fact that Digby's experimentalism did not have the methodological coherence of Bacon's, however, does not mean, as Dobbs has argued, that Digby 'did not aim at ultimate certainty in natural philosophy'.[101] For Digby, an experimental inquire of nature can indeed provide a certain knowledge, provided that experiments are guided by and imbedded into a pre-existing and all-encompassing system, which in Digby's case remained Aristotle's. In this sense, experiments are truly *ancillae philosophiae,* or, as Digby put it before describing his experiments on plants, 'I shall hereafter convince experimentally, besides the evidence of the reason that concludeth it must be so'.[102]

The third point, that is the theological upshot of the mutual relationship between experience and reason, or between science and theology in Digby's philosophy of nature, is that while God is still needed to explain nature, nature can help to explain God. We have already seen the embryo of this concept in the 1620 lecture that Digby presented at the Accademia dei Filomati in Siena, where he explained that alchemy was the only science that could provide some knowledge of the divinity.[103] In the 1660s Digby had worked out a much more sophisticated version of his argument, profoundly influenced by the 'Aristotelian atomism' and theological views elaborated with Thomas White in the preceding decades. The treatise on the vegetation of plants, in fact, is concluded by a lengthy passage on the resurrection of human bodies after death. In a nutshell, Digby argued that once we demonstrate that revivification of plants through heat is indeed possible, we can also apply this completely

---

[99] Ibid., pp. 46–48.
[100] Ibid., p. 70.
[101] B.J. Dobbs, 'The natural philosophy', p. 14.
[102] K. Digby, *Vegetation*, p. 30.
[103] See *supra*, chap. I, pp. 7–8.

'natural' process to explain the 'natural' character of the resurrection of bodies:

> ...my undertaking is, to convince that there is no impossibility nor contradiction in nature, against this great and amazing Mystery. If there were contradiction in it, it could not be true; it were not the subject of a Miracle. But if I prove that there is no repugnance against the feasibility of it, I am confident I shall not misse of hearty thanks from those sincere believers who have nothing to shake the firmnesse of their Faith, but the suspected impossibility of the Mystery.[104]

As Digby's natural science needs theology, so theology needs natural science, for without the proof that religion is indeed 'feasible' we cannot reach 'firmnesse' in our Faith.[105] The real miracle, in Digby's opinion, is the perfect harmony between natural and supernatural, without 'impossibility and contradiction'. At the end of his life, then, Digby returned to the fundamental core of the doctrine that he illustrated in his 1644 *Two Treatises*, a philosophy of nature that represented not the enemy, but the most useful ally to theology. In this respect, we can say that while Digby's political allegiance and fortune changed many times over the course of his life, his commitment to Thomas White's intellectual project never faltered. Indeed, even after death Digby remained loyal to his old master, whom he remembered in his testament as 'my most honored friend, who lived sometime with me in my house att Paris, and to whom I pay an annuity of 60 pounds a year', in addition to which he left 20 pounds.[106] Not long after writing his testament, Sir Kenelm Digby died.

---

[104] K. Digby, *Vegetation*, p. 89.

[105] On the theological concerns that inform Digby's philosophy of nature see also B. Janaceck, 'Catholic natural philosophy'.

[106] Digby's testament, written in 1665 in French with some addenda in English, can be found in BL Add. 38175, ff. 52r–62v. The part on White is at f. 61r.

CONCLUSION

An Assessment of the Blackloist Experience

It is now time to make some final considerations on the relevance of the Blackloists' contribution to the intellectual, political and religious history of early modern Europe, and I think it useful to start this brief discussion by distinguishing between two separate sets of issues. In the first place, we should discuss their contribution in the realm of natural philosophy. Secondly, we need to consider the importance of the Blackloists' political and ecclesiological theories in the context of Catholicism's place in the history of England.

As for the former, the core of White and Digby's natural philosophy was an attempt to synthesize Aristotelianism and 'new' science. Such a synthesis had two principal aims. First, Aristotelianism as a system, according to the Blackloists, appeared resilient to the blows of the new scientific discoveries, for not only did they not call into question its philosophical foundations, but they could 'make sense' only if they were integrated with Aristotelianism. Secondly, and specifically concerning Thomas White, integrating the new science into the Aristotelian framework created a strong bulwark against epistemological skepticism, which White saw as extremely dangerous for both theology and natural philosophy.

Of these two areas, the Blackloists' contributions in the latter have proved the better studied in current scholarships, and have been judged the more lasting ones. As Beverley Southgate has illustrated, Thomas White continued to be an important reference in anti-skeptical polemics during the eighteenth century, thanks in large part to John Sergeant, his disciple, who kept the Blackloist anti-skeptical tradition alive. In this respect Southgate's work has shown that White occupies an important role in the history of early modern philosophical debates and in the history of skepticism and anti-skepticism.[1] As for White and Digby's mix of Aristotelianism and new science, it is certainly true that this was quickly and irreparably submerged by the landslide of the new mechanical science, which proved able not only to make new experiments, but also to build a world-view that became utterly incompatible with Aristotelianism. Yet one of the most fascinating aspects of the substitution of the old by the new, as current historians of science have been explaining, is precisely the moment of transition between the two. If we want to understand the significance of the scientific revolution, and even the extent to which the scientific revolution was indeed 'revolutionary', a more accurate picture of the transitional period

---

[1] B.C. Southgate, *Covetous of truth*, pp. 139 and ff.; 'Cauterising the tumor of Phyrronism' and Id., 'Blackloism and Tradition: From Theological Certainty to Historiographical Doubt', *The Journal of the History of Ideas*, vol. 61 n. 1 (2000), pp. 97–114.

becomes necessary. Thomas White and the Blackloists occupy a crucial role in such a period, and they demonstrate the complexity of the intellectual efforts that brought about the definitive end of Aristotelianism as an effective way to understand the physical world.

As far as Thomas White and the Blackloists' role in politics, Beverley Southgate has argued that White's personal political reputation never really recovered after 1660, and for many years after White's own death *The Grounds* was occasionally quoted by Catholics and Protestants alike as an example of the threat posed to the royal power by certain Catholic theories.[2] Apart from occasional instances of *damnatio memoriae*, Southgate concludes, 'Blackloism as a political programme had received its death blow in 1660'.[3]

I think that while it is true that Blackloism had little short-term impact in the political dynamics of England between 1640 and 1660, it is incorrect to assume that it was of no significance in the future history of the English Catholic community in its relationship with politics. Consider, for instance, the second edition of *The Grounds*, published around 1700, about twenty-five years after its author's death.[4] While the text does not appear to have been modified in any significant way, the 1700 edition is accompanied by a very interesting dedicatory epistle and a preface. The anonymous editor, in fact, dedicated the treatise to 'the Right Honourable the Lord Clifford of Chudleigh', i.e. Hugh Clifford, third Lord of Clifford.[5] The Cliffords of Chudleigh were a very prominent Catholic family, quite influential during the period immediately following the Restoration. Thomas Clifford, Hugh's father and first Lord Clifford, was one of the main advisors of Charles II during the tense period immediately following the triple alliance and the Dutch wars, and was made a baron in 1672 in reward for his service.[6] As the anonymous editor wrote, his epistle was 'a Dedication from a Whig to a Catholick', and the whole editorial project was meant to disprove the conclusion 'that none can be Britains that are Romans'.[7]

Why did the editor pick *The Grounds* as a text that would unify Whigs and Catholics? Even though White's principle of 'the Good of the Community' led him to justify the people's right of resistance, nevertheless, the editor wrote, '[White] carries the Point of Obedience to a higher Pitch in some Respects, than most other Writers'. The reason is that White 'discovers so little Regard to Hereditary Right, in the strict Sense of it, that he makes it a Duty incumbent

---

[2] See B.C. Southgate, *Covetous of truth*, pp. 53–65.

[3] Ibid., p. 138.

[4] *The Grounds of Obedience and Government. Being the best answer to all that has been lately written in Defence of Passive Obedience and Non Resistance. By Father Thomas White, a Benedictine, Father Confessor to the Queen Mother Henrietta Maria*, London s.d. Wing proposes 1700 as the date of composition: see W1828.

[5] See J.Kirk, *Biography of English Catholics in the Eighteenth century*, London 1909, pp.45–6.

[6] See *DNB sub voce Clifford, Thomas*.

[7] T. White, *The Grounds* (1700), dedicatory epistle, unfol.

upon a Supream Governor, dispossess'd of his Dominions, to acquiesce with a new Settlement, for the Sake of Peace and Welfare of the Publick'.[8]

In a moment in which, after the Glorious Revolution, the debate over the legitimacy of William of Orange's reign again raised the question of hereditary government, the arguments put forward in *The Grounds* in favor of the necessity of obedience to a *de facto* ruler could be useful once again. And the fact that it was a Catholic theorist that proposed these *de facto*-ist arguments could serve to demonstrate the extent to which English Catholics could and should contribute to political debates. It is interesting that, in order to make White's Catholic identity more 'palatable', the anonymous editor of the 1700 edition made some relevant corrections to White's biography. He wrote that White was 'one of the Fathers of the Benedictine Order', and no mention is made of White's troubles with the Roman hierarchy. Moreover, the editor added that even though White's principles seemed to go against the Royal Cause, which, at the time of the publication of White's book, was 'languishing in Exile in Despair', nevertheless the English King recognized the fundamental soundness of the Catholic's political principles, and White 'was afterwards admitted to be Father Confessor to the Queen-Mother of England, the Grandmother of her present Majesty, and after her Decease officiated some Years at the Altar in Somerset-House; being much reverenced and honoured by all that knew him, till Death'.[9]

Although none of the information on White's biography reported by the anonymous editor is confirmed by any other source, I believe that the fact that White's political principles were re-proposed and justified after 1688 demonstrates that his Catholic arguments for the legitimacy of a *de facto* ruler, far from being 'dead', still circulated in England. That means also that through White's political theory English Catholics continued to have or to claim a role in the English political debate. It will be a rewarding task, though one beyond the scope of the present work, to elaborate on and explain the extent to which this role mattered, both for political dynamics and political theory.

---

[8] Ibid., 'The Preface', unfol.
[9] Ibid.

Appendix[1]
The grounds of obedience and government. By Thomas White, Gentleman, London 1655, printed by J.Flesher, for Laurence Chapman next door to the Fountain Tavern in the Strand

In 12°.
Epigraph: Salus populi, suprema lex esto, Tullius, *De legibus*, book 3

Dedicatory epistle [unfoliated]: To my most honoured and best Friend, Sir KENELME DIGBY.

'Sir, The many attempts you have this long time made upon me, to declare a point of philosophy, wherein partly I was ignorant, and partly loth to meddle (being mindefull of the Poet's admonition, *Incedis per ignes suppositos cineri doloso*)[2] have at the last beaten out of my resistance this little sparke of fire, or rather light, borne by the author's intention, to shine, not to burne. For, having by experience of many our debates upon single points found that such skirmishes were not like to gaine the victory of satisfaction upon your so solid understanding, I saw my selfe forced to lay before your eyes, in one platforme or designe, the most intimate and bottome principles of obedience and government. The which, I have strived to doe in the most short and summary manner I was able, not willing to bee over-curious in so awfull a subject. I play therefore the pure philosopher. I deliver the abstract notions onely, leaving to the prudence of particulars to draw such consequences, as every one's circumstances shall make necessary and evident unto him by the short hints I give. And as for your selfe, I doubt not but my time is well employed. As for others, I feare the fortune of my other writings may prove constant also to this: that it will finde, those who reade it not, or who cannot judge of it, severe censurers; and those who like it, fearfull to oppose so loud and clamorous a multitude, or at least, stonned with the adverse noise. But for this, let the eternall Providence care. To me such clamours will bee no novelties, but the content of having given you satisfaction, an abundant reward of the endeavours of,
  Sir, your true friend, and most obliged servant, THOMAS WHITE'

---

[1] Editor's Note: punctuation and capitalization have been corrected according to modern usage, but the original spelling has been left.
[2] Horace, *Odes*, II, 1, vv. 7–8. Unless otherwise noted, all italics are White's.

[p. 1]³ *The first GROUND.*
Wherein Consists the Perfection of Government

Xenophon, in his excellent Booke of the instruction of *Cyrus*, moves this question: why, of all other living creatures, which are of different matures from man, wee easily attaine to the mastery and rule, but few men are so intelligent [p. 2] as to be fit to governe men, and those few are the highest and worthiest part of mankind?[4] But, to me, the very question seems to beare the solution in its owne bowels. For, when one asks, why man is hard to be governed since he governes other creatures, hee asks, why one, who hath the power to rule others, is himselfe so difficult to be mastered. And the answer is, because the powers, by which he reduceth others to his obedience, make him apter to resist them who seeke the conquest of himself, and so renders it a higher taske to weild and manage him, then those creatures which he hath power over.

For, we need not looke into philosophy, nor study learned bookes, to know that the nature of man is inclined to have its owne will, and casteth all things which [p. 3] are under his consideration to compasse and effect it; as also, that every ordinary man's knowledge and consideration is farre beyond any we find in other living creatures, and, by consequence, is farre lesse easily masterable then any of them.

Whence we may plainly collect, that were it possible for a governour to make every single person in his dominion particularly understand, that what was ordered by the government was his owne truest interest, such an one would be the most absolute and perfect governour, and infallibly would find the charge of governing most easie and sweet, as well to himselfe as to his subjects.

This case is cleare both in reason and in experience. Reason sheweth us, that to draw any thing to action, according to its owne fit-[p. 4]nesse and inclination, is both easier to the attempter, and makes the action it selfe more efficaciously and throughly performed. He that will drive a wedge into a hard piece of wood, strives, as far as the situation gives him leave, to make his hammer fall downewards, because a weight hath, of it selfe, an inclination that way, and so both the impression is stronger and the arme lesse strained knocking, and the very fall of a weight encreasing by motion downewards. Therefore black-smithes, whose continuall labour is to use the hammer, lay their iron upon their anvile, that is, in such a situation below their heads, as is most fitting to gaine the best advantage of the descent of their hammers, which they first raise to give them scope of a descent.[5]

Upon this principle it is, that they who tutour dogges, horses, [p. 5] elephants and hawks, knowing the ordinary attractive of beasts to be meat and some kind of flattery, make them understand, to the proportion of their capacity, that to do the action they breed them for, gaines them food, to which

---

3   This, and all further similar references are to the page numbers in the original 1655 publication.

4   Xenophon, *Cyropaedia*, Book I, i, 2.

5   On White's use of the language of natural philosophy in his political theory, see *supra*, Chapter IV.

they joine also certaine motions of stroking and gentle words, that make an impression in the beast of its owne excellency, and that it pleaseth its master. In like manner, to deterre them from certain actions, cudgels, whips, and harsh words are used, which have a notabler efficacy then one would easily imagine, if he saw it not by experience.

This, now, being applyed to mankind, drives the effect home. For man, being a rationall creature whose inclination it is to worke according to knowledge, desires to know that the worke prescribed him is good, that is, good [p. 6] for him, or his good. And because if two actions be proposed, whereof the one is better for him then the other, the lesse good action deprives him of some good which the more good had brought him, his inclination leads him to do the better, and by consequence to know and dispute which is the better; which is as much as to chuse betwixt them: and this we call being *free*, or having naturall liberty to do one and not the other. So that, the nature of man is to be *free*, and to act what ever he does, because it seems to him the best.

Whence it is evidently concluded, that the perfectest way and most connaturall for governing men is by making them determine themselves to their actions, and to proceed freely, and act, as it were, by their owne inclinations. This if the [p. 7] governour can effect, hee shall finde both his intent generally performed, because the subject proceedeth with much affection and courage, and seldome or never will his commands be resisted, or their obedience repented. For, men are not wont to repine often at what themselves chuse and judge best for themselves, especially if even after the action performed and peradventure the attempt failed, yet the subject remaines satisfied that it was best for him, in those circumstances, to do what he did. Now, if the reasons were solid when the governour proposed them, such must of necessity be, for the most part, the sequell.

Experience maketh this same as manifest as reason concludeth it. What mother or nurse doth not seeke to perswade and win the yet sucking childe with gay things, with flattery and such demonstrations of [p. 8] love (that is, of the child's good) as the child is capable of? What master or father draweth not his boyes to schoole and fitting exercises, by promises and proposalls of good, as play, goodcheere, fine cloathes, and any other toyes suitable to their tempers? The stronger ages have stronger motives, as of honour, lands, offices, and the like, by which we see the most part of men led, not onely to labour, but even to hazard their lives and those very goods which are proposed them for motives of their actions.

On the contrary side, how ill do those enterprises thrive, where the actors conceive themselves either not concerned or wronged? How diligently are excuses sought out and easily found, and every cause of delay judged sufficient? How readily – if the actours be in great multitudes, as soldiers or schol[p. 9]lars – do seditions and mutinies spring up, and all disorders grow bold and spread themselves, the commander of the action hated and esteemed an oppressour and a tyrant, his officers scorned and disobeyed?

This then is, of all hands, concluded, that the proper and naturall way of government is, by making the obeyer understand that it is in his owne profit which the action aimes at, so to make him work out of the inclination of his owne will, and the dictamen of his owne understanding.

The second GROUND.
That the Nature of Man Reacheth not to the Perfection of Government.
Notwithstanding this inclination be so naturall to us, yet [p. 10] nature is not able to make it perfect in most both persons and actions. Children are not come to the ability of judgeing; some other are so grosse of capacity, they cannot bee brought to understand their owne good, at least in that time and circumstances which nature hath provided them; most spend so much of their day in some one businesse, which they have chosen either for their livelyhood or pastime, that they have not sufficient leisure to attaine the knowledge necessary for other occurrences of their life. Even the greatest wits are not capable to understand the nature of all things necesary to their owne private conditions: the Prince himself must trust the physician, the lawyer, the mariner, the soldier, the merchant, the cook, the brewer, the baker, and divers other trades and knowledges, which he hath no [p. 11] possibility to understand so perfectly as to be a master in them.

Neverthelesse, nature doth not recede wholly from her principle, in thus subjecting one man's understanding to another's, and the greater most times to the lesser. For it doth not this otherwise then by making the party subjected see, it is his owne good to trust another's skill. Wherefore, it is true that he followes his owne inclination, and is ruled by his owne understanding, and so governes himselfe; onely, hee is a degree higher, not busying his thoughts about the particular worke, but onely about chusing the master of the worke, or about his own submission, that is, his owne action, as he is a man, and his action as that of a man, and not of a physician or pilot, or such other particular discipline or quality. It remaines therefore still that [p. 12] hee is free, and master of his owne action and the commanding part of it.

The third GROUND.
That a Rationall Beliefe is Necessary to Humane Action.
Of those things to whose knowledge wee cannot our selves arrive, but must rely on the credit of others, there are two kinds: some purely to be believed, others also to be acted. As, when we informe our selves to what passed in some forreigne country, or of the nature of trees or beasts wee never have use of, wee are barely to assent to what is delivered; but when a physician telleth us wee must take a purge or keepe such a dyet, wee doe not onely belive [p. 13] him, but act according to our beliefe. Now, though in truth this second sort belongeth properly to our discourse apart, because the nature of pure beliefe is intrinsecally included in it, as a part in the whole; yet wee must first note the rrrours to bee avoided in a meere speculative assent. And these are two: one of *defect*, and one of *excesse*.

The vice by *defect* warnes you to believe no thing but what your selfe understand, that is, indeed, to *believe* nothing at all. But, were these men bound to their own law, that they should take no physick till they knew it would doe them good, at least as well as the physician doth, nor trust their cause to a lawyer till they understood the subtleties as perfectly as hee, and so in other vocations, I doubt they would have neither health nor [p. 14] wealth for physician or lawyer to worke upon.

But, because those who advance this proposition are persons of wit, I must not think they stumble at so notorious a block. Therefore, their meaning is onely that wee ought to beleeve but what we are able to understand if wee had will and leisure to study. But, even so explicated, it is a most wilfull proposition, reason being quite on the opposite side. For, let the authority which denounceth me a truth be sufficient to make it credible, and overvalue the mysteriousnesse of the object, and the higher it is above my knowledge, the more necessity there is of believing it. What is but a little above me, I may easily come to know, and so need not believe but take paines and see it. Beliefe is ordained to truths whose direct and immediate evidence wee [p. 15] cannot compasse, and therefore is more proper, more due, more requisite for such as are above our knowledge.

But peradventure these smart persons do suppose that all things which have a possibility to be knowne, are the subject of man's wit, and so take these two to signifie the same sence, that the object is such as we are able to understand, and that it is understandable, or doth not couch a contradiction in its termes, and peradventure conceive themselves able to shew contradiction in whatever they refuse to believe. If this be their meaning, the maxime they goe upon is safe; but they must be very carefull not to subsume or apply it to particular instances without much consideration. For, ordinarily, the authority is very great which by understanding men, is alledged for re-[p. 16]mote and high truths, and so is dangerously neglected, without an exact perusal and anatomy of the truths maintained by it.

There are others soe prodigall of our naturall endowments, that they will teach us a kinde of contempt of reason and understanding. In a word, their position is, that though you be certaine the proposition made (for ought you know) is false, neverthelesse you may and ought to think it true: which how to excuse, from being an irrational act and a pure folly, is beyond my skill; at the same time, to be assured it is uncertaine, and to hold it for certaine is, to mee, an impossibility. Doe I not hold that which I am certaine of? that is, that this truth is uncertaine? How then can I hold it is certaine? Put this in the mouth of a witnesse in any Court of Justice, and teach him [p. 17] that, though hee know certainly, hee doth not perfectly remember whether hee saw the man killed, yet hee may sweare hee saw it: what Justice will remain uncorrupted?

Passion and precipitation may prevail with us to judge that cleare and evident which is not so, and carry us to believe and affirm it; but that reason should make us believe what it telleth us it seeth no ground for, or not sufficient, is to me an assertion the most unworthy, the most contrary to reason, and the most biassed by interest that can be imagined. If our nature be rationall, if all our actions should be conformable to our nature, and governed by reason, there cannot bee a more pernicious proposition, then to tell us we must assent when there is no proportioned motive think wee ought to assent.

Thus much I thought fit to say concerning the errours of belief in [p. 18] speculation, because beliefe in practicall things, and which concernes our actions, depends of it, and includes it, and is, in part, regulated by the same rules. The believing of practical things begins to trench upon the subject of our main discourse, for it is the first and most simple or uncomposed degree of government and obedience, and so the very roots of both are dependent from, and to be discovered out of it.

For, wee experience by our ordinary apprehensions, that wee esteeme a physician, a lawyer, a schoolemaster ought to bee obeyed, though wee doe not acknowledge in them the power of a Lord or Magistrate. And so wee say, the scholler will never profit, because he will not doe what his master would have him; the client loseth his cause, because he would not obey his counsell; the patient recovers not, because he fol-[p. 19]loweth not the advice of his physician. And though we doe not say the doctour or counsellour commands his patient or client, yet, if we look into it, he both rewardeth and punisheth, which are the concomitants of commanding. For who obeyeth is rewarded with learning, health, and prosperity, and who disobeyeth is punished with ignorance, sicknesse, and losses.

The fourth GROUND.
Of the Vertue of Obedience, and Wherein it Consists.
Out of this we may easily understand what nature intends by the vertue of obedience, and what are the limits and lawes of it. For it is plaine, the immediante end is that our workes and all that [p. 20] concernes us may be well done, even as to those things wherein our selves have no skill, or not enough. And the more remote end to bee atchieved by this is, that our life may bee good and happy, and the end of nature arrived to by us. The conditions likewise are cleere: first, that the matter of our action bee such as our selves are not sufficiently skilfull in; the second, that our commander bee a master in that art; the third, that hee bee a good and honourable person, in whom wee may rest confidently he will deale with us conformably to his skill, and not wilfully or for his own pleasure, or interest, doe any thing against our good and profit.

If the first bee wanting, wee also our selves are wanting to our selves; for nature hath endowed us with reason to provide for our owne good by this power. Againe, it is [p. 21] non-sence and folly to expect another man should be more carefull of our good, then our selves. And suppose it were so, it were either our fault or his, and for ought to bee mended on one side: our fault if wee bee not so sollicitous as wee ought to be, that is, as much as the weight of the affaire requires; his if he be more sollicitous of our good then the same demandeth, and soe hee who professeth such a care may bee feared to bee a busie fellow, and one who aimes at his owne profit under colour of love, unlesse it bee in an evident neglect of ours, which cannot well be imagined of one who is ready to obey another.

If the second condition bee wanting, there can be no vertue in obedience, since it will nothing mend but rather impaire our life, and to the import of that action, destroy our pretence to happinesse, to [p. 22] submit our selves to one who hath no more skill then wee, nor can bee rationally supposed to bear us more love and care, or that hee will or ought to imploy himselfe in our particular businesse more attentively then we our selves.

As for the last condition, without it obedience is a plaine precipitation of our selves into misguidance and absolute ruine, and therefore a pernicious and wicked practice.

By this discourse wee may understand, it is a fallacious principle, though maintained by many, that obedience is one of the most eminent vertues, and that it is the greatest sacrifice we can offer to God, to renounce our owne wills, because our will is the chiefest good we have. For, not denying that obedience is a great vertue, it being truly in it selfe the affection to moderate the pride of our understand-[p. 23]ing, which is subject to make us think too well of our owne opinions without having evidence of the truth of them, and so hinder us from candidly seeing and acknowledging the truth (an inclination of all others most deeply rooted in our nature, and both most hard to be conquered, and most pernicious to be followed) and therefore, the vertue which tempers and moderates this passion must needs be very excellent, yet I cannot give it so high a rank, as to preferre it before all.

For, I see it is only a vertue in case of imperfection, as penance and some others are, it being grounded on this, that a man is ignorant in those matters wherein hee ought to bee obedient. But, the reason displeases mee more then the conclusion: for what signifieth this, that it is the greatest good we have and can renounce for God's sake? If [p. 24] it bee a great good, it is no vice, no excesse, but a naturall power or exercise of a power given us by Almighty God; and then would I know, why to renounce such a thing is pleasing to him. Can we think it were pleasing to God for any one to binde up his armes or legges, or cut off his hands, pretending to doe it for his sake? Hee that made them gave them us to use them according to the manner intended by nature; and, if wee doe not so, wee offend him.

There is a story of *Origen*, that he exsected his virility, thinking to please God; but the same story saith, hee was reproved by the whole Church, and excommunicated for the fact.[6] *Simeon Styletes* is reported to have chained himself upon a hill, that he might not goe thence, but he was taught that such impoten-[p. 25]cy was fit for beasts, not men.[7] So that, to renounce any natural faculty or the legitimate and fitting use of it, under pretence of pleasing God, is a folly, not a vertue.

But let us see what power it is that wee must renounce, 'our Will'. And this word doth not, in this place, signifie any interested affection or malicious resolution, but that will which followeth and is guided by our understanding, and that truth which God hath made us capable of. Therefore the renouncing

---

[6] The anecdote concerning Origen's self-mutilation and the disciplinary consequences that followed is narrated by Eusebius in his *Ecclesiastical History*, Book VI, chap. viii.

[7] White is here referring to Simeon Stylites the Elder, the first and most famous of the pillar-hermits active in the Eastern Church between the end of the fourth and the mid fifth century. On the biography on Simeon see A.von Harnack and O. von Gebhardt (eds), *Texte und Untersuchungen zur Geschichte der altchristlichen Literatur*, vol. XXXII, Berlin, 1906.

of this will, is, withall, the renouncing of our understanding, that is, of our wits and manhood; so that it is in effect to renounce our rationality, and that by which we are the image of God. If any man should take a fancy to goe upon all foure like a beast, or subject himself to bee led in a string like a beare about the countrey, would not all wise men cry out on [p. 26] him for bestiality, and thinke him unworthy the conversation of men? How much greater is the indignity of him who permitteth himselfe to bee carried in his whole course of life, and those actions that most concerne him, without using that wit or understanding which hee hath, and by the sole direction of another?

Hee can bee accounted so farre no better then a clock or watch, which tells the houre by the wit and industry of the maker, not by any sence or worth of his owne. If therefore, to renounce our wills for God's sake bee to bee accounted a sacrifice, as farre as my understanding reacheth, it is no other then that the Scripture expresseth upon another occasion, to wit, one by which the sons are sacrifed to the father, the image of God defaced to the glory of him whose imagine he is.[8] [p. 27]

The Fifth GROUND.
That Fidelity is Different from Obedience, and in What it Consisteth.
But leaving this mistake of simple devotion, of which wee needed not have spoken so much, had there not depended on it some matter of greater consequence (as the following discourse will manifest in its due place), wee are to take notice of an equivocation which may draw on some errour if not prevented. Wee use to say servingmen and waiting-maids ought to bee obedient to their masters and mistresses, whereas indeed, the vertue by which they serve is not that of obedience, but of fidelity and truth, which is manifest to him that looks into the nature of hirelings. [p. 28] For, none thinke a husbandman, who is hired to till or fence a piece of ground, obeyeth the hirer more then hee then selleth a piece of cloth or other merchandize obeyeth the buyer, because he taketh his moneys, but they are said to contract and performe their part of the bargaine faithfully and truly. So servants pay their duties, performe their bargains, and fidelity is their proper vertue, to doe it carefully and uprightly: not obedience.

For, obedience is in such actions as are the proper actions of the obeyer, which concerne his life, and by which wee may derive good if well done, and harme if amisse. Now in servants the good successe pertaineth to the master; the servants hath his livelyhood and wages, whether the event goe right ot wrong, so hee doe what his master commandeth. And hence it [p. 29] followeth, that neither ought hee bee ignorant in the action hee doeth, nor sollicitous whether his master bee either skilfull or honest: for, since what is done concerneth not him but his master, his duty is to seek to doe what hee is commaunded in the best way he can, without interessing himself about the successe. This I say, as farre as he is a servingman. But as hee is also an honest man, it may belong to him to suggest to his master what hee thinks best, and

---

[8] White is paraphrasing here a passage from Psalms 106:36–40.

sometimes, when it lieth happily in his way, to help such errours of his master as hee can, without tranching on his master's credit, still providing for his own indemnity, that hee bee not involved in his Master's either imprudence or iniquity, for by his bargaine with his master he did not renounce the care of his own preservation.

The reason of this equivocation [p. 30] is because wee ordinarily call *obeying* the doeing another man's will, and distinguish not how, sometimes, this is done with renouncing our own wills – which is in those actions whereof wee are masters, that is, our owne actions – and, sometimes, without such renunciation, as in the actions which belong to others, in which wee have no will to renounce. Now obedience as it is a vertue especially attending on the renouncing of our wills, is properly confined to the former sence, not to the other, with which it onely hath an alliance in the name, and which truly is fidelity, as we have already declared.

But, although fidelity bee a distinct vertue from obedience, yet is it nor such a stranger as not to demand a place in this treatise, especially because the kinde of obedience wee desire to look into, which [p. 31] is that by which commonwealths and communities subsist, is founded generally on fidelity or the matter thereof, which wee call promise, and in that vertue it bindes to observance. After which discourse wee shall bee prepared to venture on the matter it self of government, and to our power, declare the force of it amongst men.

Man therefore being by his nature and definition a reasonable, that is, an understanding creature, or one whose primary and principall inclination is to truth or true knowledge, and the outward carriage and action of man being naturally proportionable to his inward substance, it is cleere his chief property, by which he behaves himself outwardly like a man, is to speak truth, and to doe as hee sayeth, when his words have action following them. Hence it is, that though *honesty* (which in a [p. 32] courtlyer terme is called *Honour*, when applyed to a rationall carriage, and in a more spirituall language, *Conscience*) bee extended to many other qualities, yet it is most frequently and principally expected in his keeping his word; and in so much that tough hee have other faults, either spirituall or carnall, yet if he be *true of his word*, he, often and in ordinary conversation, passeth for *an honest man.*

Againe, this vertue of *Truth* is the principall and first engine of humane conversation, and he that hath it not is unfit to be admitted to treate amongst men, but is to be rejected and banished from all negotiation. Thus you see what engagement every one hath, both by nature and necessity of conversation, to stand upon his word or fidelity: for so we call the vertue by which we speake our mind in reference to action, and [p. 33] are constant to performe what wee say.

Yet, since malice is growne to such a height, all nations who pretend to fear of any Deity have used to make men confirme their faith and promise by the invocation of the Deity they worship, hoping religon may worke in them what nature is not strong enough to effect. This confirmation is performed in two sorts: one, when we onely call God to witnesse, as when we say: 'God, who sees my heart, knowes this to be truth, or that I meane as I speak'. The other, when we pledge our trust in God for a security, as when wee wish God may punish us, or never doe us good, if we break our promise. And this is properly an execration, as the other an oath, yet both called oaths, and agree in this, that we pledge our beliefe and feare of [p. 34] God to another, for his security.

By which it is evident, that men generally esteem religion the thing which should pierce deepest into a man's heart and affection, and the strongest Bond and tye of faith and honesty, and that he, who setteth little by his religion, hath neither honour nor honesty in him, or at least wanteth the greatest and strongest part of them, and that which ought to rivet in and fixe the naturall inclination which we have to truth and fidelity.

The Sixth GROUND.
In what consists Right or Due.[9]
The next consideration may appear too metaphysicall a subtlety for a morall treatise, yet such it is, that the ignorance of it [p. 35] is mother of many mistakes and quarrels. We ought therefore to know that a man, considered in pure nature, lookes on all other things, men and beasts, and insensible creatures, as his subjects to worke on, his onely rule being reason, which takes nothing to bee good but what is good to himself, and makes the rule of his actions, to do what is fitting for him or conformable to his, that is, to a rationall creature. By this rule he treats another man otherwise then a horse or a dog, and them otherwise then a tree or stone: for reason is a faculty to use every thing suitably to their natures, as to take a knife to cut, a horse to ride on, a man to read or write or be his counsellour. And this runs through all his actions.

But as, though a taylor or mariner governe himselfe by this rule, [p. 36] even when he playeth the taylor or pilot, yet none can doubt but the rules of taylorship or steerage are different from this seeking his owne good and applying all things to that end, so neither can any justly doubt but the art of a lawyer or counsellour is different from this principle which belongeth to all men.

And to find out the difference, wee are to reflect that he who maketh a promise to another, so it be a perfect one (which we adde to decline the question of what promises oblige, what not) puts himselfe and his promissary into a rank of agency and patiency, on a new score, to wit, that of fidelity and negotiating. So that now, not the nature of the two men, but their words, and what followeth out of them, ground their being active and passive. This power of activity is, [p. 37] in Latine, called *Jus* or *Justum*, in English, 'Right' or 'Due'.

The difference of these two arts is: one considers onely what is noble, and manly, and conscience; the other, what is according to promise and consent of parties. Whence we finde, by the vertue of a promise, a new order growne

---

[9] To put this chapter of White's treatise in the context of the early modern discussions on right see R. Tuck, *Natural Rights Theories: Their Origin and Development*, Cambridge 1979.

amongst men following out of promises, wherein three things are to be considered: the engagement of nature and honesty, the confirmation by oath, and lastly, this right and duty which ariseth from the promise. For whoever promiseth submits himselfe to his promissary, and becomes his subject, as far as the contract reaches.

The first mistake that springs from the ignorance of this difference is the great noise we heare of the Law of Nature and the Law of Nations. For we are made to ima-[p. 38]gine that nature hath bound us to certaine lawes, and not left us to the liberty of reason, where no pacts or agreements intervene, as, that men ought to give free trade to leave the seas open, to give immunities to ambassadours, and the like. For these either depend on custome and consent, or are free for every man to dispose of, according to his owne profit, necessity, or convenience of his affaires.

It is true, there is an inclination in man, from reason, to do another any good I can without my owne prejudice, and to have a desire to keepe peace with all men, but if I do not, it followes not that I wrong him, even though I do him harme or seeke his ruine, but I wrong my selfe, nature binding me to make my carriage to every one rationall and becoming a man. For he is no otherwise to me then [p. 39] a piece of cloth or wood, which I cut and shape after my owne will, fittingly for my use. And, on the contrary side, the party prejudiced or refused a courtesy gets no right over me to revenge himselfe, but nature and reason teaches him, peradventure, that it is good and prudent for him to hurt me, to prevent a greater mischiefe to himselfe, and he doth right to himselfe in harming me, because he doth an action rationall and suitable to menhood.

The different consequents of the two positions will appear in this: that, if there be, in nature, radicated such an order of right and naturally just or due (as many hold), it is a thing that reason can never infringe nor can any thing justifie what Gad hath shewed us by example, and we see wise politicians practise sometimes, when, without crime [p. 40] or offence offered, they make themselves masters of convenient places. But, if there bee no such right by nature, then reason is left mistresse to judge whether it be conformable to the nobility of man to do such an action or no.

The Seventh GROUND.
Why Men Desire to Live in Community, and of the Necessity of Governement.[10]
Not to make the foundations or under-ground workes bigger then our building, it is time to enter upon our pretended subject of *Government* and *Obedience*, and examine what it is maketh governement necessary to mankind. And, because the governement we looke upon is that of a multitude, first [p. 41] it is fit to understand why men desire to live in flocks or multitudes. Neither can

---

[10] In this and the following chapter White lays the foundation of his view of the nature and aim of government; to understand the philosophical and theoretical context in which White's view have to be put see Q. Skinner, *The Foundations of Modern Political Thought*, vol. II, Cambridge 1983 (1978), pp. 113 and ff.

any who hath never so little skill in nature doubt, but, as pleasure masters and heads all our actions, so likewise doth in this of living in society.

The first community is of man and wife. Who seeth not the power of pleasure in their mutuall society? *Aristotle*, out of experience, teacheth us that we take pleasure in conversing with handsome persons.[11] And if wee consider pleasure to be nothing but the knowledge or sence of our being well or receiving some good, and, that the immediate cause of pleasure is the impression which some naturall or apprehended good maketh of its owne presence, and that good signifieth connaturall or fitting for us; wee shall perceive that handsomenesse in our owne kinde must of necessity cause plea-[p. 42]sure in us, the impression it makes by our eyes being of the features and colour due to the perfection of our nature, a gracefulnesse, not onely of gesture and voice, but even of wit and discourse being regularly the ground of the outward beauty. So that (if nature hath not miscarried) all the parts and actions of a beautifull body are gracefull to nature, and breed pleasure in others who injoy them by conversation and, as it were, communication.

This then is the first origine of meeting and living together, as whosoever lookes into experience will easily discover. For he will finde most men burthensome to themselves when they are alone, and to seeke company to divert themselves, so to elude the length of time. I remember to have heard a country fellow complaine of the losse of a dog which was stollen [p. 43] from him, and gave for his reason, that he was to travell a whole night alone, and the Dog would have beene an excellent companion to him. Bees also, wee know, love company. Horses not onely labour, but even eate better amongst their fellowes, and we often heare sickly stomachs thank those that visit them for the good meale they have made, as if the company helped downe their meat. Pleasure therefore and love is the first combiner of men into society.

The next is, that God and nature have so managed mankind, that no one hath of himself as much as he desireth, but regularly aboundeth in one kinde of goods, and wants some other which his neighbour hath. Hence, they mutually affect society, to bee accomodated with such necessaries, as they cannot have but by communication one with another.

[p. 44] In the third place comes feare: for hee that findeth himselfe stored with those things which hee and others love is subject to feare those whom hee suspecteth able to bereave him of them, and so seeketh company of friends for protection. Nor doth any one feare to lose but what he affecteth to have, so that first love marcheth in the van, and feare followeth in the reare. Besides, it is against all generosity, and embases nature it selfe, to set the throne of feare above that of love, and agreeth neither with philosophy nor morality.

To make a step farther: granting once men to be desirous to live together, and taking notice of the passions they are subject to, and how selflove corrupteth the judgement of almost all in their own case, it is evident they can never live in quiet and content, unlesse there bee some way [p. 45] contrived of

---

[11] Aristotle treats the question of the relationship between pleasure and friendship in the books VIII–X of his *Nicomachean Ethics*.

agreement, when passion stirreth contention. They must therefore, necessarily, give consent, to end their controversies by some means. And since reason is our nature, and every one's reason freer to see the truth in another's case then in his owne, and a wise and good man fitter then a fool or knave, the most naturall way for a multitude to live in peace is to have some man or men, accounted wise and good, chosen, to whose arbitrement all the rest ought to stand, the stronger part combining to force the weaker, in case of resistance, that is, the disinterested part, which is the multitude, to force the interested, which generally are but particulars if compared to the body of the people.

Here you see the nature of government beg in to appeare. But, to make it perfect, wee must farther con-[p. 46]sider, that many commodities are necessary to a multitude, which are to be furnished by common consent, that likewise there are many forraigne enviers to a multitude which liveth handsomely and happily, and in conclusion, that to provide for goods and prevent evils in common, is a matter of so great weight and difficulty, that it taketh up the whole life of one or more men; and by consequence, these business cannot be carried on by the whole body of the community, whose worke and aime is to enjoy themselves to their proportion, in getting by their labour, those accomodations of humane life, which they esteem necessary or conducing to their happinesse. It followeth therefore, they must entrust some more or fewer to take care of the common concernements.

Such trustee are called governours, and the community is said to [p. 47] obey them. And according to the principles forelaid, you see the people are supposed ignorant of what ought to bee done for the publicke, this being a businesse requiring a man's whole time, which they neither can spare, nor doe desire to employ in this way. You see they entrust others in whose prudence and goodnesse they confide, and themselves execute what their trustee think fitting, either by practising when they are commanded, or giving a sufficient force to their governours to master such restif parties as will not obey. In conclusion, you see governement is, naturally, a power or right of directing the common affaires of a multitude, by a volunarily submission of the communities' wills to the will of the governours, whom they trust, upon opinion that they are understanding and honest, and will administer [p. 48] the commonalty by the rules of wisedome and goodnesse, as is most convenient and advantageous for the people.

It seems to mee no moderate and discreet person can doubt but a governement so ordered is both necessary and connaturall to a rationall multitude, and, in a word, such as humane nature requires, and is the best, if not the onely, that sutes to the disposition of free men and prudent.

The eight GROUND.
Of the Authority Given to an Absolute Governour, and of Other Sorts of Governement.
By this resignation of the people's will, it is also evident, the magistracy receives such an activity [p. 49] and power as, wee have explicated before, did arise out of a man's promise to his neighbour, and by consequence, that the people as

farre as they have renounced their owne will, so farre they have no power left in them to contradict or resist the orders of the magistracy.

I say, as farre as the people have submitted their wills: for since this power is in the magistrate in vertue of their wills, it cannot extend farther then the people's promise. So that if the people binde their magistrates to certaine lawes and limits, hee hath no right to transgresse such lawes, or extend himselfe beyond the prefixed limits, by his installment, and the original power given him, but above all, he cannot dispose of one chip or dispense inone [sic] the least law, farther then he apprehends it as fit and necessary to the good of the commonwealth, and, if hee [p. 50] doth, hee exceedeth his patent and power. True it is, there is a great discretion to bee used in such limits, and the prudent governour will see that the good of the community requireth many of those dispensations, which carelesse governours use out of an overweening of their owne height and power.

Having thus declared the nature and conditions of naturall governement, it is not amisse to see whether there bee any other governement, and wherein distinguished from this. And casting our eyes round about us wee quickly perceive certaine communities which pretend to a defective governement, as companies of merchants or trades-men, universities and cloysters of men and women, who pretend to employ themselves wholly to perfect their soules towards eternall beatitude. All these [p. 51] have a participation of governement, but have not the universall administration of humane goods and evills, for, power of life and death generally they have none, and are subject, for the most part, to appeals from their judgements, in matters of great consequence. Neither have they any power of peace and warre, and if sometimes any of these royalties belong to them, it is not as they are heads of such communities, but as they participate of soveraignty by priviledge, or accident.

These therefore are distinguished from the governement wee pretend to declare, as being slight imitations of it, and certaine likenesses, not the power it self, or as some art or trade is different from morall philosophy, which is mistresse of the will, and all her actions, the others being but ushers to the parti-[p. 52]cular, as it were, formes or rankes in which petty things are taught. In fine, these others are to our governement as particulars to the universall. The governement therefore which wee explicate is that which hath power, either of all things belonging to the people it governeth, or at least, of all comprehensible by nature and falling under sence and experience. The first of these wee see in the *Pope* and such *Bishops* as are withall *Secular Princes*; the second, in other Christian governements either of princes or commonwealths, where the spiritual jurisdiction is acknowledged to be higher and greater, though not commander of the temporall.

But wee seeke farther, whether there bee any supreme governement different from this wee explicate or no. And the occasion is from what wee see in certaine instances, [p. 53] that there is a kinde of command or rather subjection, which wee call slavery, exercised not onely amongst Heathens, but even Christians, who have more conformity to nature.

The Nineth GROUND.
Of Slavery and the Lawfulnesse of it.
And first, wee must looke into the notion of slavery, which signifies a subjection to command in all things, and that meerely for the Master's profit. This *all things* may either reach to the hindring him from those actions which are necessary to obtaine beatitude, or onely to corporall services, with that moderation, that the master hinders him not from such exercises [p. 54] as concerne the procurement of future happinesse.

And clearly, it is against nature for any to submit his will so farre as to renounce eternall blisse. There cannot, then, bee any obedience due to such an extremity, and, by consequence, there cannot be any power of commanding such enormities in the compasse of nature. The like I conceive of a subjection to be killed or maimed causlessely and without desert, or even tormented, nay, or so penuriously abused as to have no content in life, but perpetually to suffer sicknesse, hunger, cold, or any other notably afflictive condition, so that his life is rather a punishment then a content to him. For since life is our beeing, and since beeing is the thing most deeply recommended to us by nature, it is evidently against the inclination of nature to consent to the losse either of [p. 55] life or of the profit of life, which is, either to be well in this world or in the next. Therefore it cannot be conformable to nature to renounce either; especially, the quiet in this world being the meanes to gaine blisse in the other.

Neither doth it scare me to cast my eyes upon so many holy men and women, as have put themselves, voluntarily, upon penurious and painfull lives. For I can easily answer, that they had not displeasing lives, enjoying the fruit of contemplation, and the sweetnesse of conscience in expecting a great reward for what they did. So that they onely refused the pleasures of this world to gaine those of the next, which is very rationall. But for a man to renounce the content of this world, who either thinke not of another, or, at least, hopeth nothing out of his renunciation, this must [p. 56] of necessity be extremely irrationall and against nature, whose universall aimes are, to be well, either in the next or in this present life. But if there be no such subjection naturall, there can as little be any power of command gotten either by promise and submission of the subject, or violence of the commander, who may perforce do what he list, but can never make it conformable to nature, to use an other with such inhumane severity.

There followes yet another kinde of slavery, which consisteth in being bound to do what his master commadeth, while his master affordeth him a convenient livelyhood; and being subject to due punishment, without farther appeal, he deserveth it. And this hath no apparent opposition to nature: why, in circumstances, a man may not binde himselfe to it, and be ob-[p. 57]liged to maintaine and make good his word to his dying day. And, of such a kind of slavery, we may question, whether nature alloweth a whole people to be involved in it, or it be a thing that onely can happen accidentally in nature.

And *Aristotle* is the first man whom wee are engaged to offend in this matter, who sayes or seemes to say, that some nations are naturally masters

and commanders; others, slaves and subjects.[12] To which conceit *Virgil* seemes also to incline:
Tu regere imperio populos Romane memento et c.
Hae tibi erunt artes[13]
As if it were proper to that countrey to command. Neither doe I thinke *Aristotle's* meaning was any more, then that there was a greater fitnesse [p. 58] in some nations to command, then in others: for, himselfe teacheth, the Barbarous prisoners, whose education had been noble, should not be put to servile offices. So that, it was but a little selfe-pleasing in these two great authours, and affection towards their Countries, which made them fall into this extremity of thinking it fit that other nations should submit to theirs. Whereas, had they lived in our dayes, long experience would have taught them that, in every nation, there are men fit to governe, if education and discipline be not wanting. And againe, any nation may prove a slave, even through too much wit, if they have no goodnesse to temper it. But we must not be angry, even with great ones, if they flatter a little their Countrey, but take warning it be not our owne case, either for our Countrey, or, which is more absurd, for our selves.

[p. 59] Leaving then this question, whether any nation be, by nature, borne and designed to slavery, let us see whether, within the latitude of nature, it consists that any nation can enslave it selfe in the sence propounded. I do not here intend to engage in that question, whether one nation may oppresse another, and, by force of garrisons and armies, keepe them quiet in a legitimate course of governement and subjection, a question much different from ours, which is onely, whether a whole Nation may voluntarily submit it selfe to a governement, but which it shall have nothing of its owne, nor be able to deserve or get any thing, but bee entirely at the disposition of the magistrate it chuseth, without right or property.

That we may not walk too much in the dark, the Holy Scripture [p. 60] holdeth us out a lanthorne in the example of *Joseph*, who bought up the whole nation of *Aegypt* for *Pharaon* their King, so that he rendred him not onely the governour as before, but also absolute lord and master, and them his slaves; and this by their consent.[14] Neverthelesse, I am not able to understand reason in it. To put therefore the case clearly, the meaning is, whether a whole nation can ty it selfe so by any promise to one magistrate, as afterward to be bound, they and their children, in force of their words, not to have or dispose of their labours and goods of fortune but at the pleasure of the magistrate, and that he hath power, arbitrarily and without any farther reason then his owne will, to give what one man possesseth to another, and make any one worke and obey another, meerly because such is his pleasure.

[p. 61] That which induceth me to declare for the negative is the nature of man, whose first and maine operation is judgement and choice, and the

---

[12] Aristotle, *Politics*, I, ii, 2–22
[13] Virgil, *Aeneid*, VI, 851–2.
[14] White is here paraphrasing Genesis 47: 18–21.

matter of this is his ourward action. So that who universally renounceth his judgement in externe action, truely renounceth nature it selfe, in renouncing the end and action for which it was made. Now, that a single man may be forced to do this, I make no difficulty, for if force can take away a single man's life, much more may it take away his outward action. But when I speake of a nation, me thinks I speake of nature it selfe, for I understand a nation to signifie a thing in nothing different from humane nature, except in greatnesse, as a bit of bread from a loafe, or a paile of water from the pond out of which it was taken; and so reason cannot teach us to do that to [p. 62] a nation, which ought not bee done to all humane kinde. Now, who abhorres not to thinke that the use of judgement and will should bee banished out of mankinde? Were not that quite to unman us and bebeast our whole nature? On the other side, it being the property of reason to use every thing it knoweth, accoding as it is fitting to the respective nature of the thing, and nothing being more fitting for man in common and every one in particular, then to judge and governe in his little spheare of activity, reason can never demand or approve of the contrary to be practised universally, as is implyed in this position, that it may be done to a whole nation.

I looke not into the inconvenience of such proceeding: how base and unworthy it renders the subjects, how unfit for the service of [p. 63] the magistrate, how ready to accept of any occasion to better themselves, and the like; which are sufficient to dehort any wise governour from attempting or desiring it. Because my theame is onely upon the contracting an obligation of obedience, out of the force of their promise, and extends no further. And, I suppose, the shewing that such a promise invalidateth the principle upon which a promise grounds its constancy, is enough to shew that no promise so made can be constant and firme, since a man stands to his word, because he is a man and hath a principle of judgement or choice upon judgement, by which and according to which he is and ought to be governed. Now then, such a promise being a renouncing and bereaving him of this his manlinesse, it cannot assuredly bee maintained by manlinesse which [p. 64] is the onely or chiefe strength of a promise.

But, what must we reply to *Joseph*? What to many thousands of eminent Christians, who seeme to professe and observe, in vertue of a vow, this very kinde of subjection? As for *Joseph*, he justifies himselfe, in renouncing the vassalage of his people for one fifth part of their lands and fruits.[15] And, not to make an estimate, how proportionable the fifth of a kingdome is to the furnishing of necessaries for governing, so much at least is plain, that by his remission of foure parts absolutely, that is, for ever, he did not execute what he pretended by the bargaine; but, by the formality of acquiring all, he obtained what he aimed at, that the people should willingly contribute the fifth part of their labour and goods generally, and, in case of necessity, [p. 65] willingly obey their governour.

---

[15] White is here paraphrasing Genesis 47: 24–6

As for the speciall obedience vowed by some Christians of exemplary life, it is professedly only concerning spirituall instruction or exercise, even then when it is applyed to the knights champions of christendome. And this is expressed by the greatest Divine the Schoole ever had, in his 2 2ae *Qu. 104. Art. 5 ad tertium*.[16] So that, neither of these objections prejudice the conclusion we have setled, however the outward undiscerned shew may make an appearance to the contrary.

Out of this conclusion it is easily seen, that the Turkish, Moscoviticall, Tartarian and other whatsoever governements, setled upon this principle, that the goods and lives of the subjects are the prince's, not to defend (as our lawes go) but to dispose of at will, without [p. 66] contradiction or limitation, more then of his pleasure, neither do nor can ever breed any obligation of obedience in the subject, farther then out of feare or present utility.

It is not amisse to adde this consideration, that those tyrannicall governours exact of their subjects no lesse then to forgoe all that is deare in this world at their pleasures, like and meanes, wife and children, and whatsoever hath made impression upon them. So that, truely, there is no protection or security from them, and if they rob you not, it is because they have no occasion, not because they conceive any unworthinesse in it. Whence, no good nor profit doth, regularly and according to the intention of the pact and agreement, result to the particular, but all is the high master's, and the subject's portion is onely to [p. 67] share those scraps he shall cast down to him, as to a dog, to make him fit to hunt for his master.

The Tenth GROUND.
Why a Man is to Hazard Himselfe for the Common Good.
It is true, this debt in the subject, of hazarding life and limbs and all that is estimable in this world, is exacted, as well in just and legitimate governements as in those hideous tyrannies, but there is a recompence for it, and the good of the whole reflecteth on the part, and if one lose his life, his children and relations at last feele the sweetnesse of it, and this makes men hazard with courage, and die with comfort. And cleerly, were there not this obligation, no commonwealth could stand. What city could be defended, if the citizens would not venture their lives [p. 68] upon the walls? What army could bee managed, if the souldier would never be brought into the danger of death, or would fly as soon as the bullets began to play about his ears? All wrongs must be suffered at their hands who could expose their own lives to hurt others, and no justice maintained, or innocency defended. Nature therefore makes it most cleer that such an obligation is unavoidable, and the daily necessity of it beateth it out so flat and plaine, that wee can no way escape so manifest an evidence.

But if it bee by the direction of nature, certainly it is also rationall, and hath some principles of its truth and reasonablenesse. Now, in morality the reason of all action is the good obtaineable by it, which if lesse or not greater then what we hazard and, peradventure, lose in the attempt, it is no good nor can

---

[16] Aquinas, *Summa Theologiae*, IIa IIae, question 104, article 5.

[p. 69] bee a rationall motive of such an action. We ought therefore to seeke out this great good.

Aristotle proceeds as cunningly in this businesse as became so wise a master, and, according to his fashion, where his skill reached not to explicate the particulars, remained in common termes, telling us, that *Bonum commune divinius est quam particulare.*[17] But, in what this Divinity consists, hee no where expresses. Truly, if there were a *Platonick Idea* of the particulars goods, which might bee termed the common good, I could understand that there were a Divinity in it, but himselfe hath extinguished that flash of *Plato's* beyond reviving. I understand also that the notion of *common*, compared to the notion of *individuall*, hath a kinde of excellency by its universality, which rendreth it very august and lustrous, [p. 70] and of a higher degree then the particular. I know again the perpetuity a commonwealth pretendeth to, compared to the mortality of a single person, vesteth it selfe with a kinde of infinity, which giveth it a glorious appearance. Nay, when I see the same man work for a commonwealth, in a free way of doing it good, and againe, for a private friend, I see a vast distance between his pretended ends, and an eminent generosity in one over the other. Whence, I belive, it cometh that *Heroës* and heroicall vertues are chiefly taken in respect of doing good to whole contreys or cities.

But when, on the other side, I see the same great master teach us, that good is the same with desireable, and every one's good, what is desireable to him, I finde it is an intricate labyrinth of equivocation wherein wee endlessely erre, while [p. 71] wee think that good taken in common, should bee accounted good, truly and properly.[18] As, who would bee so wilde as to bend any strong labour here in *England* to profit the King of *Persia* or *Siam*, if hee expected no good to reflect on himselfe by it? Much lesse would any account it good to bee robbed or maimed, because it was good to another who possessed his money or was afraid of him, and yet if wee stick upon the common notion of good, without determining to whom it is good, both these must bee esteemed not onely goods but great ones, for so they are to some body, though nothing or harme to the esteemer. Then, to cry 'the common good' is a meere deceit and flattery of words, unlesse wee can shew that the common good is as great to us as wee make it sound.

Neither can the authority of [p. 72] learned nations and the many endevours of worthy men perswade us the contrary. For these nations generally were of popular governements, where plainly the common good was the good of them who were to reward the causes of it, so that it was no wonder the 'common good' should be so highly exalted and cryed up, where it was the particular good, both to them to whom it was commended, as also the commenders themselves were to arrive to their own private pretences through that notion of common good. The like is of all princes and governours, who, if they bee

---

[17] In this and the subsequent paragraphs White discusses Aristotle's position and criticism of Plato expressed in the first book of his *Nicomachean Ethics*.

[18] White is here rejecting the relativist consequences of the Aristotelian notion of good, unlike Thomas Hobbes, who used ethical relativism as the starting point of his theory of government: see R.Tuck, *Philosophy and Government*, pp. 304 and ff.

wise, conceive the common good in most circumstances to bee compared to them as their own proper good.

It remains, therefore, to see what may bee the ground on which an understanding man ought to value so highly the common good, and ex-[p. 73]pose his life and all that is deare to him, upon the score of the publicke. Cleare it is, that hee who ventures his life, ventures all this world, for if hee dies, what reward remains there in this world? *Fame* is a slender recompence, when the fruit of it (which chiefly consists in being respected in company, and having a power amongst his associates) is once passed. The good of his wife and children, that may rejoyce a dying man, but if there rest nothing after death, it is a comfort which soon expires, being indeed nothing but a flash. It is then past dispute, that for him, who expects nothing in the next world, there can bee no rationall motive of voluntarily endangering his life for the common cause, if himselfe bee not particularly interested in it.

I know philosophers reply, that there is no harme in death, nor pain [p. 74] after it, and wee are but as if wee never had been: so they dispute to take away the feare of death. But first, I would ask them, why, even in such a cause, the fear of death should be taken away? What signifieth this to a sound philosopher, to take away the love of his *Summun Bonum?* Of the end for which hee is to doe all his actions? Againe, if hee must embrace death, upon what motive must he make his consent? Shall hee propose to himselfe none? Or a lesse good then hee loses? Or entertaine frantick apprehensions of glory after hee is nothing? These are not answers for philisophers and considerate persons, but for some hare-brained fool-hardy flashes or doating oratours, who, with a multitude of fine words, can plausibly dresse up contradictions and nonsense.

This therefore remaines certain, [p. 75] that there is no good to bee expected here equivalent to the hazard of death, and consequently, none can bee rationally valiant, who sets not his hopes upon the next world. And as, before, wee made it apparent, that hee who was not constant to his religion, could have no rooted honour or honesty in him, so now it is likewise evident, hee cannot rationally bee either valiant himselfe or trusted by others in danger, farther then hee is a foole. Since then, on the contary side, the nature of commonwealths makes it beyond dispute that hazarding is necessary, it is both evident there is another life to bee expected, and that it imports good governement to plant deeply in the breast of the subjects a rationall apprehension of it. The cause therefore, and solid reason why men ought to bee valiant, is the hope of reward hereafter for doeing good to [p. 76] our neighbour here, and the commonwealth beeing our neerest and greatest neighbour, as including our friends, parents, acquaintance, and all of mankinde that our knowledge reacheth to, to performe service to it is certainly the greatest act of charity towards our neighbour, that is the highest externe act which God hath granted to us, and consequently to bee preferred before all ohers, and as such to expect a profit and recompence in the next life.

I know, it may bee objected, that in beasts also is to bee found a kinde of valour, even to the hazard of their lives for their mates and little ones, and yet no reward of the next world can be pretended for them. But wee are to reflect that beasts are not governed by any reason given to them to governe themselves by, but like clocks and other engines, [p. 77] by the wit of their makers. And therefore it ought not to bee expected they should bee addressed to that which is their individuall greatest good, as man is by his reason, but onely to what is fittest for their creator's intention, which being onely to continue them for the use of man. And this passion of audacity which wee see in them, being fit for that, wee are not to seeke a further reason for them to hazard their lives, not to draw any consequence from them to mankinde, whose propriety is to governe himselfe by the knowledge of his owne good, and not to bee forced out of that for the good of any other, so the notion of good bee rightly taken.

By this wee, in part, understand wherein consists the worth and excellency of a magistrate and his office: to wit, that all others ends being purely for the good of their private per-[p. 78]sons or family, the magistrate's aime is at the universall good of the whole eternall body of the Commonwealth, the extent of the persons, the longe and farre-sighted care, and the abstraction from his private good, manifestly exalt this function, beyond comparison, above that of private men and their intentions, and placeth it, as it were, in an orb of honour proper to its dignity.

The Eleventh GROUND.
The Quality and Rationall Power of a Supreme Governour.
Thus is our supreme magistrate our governour mounted on his throne of justice and soveraignty. Hee hath for his strength, that right the people have bestowed on him, [p. 79] devesting themselves, by this submission, from interposing in common affaires. He hath besides the strength of the people, both their wealth and swords being delivered up to him, so that, if he bee wise, he can make himselfe and his lawes obeyed. But chiefly he hath his owne prudence and goodnesse, which is supposed to be the choicest that could bee found in that people, and the credit of it to be his strength and support.

For, if we looke into it; as we see that, in the naturall generation of governement, the people truely intend to be governed by one whom they esteeme the wisest and best amongst them, so afterwars, when they apprehend their magistrate no *Solomon*, yet they still conceive he is the best they can obtaine or prudently aime at. That is, if they should attempt to change, it [p. 80] would bring greater inconveniences then their continuance under this weaker magistrate. So that, as it were, the essence and forme of his power to governe, is wisdome and goodnesse, at least, such a degree of both as is supposed and apprehended the greatest possible, according to the circumstances wherein they are. His end wee finde to bee the common good, and to that is he wholly and adequately bound, by his owne goodnesse, by the people's intention, by his owne acceptance, by the nature of the charge it selfe, and by the very forme of his life and profession. In so much that he faileth from his duty, from the expectation of his subjects, and his owne goodnesse, if he doth the least action for his private interest, or otherwise then out of his esteeme that it is for the greatest good [p. 81] of the commonwealth.

And truely, if it bee duely considered, we may plainely see that his private interest is not distinguished from the publick. For, how can it be? First, for honour, it is plaine, the welfare of his subjects is the highest honour; their knowing they are well by him, and so their love to him, his strongest security; their expressing still on all occasions content with his actions, and esteeme of his person, his greatest pleasure; and in fine, the more wealth they have, the greater commander is he: so that really, this private interest (if he be indeed a good governour) is the true felicity of his people. I doe not, by this, intend to cut off from supreme magistrats that promise and magnificence wee see usually in persons of that quality, but whereas it may be practised either for pride and vanity, that [p. 82] is, to procure and esteem of the private merit of the magistrate, or else, to facilitate the governement by the awe and reverence it printeth in the subject. I expect the supreame magistrat to be so discreet, as to understand the former is meerly a shadow or faint and fading colour, the other a reall profit and necessary instrument, and so to be embraced for the good of the people.

Neither must wee leave our magistrat here, but transplant our discourse into a new consideration. For, if he hath gotten a commission, he hath not, by that, lost the quality of a rationall, wise, and good man, but joined to that a new obligation of being now fixt upon the common good, as the effect and scope of the actions of his whole life. Insomuch that, to determine the quality of his action, we must [p. 83] make one complexe of the whole person, and aske: what a wise and noble minde, haveing such limitations upon him, by word or oath engaged in his installment, may or ought to do concerning the limitations?

And first, it is undoubted on both sides, that neither may he, without great cause, make a breach in those hedges his way is fenced with; nor, if he make some small and inconsiderable breaches, that hee violates therefore his oath. For the nature of humane action is such, as not to consist in an indivisible, but, of it selfe, to have a morall latitude: our understandins not being able to reach to such small and petty differences as nature maketh and our operations containe, as far as they depend from nature.

But, the question cometh, when some great fault discovers it selfe in the limitations, and the end of governement is prejudiced by such a defect, and neverthelesse it is no doubt but it is intention of the people or the trustees of the people to binde their magistrat to such conditions, whether, in such a case, he be bound to his orders and oath, or whether the duty of a wise and good man foth enfranchise him to doe what is truely best for the people, though it be against their wills?

The question seemeth hard, and therefore it is not amisse to note, that *truely best* signifieth that it be not onely best, if it had been fore-ordered or if it were in practise, but that it be best to be brought into practise, and that notwithstanding all dammages and dangers which are to be incurred in the setling of it, otherwise, it is clear, he ought to stand to his oath. Another caution [p. 85] is, that the magistrat doe not onely *think* it so *best*, but know it by certainty and science, otherwise hee proceedeth not wisely, to hazard a disturbance of the commonwealth upon slight and weak appearances.

These two suppositions premised, wee are to consider what it is that engageth the magistrate on both sides. And, for his promise, it is above declared, that hee is engaged to it by the connaturality and beauty of truth in man's nature. Now not truth onely is conformable to man's nature, but also that noblenesse goodnesse that bindeth man to man, which in its highest pitch, that is, as it looketh upon a commonwealth or a little mankinde, is the beauty and vertue of a governour.

Againe, I see a governour hath in himselfe, as it were, two truths, or degrees of truth belonging to his person: one, which is the publicke [p. 86] honesty, either considered betwixt him and his subject or some aliens, and this forfeited maketh his publick credit weak and unfit for the use of governement. The other is but a splendour reflecting on his own person, by which hee appeareth in the face of honour and a man of his word. For this latter it is very evident, the affection to the publicke ought to oversway it, because being but a private good it should doe homage to those vertues which carry a man to the common interest. For the former, the dammage ensueing is to bee esteemed and poised against the profit or necessity of the commonwealth. For if it bee evident that the good of the change openly and vastly exceeds the dammage proceeding from the discredit, cleerly hee is bound to admit of the discredit, to purchase the advantage accrewing by the change. But, were [p. 87] there is none or little difference, there the ballance hangs upon quietnesse side, and change is not to bee ventured on.

This seemeth so plainly and evidently concluded, that a rationall man cannot resist it. But, to those who are used to maintaine their credit by custome more then by reason, it is a *bolus* of hard digestion, to tell them they must break their word for the common good, and seemeth to bee of the same nature, with that famous definition of an *Ambassadour*, witty in *England*, harsh in other Nations, that Hee is sent *ad peregre mentiendum pro patria*, which were the equivocation of *lying abroad* is not understood, is, in verity, a scandall to statesmen, whose negotiation hangs so tenderly on their credit, that, it once being broken, they have lost a principall instrument to penetrate [p. 88] the hearts on which they are to work.[19]

Therefore, let us see whether the high magistrate (in proceeding as wee have declared) does truly force the rampart of veracity so necessary for a governement. Let us first begin with his promise, and consider what it is. Hee is entrusted to doe for the common good, and the reason why hee is entrusted is, because the entrusters conceive themselves, either through their incapacity or attendance to other impoyments, ignorant of what is truly the common good. They entrust him, therefore, with more then they understand, and so his power

---

[19] White is here referring to Sir Henry Wotton, who was reported to have written the said witticism on his way to Venice as English ambassador in 1604 (see *DNB sub voce Wotton, Henry*). Gaspard Scioppius, under the pseudonym of Oporinus Grubinius, wrote a pamphlet on this anecdote: see *Oporini Grubinii Legatus Latro, hoc est Definitio Legati Calviniani* (Ingolstadt, 1615).

is to proceed according to his understanding, though it crosse theirs. Hee then of necessity, must bee false to his oath, if hee doe not, according to his trust, act for the common good what hee evidently sees in a high degree to im-[p. 89]port it. Further, because wee know, in morall businesses, the end aimed at is more principall then the means ordered to it, and hath such a command over them that they are to bee or not to bee, according as is fitting for the end, and in the oath or promise of our high magistrate, if hee observe his limitations, he destroyeth the end for which they were put, hee offends against both his oath and fidelity to his people, if hee maintain such limitations, when hee is obliged, for the publick good, that is, when hee ought to break them.

Yes, but (replieth the man who thinketh himselfe wedded to an outward and seeming honesty in this cause) howsoever, at least hee breaketh that part of his oath, in which hee swore directly, to those limitations. Let us therefore see even that point, and ask, what was the people's will in [p. 90] exacting his oath or promise? Doeth any one will what hee understandeth and knoweth not? If one should say to another 'I give thee what is in that trunk', in which himselfe had put a suit of apparell, and, without his knowledge, his servant had taken that out and put in bags of gold to the same bulk, would any divine, or chancery judge, or prudent person assert he were bound to bestow on that promissary all his gold, which was in the trunke? I thinke not, and the reason is, because it is the will and understanding which hath the power to give strength to a promise or contract, and here the will is wanting, for hee knew not what he said, not intended to give any thing but a suit of clothes.

How many promises doe divines and lawyers pronounce null, though they were good and valid [p. 91] when they were made, by reason of the change of accidents following, which could not be foreseene? If one promise his daughter in marriage to his neighbour, and shee dyeth, is he bound to fulfill his engagement, or seeke his neighbour another wife? Nay, if the neighbour be discovered not to be the man he was taken for, not to have a competent estate and such like conditions, he may justifie the disperformance of his promise, nor shall he forfeith his credit if he doeth not keepe his word, but rather, if he do, be accounted a weak man.

Now, to come to our purpose, let it bee supposed the people were made understand, when they exact the promise from their magistrat, that such limitations would destroy their peace, and contentment: doth any one think they would binde their governour to maintaine them? [p. 92] If they would not, it is evident, howsoever their mouthes pronounced the words, their hearts were ignorant and inculpable of such an exaction, for they knew not what they did, thet understood not nor meant what they spake.

But suppose that truely they knew the incommodities that were to follow, and yet they would have them observed – for this happeneth often in this our subject, that some (especially great men, and sometimes the populace) understand the inconvenience of a law, and yet for private interest will have it maintained: what then is the duty of the supreme magistrate, who is sworne to maintaine the said lawes? The question is clearly answered by the condemnation of *Jephthe*, who, when he had rashly vowed to sacrifice the first thing that he met him from home, did impiously murther [p. 93] his daughter.[20] All understanding men know, a wicked oath is not to be observed. He that should give a mad man a sword, because he had vowed or sworne it, deserved to be hanged for the murthers by him committed. Now, an ignorant and wilfull man, what is he but a mad man? Or what is madnesse but a wilfulnesse in doing evil? If the action be naught and such as the exactor cannot, with reason, desire, he cannot by any other oath bind a swearer to it. Now, to observe conditions which shall ruine the governement and destroy the end for which they were instituted, is an action contrary to all reason, and to which the promissary cannot binde the promiser, in any wisdome and goodnesse, he is therefore bound, rather to the destroying then fulfilling such conditions; neither is he therefore perjured, but were ra-[p. 94]ther unjust and wicked, if he observed them. This so resolved, it appeareth plainly, that no supreame magistrate can bee bound to any lawes contrary to good governement farther then either the danger of changing them, or the not cleerly seeing them to be such, may hold his hand.

The Twelfth GROUND.
Who is Such a Governour, and the Subjects' Duty Towards Him.
Wee have long talked of a supreame governour; it is time we should point him out, that he may bee knowne. And, since all agree that there are three sorts of governement, monarchy, aristocracy, and democracy, when [p. 95] they are simple, there can bee no doubt who is the supreame magistrate. Now, mingled they may bee, all together, or some two of them. And againe, their mixing may bee either continually, as when all parts mixed are so often engaged that their authorities run jointly, or else some are continuall, others but at certaine termes.[21]

If monarchy bee mixed, either with aristocracy or democracy, so that they be continually joint actors, the monarch is but a servant, and the other part the master, as is to be seen in the *Italian Doges*, and the *Lacedaemonian* Kings, for his force is nothing, compared to his consort.

If democracy and aristocracy be so mixed, the quarrell is more ballanced; and because it is a governement divided in it selfe, and therefore dangerous, no doubt but, [p. 96] if the aristocracy get power enough, she is in the posture of supreame authority. The example of this wee have in the *Roman Commonwealth*, in the time, specially, of *Sylla's* conquest, when, if he had setled the State in the Senate, there had been no feare of *Caesar* and *Pompey's* mangling that *Commonwealth*, as afterwards fell out.

---

[20] Here White is summarizing the story that can be found in Judges 11: 29–40.
[21] In this discussion of the three fundamental forms of government and of the possibility of a mixture between them White engages in an interesting elaboration of Bodin's arguments against mixed governments, see J. Bodin, *Les six livres de la republique*, Paris 1583, Book II chap. I. On the concept of mixed government see J.M. Blythe, *Ideal Government and the mixed constitution in the Middle Ages*, Princeton 1992, and J. Franklin, 'Sovereignty and mixed constitution: Bodin and his critics', in J.H. Burns (ed.), *The Cambridge History of Political Thought, 1450–1700*, Cambridge 1991, pp. 298–328.

Monarchy and democracy can hardly be so mixed, that democracy be perpetuall, and monarchy by spurts. For that is not monarchy, the said monarch being nor long enough in power to be accounted a setled magistrate, as wee see in the *Decemviris*, *Tribunes* and *Dictators* amongst the Romans; so that, the monarch hath not the power in his hand to change any thing, which is the case we aime at. And the like is of aristocracy; when its employment is the ordinary and con-[p. 95]tinuall, and monarchy onely by turnes and seasons.

There remaineth onely monarchy in continuance, compared to aristocracy and democracy at certaine turnes. And in *both*, it is cleare, the monarch is the supreame governour in ordinary, and so the magistrate of whom we speake, who may alter the inconveniences, if occasion serve. As for the people, they are but a weake part, if the governour be wise, so that he is, by his posture, in the state of doing that good to the commonwealth which his judgement and conscience dictate to him to be necessary. The comparison to aristocracy is much harder, every one of the aristocracy being, generally and regularly speaking, a petty monarch, and the whole of them easily assembled, and, when so, having the power in their hands: so that the [p. 96] monarch is not (by vertue of his ordinary condition) in a posture to bee able to rectifie what he seeth necessary to be altered, therefore he is not the man wee call the supreame magistrate, but the assembly of the nobility, whereof he is but an eminest and considerable one.

The subject, being correlative to the magistrate, requireth upon that title, to be reflected on, but much more because the nature of the magistrate cannot be well understood, unlesse the duty of the subject bee joyntly declared. We must therefore declare, or seeke out at least, what honour and conscience obligeth the subject to; and, to performe this, wee must reflect upon his motive of obedience, which, as is before insinuated, was grounded on the love and necessity of living in community, that, from it, he may receive good, and, by [p. 97] its protection, secure himselfe against evill. To this end he entrusteth the charge of the common administration to the magistrate, taking himselfe as one unskilfull or unable for such employment. Wee see therefore, the end of the subject in his obedience, immediately, is the publick good or the good of the commonwealth. A farther though more cordiall and deep in the subject, is the good he is to receive out of the commonwealth being well, which is nothing else but that the particulars of the commonwealth be so. Evident then it is, that the immediate motive which the subject is to propose before his eyes, in his obedience, is the good of the commonwealth; that is, the very same motive the magistrate ought to have in administring, and which hee had when first, in his owne person or in his forefathers, he submitted [p. 98] himselfe to this rule.

Wee know, by consequence, how excellent a virtue this act of obedience is, having a motive of so great a price and high elevation above other ordinary employments, which reach no farther then to his private good. But, herein the same vertue is lesse in the subject then in the commander, that, because the common good is the very private good of the commander, therefore it is not related to any private good of the same nature, and so not commanded or limited by any other, as in the subject it is by the end of his idioticall good.

The next thing that occurreth is the subject's fact by making this trust, and that is, that he hath made away all power of judgeing and caring for the common good, farther then by the eyes and hands of the magistrate, his trustee, other-[p. 99]wise they have not made him supreame governour; so that, if he thinketh or judgeth any thing to goe amisse, or interpose his opinion, in any reall and effective way, even so farre as to disgust himselfe or any other against the governement, he breaketh his promise and engagement to his governour. Much lesse is it in his power to recall the trust and seeke any way to take it out of the hands of his soveraigne. As for his oath of allegiance, I believe every man sees, it takes its strength from these two; and, by consequence, is to be understood to reach whither they carry it, and strengthen the obligation that they ground, but not to extend it selfe to what they doe not; onely what they begin and, as it were, make, the oath doth, by religion and reverence to God, enholy and consecrate, and so give it the greatest strength that [p. 100] falleth upon humane liberty.

By this discourse, we learn that the magistrate's security, from honesty and conscience, is the greatest that humane nature can frame, being grounded upon the noblest vertue, fortified by the vertue of veracity so naturall and principall as is above signified, the subject having made as great an alienation of his propriety to governement as will can ratifie, and lastly, elevated it above his owne soule by the invocation of him who is master both of soule and body, of time and eternity. Whence, nothing but the frailty of humane condition can prejudice a governour once estated legitimately in his seat of justice, nothing can make a subject more delinquent, then to work against this duty of obedience: no wonder, therefore, if rebellion be connumerated with soothsaying and idolatry [p. 101] and obedience preferred before sacrifice, even in the sight of God.

The Thirteen GROUND.
Of the Qualities of Lawes and Commands, in Respect to Obedience.
Out of what hath been said concerning the subject's obligation to obedience, wee may understand a distinction made by many, of the validity and lawfulnesse of commands. For, the lawfulnesse to a soveraigne commander, is no other then that hee truly thinketh it to bee for the good of the common, that is, for the greatest good, all things considered; which if hee doth, it is, by the former discourse, lawfull for him to command what he pleases, without [p. 102] reproach of conscience or honour to him. And on the other side, if hee swerve never so little, hee so farre breaketh his trust, and the greater the abuse is, the greater also his fault and shame. But, the subject is to remember that hee hath put his confidence in his governour, as beeing himselfe ignorant and not having leasure to look into the depth of the policy, and therefore hee is to think and judge well of his magistrate's counsells, and make account hee doeth not understand the bottome of them, and so bee prompt and forward to obey.

The validity of the command consists in the obligation the subject hath to performe it, and this may faile in two degrees: one, to the not fulfilling the command, by avoiding it; the other, by resisting it. This latter is no waies in the subject's hands, unless it be in such a case as [p. 103] his oath of allegiance and obligation to the good of the community cease or bind not. The former can never happen as long as it can be presumed to be the commander's will this subject, in these circumstances, should perform this command, for so long his trust obligeth him not to faile. But, because a governour many times is not rightly informed, nor can a law reach home to all particular accidents, it is very incident that, in some speciall cases, the subject may presume it is not the magistrate's will he should be bound to this particular service. And this is so ordinary that, amongst us, there is a particular and highest court, to declare when wee are not bound to the written lawes.

Yet it is not necessary to believe that even that court is able to satisfie all cases, or that private men are bound not to avoid a law without having [p. 104] recourse to that court, or to obey all decrees of that court if they can prudently avoid it, because no court (especially amongst refined pleaders) can bee without many formalities, which are not the substance of justice, and therefore may prudently bee declined, neither honour nor conscience obliging to such proceedings. But they must ever have for their rule, that the lawmaker intended not to include them, in these circumstances, within the compasse of his law.

Some make us a threefold division of lawes' the first absolute or commanding; the second permissive; the third they call penall lawes. The first they averre to bee obligatory, because directly intended by the law-giver; and of this sort is verified what wee have newly discoursed.

The second (were it expressely [p. 105] the sense of the law to permit a thing) is also of the former kinde and onely distinguished in the matter, for it would make the thing permitted truly lawfull. But this is not the writers' meaning, for they doe not conceive it was the lawmaker's intention to allow of the practice, but onely not to punish it, or to ordaine somewhat in supposition of the case. As when usury is limited to such a rate, that greater is forbidden, but to such a rate is so permitted, that he that hath borrowed is bound and compellable to pay so many in the hundred, but no man is bound to borrow, nor as they say, *allowed* to take interest, though the law constraine the borrower to pay.[22] But, how the law can force the one to give, and yet not allow the other to take, is to mee, a hard proposition and like a riddle, and therefore, I believe, [p. 106] the law it selfe is to bee condemned or the practice to bee justified, and that truly there neither is nor can bee such a kinde of law, as shall compell a thing to bee done and not approve of the doeing.

The third sort also seemeth to mee no lesse contradictory: for though I confesse there are penall Lawes unquestionably, that is, such as constitute punishments for offences, yet these Masters meane not such, but under the cloake of the name, teach disobedience to certaine Lawes, perswading us the Law-giver's intention is indefinite, that either a man should doe such a thing, or suffer such a punishment if hee be discovered to have committed the fault,

---

[22] On the legislation concerning usury in early modern England see N.L. Jones, *God and the Moneylenders: Usury and the Law in Early Modern England*, Oxford 1989.

which is directly against all goodnesse. For first wee are to consider whether the thing commanded bee usefull to the commonwealth: if so, it cleerly argues it is the direct [p. 107] will of the lawmaker. Againe, it is to be looked into, if it be universally neglected, what dammage accreweth to the common, and this also will assure us, by the necessity of it, that it is intended for the common good, and therefore to be executed to the possibility of the subject. Againe, how unworthy a thing is it of a governour, who is supposed to be all equity and goodnesse, to ly at the catch with his subjects, to entrap them for a thing he doth not aime to have done? Besides, the name of punishment supposeth a fault, so that, the law must be supposed to speake improperly, which, in its dogmaticall way of proceeding, is absurd.

Yet doe I not deny but lawes may bee made indefinitely, as, to command every townesman to march or pay so much monies, lea-[p. 108]ving it to his liberty to do which hee listeth. But this is no penall law, nor hath it any likelyhood of one, but is meerly a disjunctive command. Neither likewise do I entrench upon such orders in communities, which being almost impossible to bee rigorously observed, have some other obligation annexed to the failing, to be performed by the conscience of the Delinquent, whether discovered or no. For, this clearely remaineth voluntary, and is ordered to make the failing rare, and to acknowledge a defect and fault in the not observing, and so hath not that crossing of the will, and that force which one feeleth when he is discovered and, by authority, chastised. So that, in conclusion, there is but one sort of law in all these, and that binding the subject, in force of his promise and oath, to the proportion of [p. 109] his concurrence to the common good, by his act of obedience.

The Fourteenth GROUND.
In What Conditions the Subject May Resist Governement.
Now, to returne to the former part: it is evident, if it be rationall to resist to the governement, it will be lawfull also to break and remove it, for these two actions are of the same nature, and, in truth, pure resistance and disobedience is the annulling it. For, governement, consisting in the power of commanding, that is, of having no resistance, to resist is not to acknowledge it, but maintaine there is no such power, at least, in this case; that is, to take it away in this case; that is, to set another judge or knower when obedience is due and when not; that is, not to keepe the subject in the nature of ignorance, in which is grounded his being a subject. This being the nature of this disobedience or resisting, the magistrate is bound with all his strength to crush and breake it, and, by consequence, it draweth along the concussion of the whole state, if the subject bee able to make good his resistance. Out of this it is cleare, that a subject may not use this resistance but in case when it is fitting to attempt the dissolving of the governement.

It followes first, that it cannot be done, but when the occasion is greater then the value of the publick peace and good of the commonwealth. No man therefore can justly attempt such a disobedience to [p. 111] save his owne life and goods, or the life and goods of his owne family, how great soever, if contained within the bounds of a private family, or but a part of the commonwealth. Now, how farre this extendeth, I dare not subtilize, it being a kinde of morall consideration and a prudentiall esteeme to weight it in particular, the common notion reaching no farther, then that it be not so notorious a part of the commonwealth, that it bee a homogeneall part of it, such as is fit to make a commonwealth of it selfe, to determine whose nature, is not the intent of our present embarquement.

The next consideration is, that neither an universall harme, if moderate and such as may bee supported with lesse dammage then followes out of the state, is a sufficient cause of resistance to the soveraigne [p. 112] magistrate's command. As for example, an enormous taxe, such as was thought to be that which revolted *Guienne* from *Edward* the third of *England*, or the *Low Countries* from *Philip* the second of *Spain*, as both their wars may well testifie,[23] in which the taking of any one towne was of more consequence then all such a taxe would have been. How farre this also reaches is not for mee to esteeme: who should aske me, if the governour exacted for one time all the subject had, so there remained a ground to worke upon of new, and within a little time to live contentedly, I should be troubled to confesse it were a sufficient injury to take up armes against him, because I cannot judge which were the greater mischief to the subject.

Thirdly, if the wrong be of that nature as to ruine the whole commonwealth, yet not suddenly but [p. 113] after many yeeres, if often repeated, I cannot allow it a sufficient cause of open resistance. The reason is cleere: for, on the one side there is no inconvenience so small but (in processe of time) may grow to bee the ruine of the commonwealth, if it bee often repeated and so excessively multiplied; and on the other side, long time breeds so great changes or, at least, is subject to them, that the pure nature of the offence is not able to justifie a rebellion and breach of unity in a commonwealth, and so, not the resistance to the governour. How much the time in which the ruine would follow should bee, to make it a sufficient cause, who can judge? Onely this wee see, that what will not ruine in a set time, wil never doe it, and I have seen people live happily, where it was said, they paid the value of their whole subsi-[p. 114]stance to their magistrate once in seven yeers. Nor doe I pretend, by these instances, to set any rule for enfranchising the subject, more then this: when *evidently* the tyranny of the governour is greater then the mischiefe hazarded. When ever this happeneth, bee the materiall conditions what they will, the subject is free, and if this bee not, whatsoever the circumstances bee, the subject ought not to stirre. For, this and this onely is the finall cause measuring all attempts, *what is best for the people;* and knowne it is that, if it bee not evident to bee better to stirre it, it is evidently better to remaine quiet, for, not-a-cause is sufficient

---

[23] Here White is referring respectively to the Dutchy of Guienne, over the possession of which England and France fought during the Hundred Years' War; and to the revolt of the Spanish Netherlands against Philip II, which started at the beginning of the 1560s and formally ended in 1648, when, in the context of the Peace of Westphalia, Spain recognized the independence of the Dutch republic.

for not changing, but, for a change and such a change, it ought to bee a *clear and evident abbetterment*.

There is further to be looked into what part of the commonwealth it [p. 115] ought to bee that is sufficient to justifie such a quarrell. For, as there is no doubt, but the whole commonwealth, that is, such a portion of it as makes the governour's party inconsiderable, is sufficient, so, there will bee lesse doubt on the other extreme, if the number resisting bee a pure single part, it is not sufficient to proceed to this extremity. The question then is, whether the party rising ought to bee the *major* or equall or, at least, inconsiderable lesse then those who side with the magistrate. But here wee must observe the greatnesse of the commonwealth divided. For if such parts bee of themselves, nothing considered but the quantity or the number; it cannot bee doubted but that will suffice: now what the quantity is, belongeth to another science.

Besides all these considerations, [p. 116] there remaineth another that it can bee effected, for who is to attempt an action, ought as well to weigh the cost of compassing, as the worth and recompence when it is compassed. So that, unlesse the hazard of missing and the labour of obtaining, beeing both added into the ballance with the present quiet, bee all overswayed, it cannot bee prudently done to engage for a change.

Some will tell mee, never did people expect with so much patience as I require, and your gallants, who pretend to generosity, will exclaime, it is better to dye in the field then suffer such indignities. Nay, some will think or, at least, vaunt it fitter to lye in prison or rot in a dungeon, or seeke his fortune in *Barbary*, then to be under such a slavery. My answer to these last gallants is, that they should first [p. 117] try what it is to rot in a dungeon, or wander amongst Barbarians, before they engage themselves and other ignorant persons in such adventures. To the second, that I understand not those spurgalls of honour, which disquiet their fiery humours: I onely discourse of what is fitting to make a sweet and contented life, to them who thinke it consists in enjoying naturall goods of science and vertue for our mindes, and the accomodation of our sences for our bodies. Those high and aereall goods of honour, and vapouring words I esteeme as *Ajax* (when his eyes were open) at his death: '*Vertue* (said hee, meaning honour) *I followed thee as a thing, but I finde thou art but words*'.[24] To the formost, I answer, I doe not averre men either have been wise or will bee so wise, onely endevour to lay before them what it is to bee [p. 118] so, let them look to the exercise. Neither on the other side doe

---

[24] White has not given here an exact quotation, and therefore I have not been able to trace this reference conclusively. I suspect, however, that this is White's own rendering of Sophocles' *Ajax*, which in seventeenth-century England was known only in Latin (among the most important Latin translations was *Sophoclis Tragici Ajax Flagellifer… I. Lonicero autore*, Basileae 1533, which was staged at King's College, Cambridge, in 1564, on the occasion of the Queen's visit. Elizabeth, however, did not actually see the play, see R.R. Bolgar, *The Classical Heritage and its Beneficiaries*, Cambridge 1958, p. 524; and B.R. Smith, *Ancient Scripts and Modern Experience in the English stage 1500–1700*, Princeton 1988, pp. 214 and ff. The first English translation of the Sophoclean tragedy was published in 1714: *Ajax of Sophocles. Translated [in verse] from the Greek, with notes, by Jackson and N. Rowe*, London 1714).

I justifie the Prince who putteth his subject to such extremities, or think it prudence in him to doe it, or that he doeth not deserve all the mischiefe which may light upon him for it: I leave both to the force of nature, to their wit or folly, and to the force of reason or passion which governes in persons and present circumstances, keeping my self in the common notions which belong to science.

Still there remaines one difficulty, which may breed great variety in the resolution, and it is: who is to bee judge, whether the neglect of the magistrate bee so great, as to deserve resistance? For, if the magistrate himselfe bee endowed with that power, it is a folly to thinke that circumstance will ever come; and, if it belong to the people, [p. 119] such hot-spurres, as wee spake of, will make it come long before the season bee ripe for it. But, the truth is, this question seemeth in a manner superfluous, for it supposes, there is a question and ambiguity to bee decided, and by the conditions put, it is cleer there can bee no question of the necessity of the resistance, for they are such as to put the question beyond all ambiguity in the very conscience of the magistrate, the objects beating on the subject in every one's particular beyond denyall and dispute. And besides, as long as truly there is any disputablenesse, the trust reposed in the magistrate makes him judge: for beeing entrusted as a man both knowing and good, and the people taking themselves as ignorant in what they trust him, cleerly hee remains sole judge, as long as there remains a case to be judged. And [p. 120] therefore his either ignorance, or carelessenesse, or Tyranny ought to bee so evident, that it bee beyond all question, or else the subject must have patience for his owne good, which is his aime in putting himselfe under governement.

The Fifteenth GROUND.
Wherein Consists the Power and Liberty of the Subject.
Yet may some think, on the other side, that the doctrine delivered contradicts it selfe. For, it beeing before determined, that the people hath alienated all right of judging or medling in governement, how can it ever happen that they should have a right to interpose againe, or that such circumstances can possibly [p. 121] fall out in which they may resist the magistrate? And this objection is so much the stronger, by acknowledging so great a power in the magistrate of breaking all lawes and limitations of governement, by the force of reason placed in the circumstances of power and authority, as hath been declared; whence it seemes, since that authority in the magistrate cannot consist with an opposite auhority in the subject, to bridle and curb him, they can never have this power to resist.

And the truth is, the people acteth no what it doeth in such a case, by any authority acquired, but by the force of nature, the same force by which the magistrate overswayes the lawes, but in other circumstances. And first that the people hath no authority to oppose their superiour is manifest, for authority is a thing instituted by consent and de-[p. 122]pending on promise, but here is no need to consent nor any thought of it, here is no publicke meetings or *Ligues*, and if there were, they would bee of no value against a former tradition of their wills to their magistrate. It cannot bee therefore, that the people proceed by any such contract.

Whence is it then that the people come to any such power? The answer is, as, when they first instituted governement, they did it in the force of nature, without having any other Power then the pure force of rationality. So, if by any circumstance they be devolved into the same state of anarchy, that their promise made bindes no more, then rationality teacheth them and giveth them, by force of nature, to institute another governement. Now, the excessive disorders, expressed in the forementioned conditions, make it [p. 123] evident they are not in a governement, that is, in a conspiracy to the common good, which is the offence of governement, but in an anarchy, and therefore remitted, by the evill managing or insufficiency of their governour, to the force of nature to provide for themselves, and not bound by any promise made to their governour, the whole end and intention of their promise being, purely, to submit to governement, that is, conduce to the common good and safety, which having failed, there is no more obligation in their oath or promise, then if they had never made them. This is, therefore, the ground of the people's opposition, and onely circumstance to justifie their breaking their oath and promise: so that, in truth, the magistrate, first, by his miscarriages, abdicateth himself from being a magistrate, and proveth a brigand and robber in [p. 124] stead of a defender, and the people, in the way of naturall preservation of themselves, make resistance against him.

I should passe farther to the change of governement, did not the loud and universall cry of all common people, especially of our northerne countries, diverting my pen, force me to attend their importunity. They say, this doctrine delivered ruineth their liberty, and people are but a knot of slaves and galley-birds, if this be the course of governement.[25] They must be satisfied, or, at least, their courage allayed, by reason, if it be possible. For this word *liberty* prints it selfe in such a letter, that it leaves unstudied no man, as one speaketh. The *Pelagian* thinkes he hath lost his naturall liberty, if it may be commanded by God's omnipotency. The wordly man accounts himselfe a [p. 125] slave, if rationall governement be conserved: he must have license to commit wickednesse and ruine governement, or else he is in chaines. Let us then repeat the nature of governement, and see wherein consisteth the liberty of the subject, that we may know when he hath it, and what belongeth to it.

The people (we said) to fall to their owne businesse, and the improving of nature, chuse one or more to manage the common interests, holding them wise and capable, and themselves unskillfull, and this with a great deale of reason: for nothing but experience, and much debating is able to beget a sufficient art or knowledge, in such subtile points and turnings. Besides, they esteemed a few fitter for resolution, and easier to agree then their owne multitude, where so many private aimes are hard to be avoided, and if nor pre-[p. 126]judiciall

---

[25] White's refers here to Buchanan and the Scottish monarchomas, see Skinner, *The Foundations*, vol.II, pp. 338 and ff; J.H. Burns, 'George Buchanan and the anti-monarchomachs', in N. Phillipson and Q. Skinner (eds), *Political Discourse in Early Modern Britain*, pp. 3–22.

to the common. Upon these grounds, it is plaine, out of the very nature of Governement, that they reserve no power in themselves to consult of common businesses. For, how absurd is it that he who hath no skill shall give councell, or sway the resolutions of those whose art and posession it is? Or, what wise man could undertake a governement with truth and honour, if, in his greatest difficulties, he must depend on the advice, or rather wilfulnesse of an ignorant rabble?

Let us look now what is left for the obeying party, and we shall finde, it is to governe their private affaires, as farre forth as they fall not within the verge of the common good or harme. But, once put that the private man's business either hinders, or is necessary to help the common designes, and, as evident as it is that the common is to be pre-[p. 127]ferred before the particular, so evident it is, that even his proper businesse is not to be managed, so far, by his private understanding and liberty. If the souldier, when he is commanded to stand *perdue*, should have his private considerations allowed him, what could the army doe? If the citizen, being commanded to watch his turne upon the walls, might bring an excuse that he had no body to look to his shop, the city would soone fall to the enemies' prey. Private interest, then, must yeeld, when the publick is concerned, or else no governement can be hoped for: and, he that will leave matters of great consequence to the resolution of the governed party, must make them governours.[26]

Wherein then consists the liberty of every subject? In not being controlled in his private affaires. It there be not justice administred both [p. 128] against robbers and riotous oppressors, the citizen is not free; if he be molested in his domestick manage, otherwise then when the common demandeth his assistance, he is not free. But, for serving the common, it is the freest act he hath: it was his choice to elect it, it is his good to conserve it, and will be his destruction to infringe it. As it is no liberty to have an immunity to hang or maime himselfe, or his wife and children, or to commit any other unnaturall act, no more is it to be esteemed liberty, to have the priviledge to substract himselfe from the service of the commonwealth. They are therefore seditious spirits, who, using the name of liberty, provoke the subject against the magistrate; and in themselves, ordinarily, it is either ignorance or faction, which is the true mistresse of such attempts. Nor can it be feared, that [p. 129] governement, carried connaturally and as it ought to be, doth any way prejudice the liberty of the subject, what seisures soever it makes either upon goods or persons.

---

[26] On the question of the relationship between private interest and public good see J.G.A. Pocock, *The Machiavellian Moment: Florentine political thought and the atlantic republican tradition*, Princeton 1975, and id., *Virtue, Commerce, and History: essays on political thought and history*, Cambridge 1985. For a different opinion and a discussion of Pocock's theses see S. Pincus, 'Neither Machiavellian Moment nor Possessive Individualism: Commercial Society and the Defenders of the English Commonwealth', *The American Historical Review*, vol. 103 n.3 (1998), and Id., 'From holy cause to economic interest: the study of population and the invention of the state', in A. Houston and S. Pincus (eds), *A Nation transformed. England after the Restoration*, Cambridge 2001, pp. 272–98.

Yes, but governours will exceed the moderation of the true lawes of governement. First, the commonwealth hath a presumption of their goodness to the contrary. Secondly, admit they doe, must we seek to remedy it by a greater wound which is, by taking away the life and soule of governement? Againe, the oppression is either in common upon all, or in particular upon some few. If in common, it is almost impossible to be heavy upon every one, for many little summes easily rise to a great one, and many hands make light worke. If the wrong be done to particulars, wee ought to consider that accidentall harmes cannot be prevented neither [p. 130] in nature not in humane affaires, and so are objects of pity rather then of hope to be amended, and to be tolerated rather, in respect of the great good which is in the common peace, then expose all to such confusion as must be, and ever hath beene where the governement is, in part, placed in unexperient hands.

This, therefore, is resolved, that the plenitude of power in the governour hinders not the liberty of the subject, which is to bee contained within an inferiour sphere, and the sphere it selfe within the sphere of governement, and to be carried by it, as the private good by the common, when the necessity of the publick requires. Likewise, the propriety of right of the subject is to bee taken, not against the governour or common right, but against the encroaching of another party, as whoever understands what common [p. 131] and particular signifie, easily understands that the common and particular are not two, as the part and the whole make not two, because the part is included in the whole, but part and part make two, because one hath no community with the other. Therefore, it stands not with reason, that any private person should claim a right against the commonwealth, or the governour, which is all one, for so he makes the commonwealth a part distinguished from himselfe.

The Sixteenth GROUND
Of the Dispossession of a Supreme Former Governour, and of his Right.
This rubb being taken away, our march is free to consider the action of the change of governe-[p. 132]ment: by what it is effected that the former governour remaineth no longer in his authority, and the new one beginneth to have the power. For, we speake of a supreme governour whose power is sworne to, and so fortified, by an allegiance due from the people, and a right obtained by himselfe. And, we may presently reflect, that our former discourse, 'Of the people's resistance to a soveraign magistrate', reached not to the resolution of this. For, there we supposed magistrate to have behaved himself so unworthily, that he was truely no governour but a tyrant and robber, and so had really deposed himselfe, and disannulled the subjects' oath and obligation by renouncing, in deeds and practise, the nature of a governour. Now, our question supposeth the governour not to have come to that extremity, but, either to have been good or in-[p. 133]nocent, or that it is doubtfull whether his excesses deserved expulsion, or, at least, if they did deserve it of themselves, yet the circumstances were not fitting for it, but the expulsion happened either by the invasion of a stranger, or the ambition of a subject, or some popular

headlesse tumult; for these three wayes a magistrate comes, forcibly and unjustly, to be outed of his power.

And first, if the magistrate have truely deserved to be dispossessed, or it be rationally doubted that he hath deserved it, and hee bee actually out of possession. In the former case, it is certaine, the subject hath no obligation to hazard for his restitution, but rather to hinder it, for since it is the common good that both the magistrate and the subject are to aime at, and clearly, out of what is expressed, it is the common harme, to admit againe of such a magistrate, [p. 134] every one, to his power, is bound to resist him. If you say, he may or will repent and amend, that importeth not our question, or whether he be to be restored, but whether he be to be chosen of new. For, since it was meerely his possession and the interest of not changing or troubling the commonwealth which obliged the subject to maintaine him, it being supposed his owne desert did condemne him, this change and trouble of the commonwealth being now turned on the other side, and another in possession, clearly neither he hath any right left, nor the subject any obligation to maintaine but rather oppose him. Now, if this desert be doubtfull, then it is also doubtfull whether he hath right ot no, and certaine, that the common good is not to be disturbed for it, nature teaching that wee need no reason to be quiet and remaine where [p. 135] we are, but that to make a change we must see a strong cause and motive.

The next case is, if he be innocent and wrongfully deposed, nay, let us adde, one who had governed well and deserved much of the commonwealth, yet he is totally dispossessed, and so, that, it is plaine, in these circumstances, it were better for the common good to stay as they are, then to venture the restoring him, because of the publicke hazard. It is cleare, in this case, there is a comparison betweene the generall good of the commonwealth, on the one side, and the particular of this man or family on the other. Let us, then, put the case on his part, and see, if he be generous, if he hath setled in his heart that every single man ought to preferre the common interest before his particular safety, profit, or honour, if [p. 136] hee bee fit for a governour, that is, one that is to espouse the common good as his owne individuall, what he will, in honour and conscience, resolve, whether hee bee not obliged absolutely to renounce all right and claime to governement; and, if he does not, hee bee not worse then an Infidell. For, if he that hath no case of his domesticks, be reputed so, with how much more reason, he that is ready to plunge a whole Nation in blood for his owne interest?

Let us cast the accompts on the other side, and see that the subjects' aime ought to be the publicke peace, and quiet enjoyment of their lives and interests: it will appear that, if hee bee bound to renounce his claime, they cannot be obliged to maintain it, and besides, that they are wilfully blinde, if, where the whole concernements of them-[p. 137]selves, their wives and children lie at stake, they will venture all for an aereall fancy, without regard to the *end* of governement, publicke peace, meerely for the *meanes*, this man's governement, without whom the end may be obtained. It cannot, therefore, be rationall on either side, for a dispossessed governour to be restored with hazard, unlesse it be certaine the succeeding governement be a pure tyranny, and so the dispossessed person necessary for the quiet and peace of the commonwealth, and therefore, that both sides pretend the good of the commonwealth, as well hee that is to be restored, as those who seek to restore him.

But some cry: 'He had right, he hath not deserved to lose it: justice must be done whatever follows on it'. Happy they that are unfortunate [p. 138] in so good a cause, they shall not lose their reward, however it fares with them now. Well for them, if this plea will serve them in the next world! Nor will I dispute whether the evidence of what I deliver be so great as the ignorance may not excuse them: that question belongs to the Tribunall of God onely. I must say that, before men, who are clad with flesh, and whose hearts cannot be pierced by other men's guesses, the law is, that not onely the intention bee good, but also the action be intelligent and prudent, otherwise we are subject to believe that some vanity or secret hopes doe byass the actor and make his proceeding irrationall. I must also tell them, that this principle, *Fiat justitia et ruat coelum*,[27] is seldome practised amongst the wise, who all agree the charity and [p. 139] prudence ought still to moderate the rigour of justice. It is also too metaphysicall for a morall way, to thinke that justice is a *Platonick Idea* in the concave of the moone, no waies to be changed by circumstantiall occurrences. Whereas, the truth is, justice is but a partiall and commanded vertue, and that which governes in man is reason or his owne nature and inclination to make all his actions connaturall and fit for a rationall creature, and so may consult whether justice be in some to bee administred, and pronounce that *Summum jus est summa injuria*.[28]

But the capitall in this matter is, that truely there is no justice on either the magistrate's or people's side, to binde to the restoring him: both these depending on the promise made, and the force of the [p. 140] promise being none, since the ground of it is changed. For, the substance of the promise made to a magistrate, is, to obey him as a magistrate, that is, as farre as is fitting for the commonwealth and peace, he being nothing but the instrument of the common good. Now, take away the fitnesse for the commonwealth, and that which gave strength to the promise is gone, and the promise it selfe is no more a promise, nor can any obligation arise for it. Who knows not, that the promise of any man depends on his intention, his intention on his knowledge, his knowledge reacheth no farther then his consideration and present memory when he maketh the promise? So that, in nature, a promise reacheth onely to presupposed and thought on circumstances: and who, when he sweareth to a magistrate, expecteth to see [p. 141] him dispossessed and turned off?

Nature annulleth promises, as when we promise to come such a day, and either die or are imprisoned before. Morality annulleth them, as if we promise to run such a horse against another a month hence, and the horse in the meane time falleth lame: who will condemne the master for not venturing on such a race? Is not the man better then his word? If then the man himselfe bee lesse

---

[27] This Latin maxim was adopted by Ferdinand I, Charles V's successor to the throne of the Holy Roman Empire, as his motto.

[28] Cicero, *De officiis*, I, 10, 33.

then the common good, which he must violate by keeping his word, can his word be greater? But a promise must many times bee kept even with losse of life? I deny it not. But, first, I must bee assured it is a promise, which before I have declared to bee none, for our case is a case of nature, not of law, we admit no presumptions, nothing what he meant to doe or should have done: wee onely regard [p. 142] what was done. Secondly, if it were intended to be so promised, it was wicked and irrationall, for to promise to regard a private man's good against the common is unnaturall and wicked; therefore, it never was a promise, can never binde as such, nor be professed with honour, either to be made, or, if made, to bee kept. I need not insist upon the confirmation of a precedent promise, and there were no promise, there can be no oath, to have the nature and force of an oath.

So that, this is manifest, a magistrate actually dispossessed hath no right to be restored, nor the subject any obligation to seek to restore, but oppose him. For, what is man, or rather mankinde (for, so we have stiled a nation) better then a herd of sheepe or oxen, if it bee [p. 143] to bee owned, like them, by masters? What difference is there betweene their master's selling them to the butcher, and obliging them to venture their lives and livelihoods for his private interest? Wee know it is naturall, that the part should venture for the whole, but that the whole should venture the losse of it selfe to save the part, I cannot understand. The governour is the highest and noblest part, yet but a part; the people is the whole, the end (though not by office, yet by worth and dignity), the master and lord, for whom those who are lords by office are to be vested and devested in lordship, when it is necessary for the common good. Who think otherwise, deserves not the name of a man. [p. 144]

The Seventeenth GROUND.
Of a Supreme Governour Dispossessed.
But one will object, if hee were wrongfully dispossessed, hee suffered wrong; it cannot then but bee reason hee should have reparation. And this cannot bee denied. But beside the governement taken from him, hee was peradventure injured in his reputation and spoiled of such aliments as are fit to maintaine him according to the quality of his birth and education, and for these, hee may, as a private man, demand reparation, but so, as still to remember he is a denizen of that Countrey, a member of that people, and compared to it as a particular to its universall, and may demand his share, yet so that if it cannot bee [p. 145] obtained without the concussion of the publicke, hee is to renounce it and sacrifice that interest to the good of his Countrey.

Likewise, on the opposite side, the commonwealth may demand reparations against the dispossessed magistrate, who abused it or his subjects during his governement, not touching any thing hee did upon intention of the publick good, though it were breaking of known laws or any injurious violence offered, with pretence of serving the commonwealth. For, the trust put in his hands vindicates him from all such actions, as long as they beare the face of any intention of the common good. But, if, for private men's satisfaction, or his owne lust or covetousnesse hee did any wrong, of that hee may bee asked an account, not while hee is in governement but after the dispossession, [p. 146] when now the common distemper followeth not the prosecution of such riots, and so, his publicke protection beeing gone, hee is but a private man, and consequently, by the force of nature, subject to a stronger; obligations of common good and former promises beeing now faded away, and hee left in the condition of a stranger, saving that his demerits follow and pursue him, if other merits doe not counterballance them and exempt him.

Againe, when hee is to bee judged, he cannot bee proceeded against by law, which can judge none but the offenders against it. Now wee have had often occasion to declare that the chiefe magistrate is not under the law, the common good for which the lawes themselves were made, beeing committed to his trust, and the end hee is to look af-[p. 147]ter beeing higher then the lawes, which are but a part of the meanes to arrive at that end, and therefore inferiour and subordinate to it. But those who could put their owne agreements, that is, the lawes under his feet, could not put nature under them, nor authorise him to doe any irrationall or unhandsome action. Therefore, when the structure of the commonwealth is dissolved, that is, disjointed from him, then any who hath suffered wrong in the fore-declared manner may bee party against him and proceed as if there were no commonwealth, by the law which, in a wildernesse, warranteth us to kill a tyger or robber that seeketh to kill us, not pretending law for our action, but that it is manlike and rational.[29] Neither ought it bee called punishment that is done against a dispossessed magistrate, but rather revenge, or some [p. 148] other name that includeth no order to law.

By this wee understand the truth of that famous question: whether a soveraigne bee under the lawes. To which is ordinarily answered that hee is, as farre as his example and direction is necessary to his subjects, but not so, that the law, as such, hath any superiority or force upon him. To declare this more plainly, wee must remember, the rule of his action is 'To doe what reason teaches a man in his posture ought to doe', that is, what is fitting for the publicke. Now generally speaking, the common good requireth that the lawes bee observed betwixt fellowes of the same commonwealth; wherefore nature teacheth him to give example of that observance, as farre as his publick office permits.

Besides, in the very person of the [p. 149] soveraigne are to bee distinguished, his beeing one of the commonwealth, and beeing the head or magistrate, so that, though his beeing a magistrate exempts his publicke actions and also his person and private actions from the inquisition of the law, yet it doth not exempt his private actions from the proportion to those of the subjects, that is, from being good or bad, because like or dislike to the actions which the law commandeth or forbiddeth. So that, he is not, even in his private actions, subject to the lawes at his *rule* for *that* is onely reason, but, as they are a kinde of way chalked out to him for the materiall part of his action, as the architect frames his house for him, or the gardiner his walkes: that is, the lawes are to him as an art under him, an art to shew him what is to bee done,

---

[29] For an ananlysis of this passage, see *supra*, Chapter IV, pp. 70–73.

not to command or [p. 150] punish him for not doing; nay, not so much as necessitating him to doe, at least, universally, whether the businesse be purely betwixt subjects, or betwixt himselfe as a private person, and his subjects.

For, the principle of common good beeing higher then the art of making lawes, may, nay ought in some cases, differ from the prescriptions of the law. Yet this must not authorize him to dispense frequently with the law, the governement beeing not possible to bee good in which there is no constancy. But, if the circumstances require any law to bee often forced, the law it selfe ought to bee limited, that the practice of the subject may bee firme and customary, which is that maketh the law please. Thus in conclusion, though the magistrate bee not commanded by the lawes, nor personally subject to them, yet [p. 151] reason (which is his rule) bindeth him to observe them as the good of his people, and (ordinarily speaking) essentiall to his end, which is the common good. The lawes therefore are his matter to work on, or instruments necessary to work by, not his rule or mastering directions.

There remaines yet untouched the question that seemeth most troublesome to many, when the change of the governement is valid, and such as the subjects' obedience is due to the new magistrate and to bee substracted from the old, how unjustly soever hee were bereaved of it. And, others have sought by terme of yeers to decide the difficulty: among whom, one was Pope *Urban the eight*, an intelligent and generous Prince and well versed in politick governement. Hee published a decision that after five yeers [p. 152] quiet possession of an estate, the Church was not bound to take notice whether the title were lawfull or no, but acknowledge the possessour, in Ecclesiasticall businesses. So much hee said for aimes' sake.[30] But wee must proceed upon other principles, that is, the forelaid and main *basis* of our discourse, that the common good ought to bee the rule of the magistrate's title, and the subjects' obedience.

Out of which this followeth, that when ever (considering all things) the common good is cleerly on the possessor's side, then the dispossessed hath no claime. Neither ought wee expect till wee have assurance, that it will not bee better for the subject if the late owner (after great dangers), gaineth his former power, for first, this it selfe is uncertaine; secondly, the success of endevours to restore him [p. 153] must bee hazardous; thirdly, many and great mischiefs, during the time of the attempt, are altogether unavoidable, and all this to bee ballanced against those uncertaine hopes. Nor, againe, must wee expect that the wills of all the subjects concurre, actually, to the acceptance of the new governour, for that is either impossible or of so long expectation, as to ruine all dissensions and jealousies in the meane time. Nay, the vulgar sort are so easily led by fancy, that they understand not the common good, nor what they whould wish.

But you may demand: 'How shall it bee knowne when the common good holdeth it selfe on the possessour's hand?' I answer, wee must first see who

---

[30] Maffeo Barberini was elected Pope as Urban VIII in 1623. During his important pontificate, which coincided with the Thirty Years War, the Roman Inquisition condemned Galileo. In 1642 Urban VIII issued the Bull *In eminenti*, which condemned Jansenius's doctrine. For more information on Urban VIII see L. von Pastor, *History of the Popes: from the close of the Middle Ages*, 40 vols, London 1886–1936, vol. 29.

are the common, whose welfare is to bee preferred before private interests. And presently it appeareth that, dividing [p. 154] the whole people into governours and governed, the governed part is the publicke to whose good the governours are to direct their paines, and that these are they that spend their lives in seeking their owne profits, either by improving the land, or in arts and handicrafts. Whence it followes, when their good stands on the possessour's side, then cleerly hee begins to gaine right and power, and this is plaine to bee, when the merchant, the husbandman, and tradesman, with their appendices, are in an undisturbed practice of their functions, and begin to bee afraid of change upon the noise of an invasion.

This resolution could not bee doubted, were it not that one might object, that what is said seemes true, abstracting from circumstances, but it ought to bee considered, that [p. 155] such men see nothing but the outward appearances of what passes in humane negotiations, and so there may many circumstances lie hidden from them, which would make them thinke or wish otherwise if they knew them, as for example, home-discontents, and forraigne conspiracies, which if understood, would make these honest men preferre a warre, after which there is to follow a peace farre exceeding the present quiet and such a one as deserves the intervening disturbance and dammages.

And indeed, I allow these men understand not such mysteries of state, nor penetrate the value of the hazard: but, if they doe not, why are they not also exempted from engaging on those motives? And then the rest of the commonwealth will bee but so many private men, who must follow the common. Againe, [p. 156] if they think themselves well, they manifestly consent to the present governement, and therefore cut off the title of the dispossessed governour. Besides, who can answer they shall be better by the returne of the dispossessed party? Surely, by common presumption, the gainer is like to defend them better then he who lost it.

But, let us overslip this opportunity and end of the common good: how long must we expect, till it shall be supposed the right of the former magistrate is extinct? Some ages? As wee kept our title to *France*, and *France* did to *Sicily* and *Naples*, or at least some generations?[31] As the durance of the *Spaniard* warres upon *Holland*, or till the former magistrate declares the relinquishment of his right? Or, till his followers are weary of inventing new devices, to blind and ruine their unwary friends? [p. 157] All these are soone discerned to bee meere uncertainties, and rather nets to catch fools and bring them to the ambitious desires of some few men, then any grounded reason. But, what if an open enemy should come, could or ought the subjects joine against him with their new magistrate? If not, the whole publick must perish; if they may, then the case is the same against their old magistrate, since his right stood upon the

---

[31] Here White is referring to the claim of the English king to the French throne that started the Hundred Years' War, and to the Angevin domination of the Kingdom of Naples and Sicily that lasted roughly between the beginning of the fourteenth century and the mid fifteenth century, when the Aragonese kings reclaimed the territories.

common peace, and that is transferred from him to his rivall by the title of quiet possession.[p. 158]

The Eighteenth GROUND.
The Objection of Divines Answered.
Reason hath plaid its part, but authority cannot be silenced unheard. Let us therefore hearken to what it said. And, first steps up the Divine to preach us, out of Scripture, the duty wee owe to priests and kings, no lesse then death and damnation beeing the guerdons of rebellion and disobedience.[32] The Lawyers come yoaked from the Popes' and Emperours' Court, taking for maxime, *Tempus non occurrit Ecclesiae et Regi*.[33] The practice seems to confirme the same, wee seeing both some noble men and divers cities make protestations against the possession of others for many years and ages. But, which is [p. 159] more, they will speak reason too at least, by the Divine's mouth, who telleth us, that God, by nature, is high lord and master of all, That whoever is in power receiveth his right from him, that obedience consists in doing the will of him who commandeth, and concludeth that this will ought to bee obeyed till God taketh away the obligation, that is, till hee who is to be obeyed himselfe releaseth his right.

The Authorities they cite out of Holy Writ are, for the most part, meere commands to obey where obedience is due, without specifying what or when it is due. This command is extended to wicked and evill governours as well as good. One place there is, where *Samuel* denounceth to the people the evills that will come to them by power of the King, and calleth them *Jus Regis*, or, as the Hebrew text, *Judici-*[p. 160]*um Regis*, or, *Legem Regis*, and afterward, *Regni*.[34] And these words are, in two sences, true: one, that the king would do the wrongs there mentioned, by force; the other, that the people, since they would have a king, ought not to resist him when hee did such things. Yet doe I not deny but, if the particulars there mentioned bee interpreted gently, all that is there recited might, with justice, bee practised by a king: as, when it is said hee should take away their vineyards and olive-gardens, it may bee understood, upon confiscation and by other lawfull wayes. Besides, they may peradventure alledge that God, by his speciall command, transferred the Kingdome from *Saul* to *David*, from *Roboam* to *Jerobam*, and some others.[35] But, they should also let us know, what they deduce from hence: For in such changes, God gave no [p. 161] new authority or power to such kings, but the same their predecessors had, so that, in fine, all that is brought out of Scripture falleth short of proving that no time can make void the right of a king once given him from the hand of God.

---

[32] Here White is referring to Romans 13:1–7.
[33] Here White is referring to the English common-law rule which exempts certain governmental bodies from statutes of limitation (it literally means 'Time does not run against the Church or the King').
[34] Here White is referring to the episode narrated in 1 Samuel 8: 10–22.
[35] Here White summarizes the narrative that can be found in 1 Samuel 2.

The reason of this weak way of alleadging Scripture is, that when they read that God commandeth or doth this, they look not into nature to know what this commanding or doing is, but presently imagine God commandeth it by expresse and direct words, and doeth it by an immediate position of the things said to bee done; whereas in nature the commands are nothing but the naturall light God hath bestowed on mankinde, and which is therefore frequently called the law of nature. Likewise, God's doing a thing is many times onely the course of naturall second causes, to which be-[p. 162]cause God gives the direction and motion, hee both doeth and is said to doe all that is done by them, as truly as the weight of a Jack turnes the meat upon the spit, and the spring of a Watch makes the clock of it strike: a notion not onely of a large extent and usefulnesse in it selfe, but, which gives mee just occasion of complaining against these verball and winde-blowne Divines, as the bane of Christendome and Christian doctrine.[36] For, whereas the Scripture is a book enriched with all science and depth of learning, this sort of 'Grammar Divines', without either logick, philosophy, or morality, meerly by the vertue of their Dictionary, and such like lip-learning, undertake to bee interpreters of the sacred Bible, and in stead of the sence of the letter, obtrude to the readers their owne low and many times phreneticall fancies. [p. 163] Let us instance in our present question. The first position they take is, that God is lord and master of all things. What seems, nay truly is more conformable to Scripture and reason then this assertion, as it lies in words? And yet many not looking into the nature of God and rationall and intelligent substances, make a shift to pervert it into a meer blasphemy. For, if the sence bee onely this, that God is omnipotent and no resistance possible in any creature to his absolute will, nothing is more certaine, nothing more holy. But, this is not the meaning of the Divines; but, that there is an attribute or notion in God of being lord and master, to which they do not say we cannot, but, ought not resist, and rather admit that wee can. And herein is the first faltring, that, in effect, they deny the Omnipotency, and reduce that which is a [p. 164] true physicall power to a morall obligation. But this is not all.

The next point is, that, even if this morality were founded in that great nature of beeing, and beeing intelligent, which is in God almighty, and that they also held his commands were to bee obeyed, because they proceed from an understanding which cannot erre, and which is essentially the very order and well beeing of all creatures, the former would seeme pardonable. But, they will have it quite contrary, that therefore things amongst creatures goe well, because not reason, not the eminentiall beeing of themselves in God is their off-spring, but because a high and overpowering will or voice commandeth it so. A position in respect of God, absolutely blasphemous, as far as it makes him worke without the guidance of his understanding, that is, like [p. 165] the lowest order of creatures, as stockes and stones, et c. It is againe afflictive and vexatious to mankinde, taking away that sweetnesse of obeying, which

---

[36] On White's interpretation of God's intervention in natural phenomena, see *supra*, Chapter II, pp.31 and ff.

consists in the perswasion that because creatures are the participation of God's owne nature, every one in its degree and mankind in the first and highest place, therefore all God's command and governement, are most conformable to their good, as it were salves to their sores, and allurements to the bringing them to their final end and perfection.

But, that which is more to our purpose is, that, upon this blasphemy against God, they build the greatest inconvenience that, peradventure, is to bee found in man's nature, to wit, that God gives to all in power the likeness and participation of this irrationall dominion which they conceive in [p. 166] him, and that truly there is in superiours a kinde of dote or free gift of mastery derived from God, in vertue whereof hee is master of the inferiours and what belongs to them, either wholly or in a certaine measure, according to the extent of the power given, that, lawfully and validly, he may dispose of all or a certain part of the things under his charge, meerly because such is his will and pleasure, and that the subject ought to be content to let him doe his will, upon this score, because it is God's will that this man's will should be fulfilled. Which doctrine, though it bee manifestly against Christ's directions left to his disciples, and the practice of all good men, yet, because this treatise doth not pretend to Divinity, I will onely insist upon its naturall inconveniences.

As first, that it is not connatu-[p. 167]rall to mankinde, which, consisting, for its better part, in understanding, is not governed conformably to its disposition, unlesse it be so guided that the understanding be principall and satisfied in it selfe and leader to the will and action, which course of proceeding when it is observed, then is a man truely a man and his action goes on with sweetnesse, as is before declared. Againe, it maketh the governour proud, insolent, and carelesse. Proud, because hee taketh himselfe to bee of another orbe then his subjects, that they are all slaves and beasts, himselfe onely master, himselfe onely intelligent and a man. Insolent, because fully perswaded, by this doctrine, that he can doe them no wrong, that they are bound to suffer what he layes on them, that his pleasure is and must be their content and rule. Carelesse, because [p. 168] he thinks he hath no account to make, either to God or man: not to God, since he hath submitted the people to his will and disposition, and therefore he being incapable of doing them any wrong, cannot bee charged with any crime. Much lesse is he sollicitous to content his subjects, in whom he taketh it for an insolency to repine at any thing, and esteemes it their duty to commend all he does, and to have his authority for their rule to judge all things by.

On the other side, the subject becomes base, restive, ambitious. For, the worth and dignity of man, which is his liberty or guidance of himselfe, being taken away, it followes, he must be servile and flattering, a slave, a body without soule and understanding. The more wordly and rustick part must, of necessity, grumble and feele it harsh [p. 169] to see their labours disposed on to people, of whom they have opinion that they are idle, vicious, and unworthy, and therefore desire liberty from such a yoke, and to become masters of their owne goods and labours, and are easily susceptible of propositions tending to that purpose, when they come from faire tongues. Lastly, the higher spirits have governement in admiration, and take it for the onely happinesse, and therefore have their hearts wholly bent, how, by flattery, by cunning, by force, to arrive to this power to depose him that is in possession, and sit downe themselves in his seat of glory. If their hopes mount not so high, for the impossibility of the fact and the remotenesse of their quality, then their aime is, by adulation and compliances, to come neere the highest, to bee participant of his authority, [p. 170] and have the like power to rob and oppresse, which they esteeme vertuous and glorious in him, and not unjust but fitting in themselves, as farre as they can doe it by he participation of that dote which God hath bestowed upon the highest magistrat.

Lastly, we must looke into the lame proceeding of the common good and publicke actions of such a governement, where the subject, by the consequence of this doctrine, is set eagerly upon his owne interest, thinkes all lost that is done for his, not governour or protector, but lord and master, and therefore alienated from him. Whence, it must come to passe that, what he can cousen, what hee can excuse, what hee can delay, hee is still forward to, and, by a secret instinct of nature which abhorreth such a governement, thinketh it well [p. 171] done, though he cannot give an account to justifie his action. In a word, who sees not this commonwealth to be a kingdome divided in it selfe alwayes in affection, and very neere in outward action, wanting thereunto nothing but an occasion, and some head to manage the sedition? Who sees not that the whole governement is violent, and so may indeed continue whilst actuall force hangeth over it, but hath not the possibility of a naturall duration and length. [p. 172]

The Nineteenth GROUND.
The Authority of Lawyers Insufficient in this Question.
The *Divines'* errour being thus discovered, our plea against the *Lawyers* will be of lesse either debate or consequence, for this question belongeth not to their science or employment. The maximes, the rule, the highest tribunall of their judgements is the text of the Law, the agreements of men, and, at most, to declare the lawmaker's intention. But, to judge whether the lawmaker's intention be conformable to nature and such as it ought, whether he exceedeth his power, whether hee bee master of the lawes, and the like, is beyond the verge of their jurisdiction. Therefore, no-[p. 173]thing is more absurd, then to demand that lawyers should plead cases between the soveraigne magistrate and the subject, where the common good and governement is interessed. For, there, things are not to be carried by the Dictates of *Justinian* or *Lancelotus*,[37] or the command of *Caesar* or *Peter's* successours, but either by science of politicks, or the certitude of faith and tradition, which are the onely two rules a high governour hath. If the Divine findeth any thing contrary to the knowne

---

[37] White is here referring respectively to the *Corpus iuris civilis* compiled under the emperor Justinian in the 6th century and to the work of Giovanni Paolo Lancellotti, a sixteenth-century canonist and jurist who was the author of a very influential compilation of canon law entitled *Institutiones Iuris Canonici*, published in Perugia in 1563, see J.F. von Schulte, *Die Geschichte der Quellen und Literatur des canonischen Rechts*, 3 vols, Stuttgart 1875–80, vol. III, pp. 451 and ff.

law of God, he may speake. If the philosopher finde any thing against the nature of man, his mouth is not to bee stopped. The lawyer, what can he say? It is against the agreement heretofore made by the governement of the countrey? The governour may reply: 'Yes, but what you say is against the present [p. 174] good of the countrey, with which I am entrusted'. Is the countrey made for the lawes, or the lawes for the countrey? The lawes therefore must give place, where the good of the people is against the former resolutions. If any law be repealed by the authority which made it, or by another equal, is it the lawyer's part to plead what was law before, or what is now? When a supreme governour speaketh as such, as declaring what the present necessity requires, if any former law bee against it, it is by his declaration annulled: it was law before, but it is not now. But the lawyer will reply: 'There is no law in the land which giveth such authority'. It is easily answered: it is not a case for which a law is to bee made. See the Romane governement: when there came an exigence of desperation, all their [p. 175] magistrates, all their formes ceased, a Dictatour was made, whose word was law, nor could any man appeale to law. Such is the case when the high governour pronounceth against the law, for hee ought not to doe it, but when the law standeth not with the good and safety of the subject, and when hee doth, law is not to be pleaded against him.

Againe can any law be enacted of what shall bee done in case of a conversion of the governement? It is clearly a folly to pretend it. The ordering of the commonwealth is, then, in new hands, the former's power is expired, and to prescribe rules to them who will assuredly be their owne judges, is a piece of great simplicity. The lawyer may peradventure reply: 'There is no power in the land to repeale the former lawes or to op-[p. 176]pose them'. I thinke hee will bee wiser, yet, if hee doth say it, I aske him: 'Who made the former lawes? Was it not the people, by themselves or their deputies? And which is the stronger, if they make them by their deputies, or by themselves?' Certainely, it will be answered, 'by themselves', for the deputies have no power but what they impart to them. Is it then possible to put a case, in which there is no power in a countrey to repeale lawes? Evidently, who sayes so must say there is no people in the countrey? For, if there be people, there is in them a power to dispose of themselves, more strong then in deputies.

But the lawyer may say: 'The people cannot speake their mindes freely'. I answer: 'Certainely, they not onely can, but cannot chuse but speake their mindes, in the case [p. 177] we put'. Who knoweth not that liberty and speaking of one's minde belongeth to all circumstances a man can be put in? The merchant that, in a tempest, throweth the precious fruits of his venture and labour into the Sea, doth not he doe it freely and willingly? The *Hollanders* of late made a peace with the *Spaniard*; wee, both with the *Hollander* and the *Dane*, and are pretending to others: in any of these, were all parts pleased?[38]

---

[38] Here White is referring to the 1648 Peace of Westphalia, and to the 1625 Treaty of The Hague between Denmark and the Netherlands, and later France and England, which was intended to provide economic support for the Danish king, involved against the Catholic powers in that phase of the Thirty Years' War.

Did no party agree to somewhat which hee would not have done, but in consideration of his present circumstances? Or, was there ever peace made after a warre, but one part grudged at somewhat? Must none of these be accounted freely done? Must none of these promises binde, and be kept, upon honour and veracity? This is to destroy all commerce of mankinde, nay, not to [p. 178] allow man so much wit as to know what is fit for him to doe in time of necessity. If then the people speake, in one circumstance, something that they would not in another, it is not to be said they speake not their mindes, but that, according to circumstances, they alter their mindes, as all wise men doe. They agree and submit to the present conjunctures, not because they are not free, now as before, but because circumstances are changed, and now render it fitting. But, I said that, in the case I put, they could not chuse but speake. My case was, that then a governour is acknowledged, when the people casting off the care and thoughts of innovation, fall to their trades and manufactures: can it be denied that by so doing they acquiesce to the present governement? Which if they doe, can it be questioned whether [p. 179] they consent or not to the repealing of all such lawes as cannot stand with the present governement? Such lawes therefore are repealed, not by deputies, but by the deputants and masters of the deputies. The lawyer, therefore, must either proclaime the present governement none, or not plead law against it, for it is pure folly to admit both, that is, faire and full contradiction. In a new governement, all lawes prejudiciall to it are annulled, by the pure admission of it. Other *indifferent* lawes so goe on, as to bee subject to its judgement, whether and how farre to stand, but a wise governour will continue them as farre as hee can with prudence, because innovation is contrary to the sweetnesse which is in custome, as in a kinde of nature. [p. 180]

The Conclusion
Bee this then so resolved, that God himselfe hath no irrationall and dead title of Lordship over his creatures, but onely his all-right-setled understanding, and irresistible Omnipotency. And, as hee hath none in himselfe, so likewise not given any to those hee hath put in authority, but that their power is either in the submission of the subject by promise and agreement, or in the rationall disposition of the magistrate, which maketh him work what is conformable to humane nature. And the obedience or obligation to obey in the subject is out of this, that hee hath entrusted the magistrate with the governement, and is, by that, to suppose he doth regularly what [p. 181] is best (all things considered) for the common good.

That, by consequence, the title of the magistrate begins and dies with the good of the commonwealth, and holdeth purely so long as it is good for the people. That, no lawes made by the power or agreement of men, can judge betwixt subject and soveraigne, in dispute of the common good and governement, but onely the Tribunalls of God and Nature, or Divinity and the science of Politicks, and therefore, the maximes of law have no force in these questions. Now, if princes lose their pretences by the force of nature, it is ridiculous for private men to build hopes, upon rotten titles of ages long passed, upon weak maximes of law, after nature, by her revolutions, hath cast all law and mortall acts and agreements.[p. 182]

And so is finished this small Treatise, to the profit of them who are able and willing to make use of it. Some, by the method I have used, something new in morall discourses, may imagine the doctrine I deliver, to bee more subtle in explication then solid in practice, but let them either looke into the causes of governements, or the effects: they will see nature and practise both conspire to give testimony to the truth. The cause of all morall effects, if morally carried, are the end and intention for which they are sought and endeavoured after. This is manifest to bee the well-being of particulars under a governement. The practises, which are the effects, will shew that governements breake when it is not well with the subjects, but they are oppressed by the governour; that wise and good governours are for-[p. 183]ced sometimes to breake disordered rules which hinder their free administration; that people, as it were, forced by naturall changes, violate the promises made to their governours, cast them off when they think them pernicious, and proceed against them, *per viam facti*, as they speake in the Schooles, not by lawes, which cannot bee made for such matters. These are, in a manner, the whole subject of the precedent discourse.

FINIS

Selected Bibliography

Manuscripts

British Library, London
   Additional Mss. 4106
   Additional Mss. 10575
   Additional Mss. 38175
   Additional Mss. 41486
   Egerton Mss. 2541
   Harleian Mss. 4153

Bodleian Library, Oxford
   Rawlinson Mss. A36
   Rawlinson Mss. D1104
   Ms.Locke F.14
   Gough Norfolk Ms. 15

Westminster Diocesan Archives, London
   Old Brotherhood Mss. II.130
   Westminster Archives Mss., volumes XXX and XXI

ACDF, Rome
   Stanza Storica SS 1-e
   Stanza Storica SS 2-a
   Stanza Storica SS 2-b
   Decreta Sancti Officii
   I I (ii) 32, Decreta Congregationis Indicis

ARSI, Rome
   Provincia Angliae, Epp. Gen.II, 1 (1642–1698)
   Anglia 34

BAV, Rome
   Fondo Barberini Latini 5406

Printed Primary Sources

A Collection of the state papers of John Thurloe, ed. by T. Birch, 7 vols, London 1742

A copy of 1. The letter sent by the Queenes Majestie concerning the collection of the recusants mony for the Scottish warre..., London 1641 (WING C6196)

[ASSHETON, W.]: *Evangelium Armatum*, London 1663 (WING A4033)

[AUSTIN, J.] *The Christian Moderator*, London 1651 (WING A4243)
—— *The Christian Moderator, the Third Part*, London 1653 (WING A4248)
BALL, W.: *State-Maxims*, London 1656 (WING B595)
BAXTER, R.: *A humble advice*, London 1655 (WING B1284)
—— *A Holy Commonwealth*, London 1659 (WING B1281)
—— *A key for Catholics*, London 1959 (WING B1295)
BELLARMINO, R.: *Controversiae*, Venice 1603
BODIN, J.: *Les six livres de la republique*, Paris 1583
Correspondence of Descartes and Constantijn Huygens 1634–1647, ed. by L. Roth, Oxford 1926
CLARENDON, E.H. (Earl of), *A letter from a true and lawfull member of Parliament*, s.l. 1656 (WING C4424)
COKE, R.: *Justice Vindicated*, London 1660 (WING C4979)
—— *A survey of the politicks*, London 1662 (WING C4982)
DESCARTES, R.: *Principia Philosophiae*, in *Oeuvres*, ed. by Adam & Tannery, Paris 1897–1957, vol. ix
DIGBY, K.: *Loose fantasies*, ed. by V. Gabrieli, Florence 1968
—— *Two Treatises: in the one of which, the nature of bodies; in the other, the nature of mans soule; is looked into*, Paris 1644 (WING D1448)
—— *A Discourse concerning Infallibility in Religion*, Amsterdam/Paris 1652
—— *A late discourse made in a solemne assembly of Nobles and Learned Men at Montpellier in France by Sr. Kenelme Digby*, London 1658 (WING D1436)
—— *A Discourse concerning the vegetation of plants. Spoken by Sir Kenelme Digby at Gresham College, on the 23. Of January, 1660*, London 1661 (WING D1432)
—— *A choice collection of rare chymical secrets and experiments in philosophy*, London 1682 (WING D1425A)
FALKLAND (Viscount of, Lucius Cary): *Sir Lucius Cary, late Lord Viscount of Falkland, His Discourse of Infallibility*, London 1651 (WING F317)
GASSENDI, P.: *Animadversiones in Decimum Librum Diogenis Laaertii*, Lyon 1649
—— *Exercitationes Paradoxicae adversus Aristoteleos*, in *Opera omnia*, Lyon 1658, 6 vols, vol. IV
—— *Syntagma Philosophicum*, in *Opera omnia*, vol. II
GRANT, W.: *The vindication of the Vicar of Istleworth, in the County of Middlesex*, s.l. 1641 (WING G1525)
HARRINGTON, J.: *The political works of James Harrington*, ed. by J.G.A. Pocock, Cambridge 1977
—— *The commonwealth of Oceana*, ed. by J.G.A. Pocock, Cambridge 1992
The Hartlib Papers, (Sheffield 2002)
HMC, Hastings Paper, 3 vols, London 1928–1934
HOBBES, T.: *Thomas Hobbes: critique du 'De Mundo' de Thomas White*, ed. by J. Jacquot-H.W. Jones, Paris 1973
—— *The correspondence of Thomas Hobbes*, ed. by N. Malcolm, 2 vols., Oxford 1994

SELECTED BIBLIOGRAPHY

—— *De cive*, ed. by R. Tuck, Cambridge 1998
—— *Leviathan*, ed. by R. Tuck, Cambridge 1996
—— *Elementorum philosophiae sectio prima de corpore*, London 1655 (WING H2226)
—— *Six lessons to the professors of the Mathematiques*, London 1656 (WING H2260)
HOLDEN, H.: *Divinae fidei analysis*, Paris 1652
—— *The analysis of divine faith*, Paris 1658 (WING H2375)
—— *A Letter written by Mr. Henry Holden touching the prohibition at Rome of Mr. Blacklow's [that is, Thomas White's] book, intituled Tabulae Suffragiales*, s.l.s.d.
—— *Doctor Holden's letter to a friend of his, upon the occasion of Mr. Blacklow's submitting his writings to the See of Rome, together with a Copie of the said Mr. Blacklow's submission*, s.d. s.l., (WING H2377)
—— *A Letter written by Dr. Holden to Mr. Graunt concerning Mr. White's Treatise de Medio Animarum Statu*, Paris 1661 (WING H2379)
PUGH, R., *Blacklo's Cabal*, s.l. 1680 (WING P4186)
[PERSONS, R.] R. Doleman, *A Conference about the next succession to the Crowne of England*, s.l.1594 (STC 19398)
PRYNNE, W.: *A true and perfect narrative*, London 1659 (WING P4113)
SANDERS, N.: De Visibili Monarchia Ecclesiae Libri Octo, Louvain 1571 (see STC 21691 and A.F. Allison-D.M. Rogers (eds.), *The Contemporary Printed Literature of the English Counter-Reformation between 1558–1640*, 2 vols., Aldershot 1989–94, vol. I n. 1013)
[SERGEANT, J.], *A Vindication of the Doctrine contained in Pope Benedict xii, his Bull, by S.W. a Roman Catholic*, Paris 1659 (WING S2599)
SPANHEIM, F.: *Friderici Spanhemii Epistola ad nobilissimum virum, Davidem Buchananum*, London 1645 (WING S4799)
The Douay College Diaries, Third, Fourth and Fifth, 1598–1654, 2 vols., Publication of the Catholic Record Society nn.10–11, London 1911
The first and second Diaries of the English College, Douay, ed. by T.F. Knox, London 1878
The letters and memorials of Cardinal Allen (1532–1594), ed. by T.F. Knox, London 1932
The Queens closet opened. Incomparable secrets in Physick, Chirurgery, Preserving, Candying, and Cookery, London 1655 (WING M96)
The works of the most reverend father in God, William Laud, D.D., sometime Lord Archbishop of Canterbury, 7 vols, New York 1975
WALLIS, J.: *Elenchus Geometriae Hobbianae*, Oxford 1655 (WING W579)
—— *Due correction for Mr. Hobbes*, Oxford 1656 (WING W576)
—— *Hobbiani puncti dispunctio*, Oxford 1657 (WING W588)
—— *Commercium Epistolicum de Quaestionibus quisdan Mathematicis nuper habitum*, Oxford 1658 (WING W564)
WARD, S.: *A philosophicall essay*, Oxford 1652 (WING W823)
—— *Vindiciae Academiarum*, Oxford 1654 (WING W832)

—— *In Thomae Hobbii Philosophiam exercitatio epistolica*, Oxford 1656 (WING W822)
WHITE, T.: *De Mundo dialogi tres*, Paris 1642
—— *Institutionum Peripateticarum*, London 1647 (WING W1831)
—— *Villicationis suae de medio statu animarum*, London 1653 (WING 1847A)
—— *An Apology for Rushworth's dialogues*, Paris 1654 (WING W1809)
—— *Tabulae suffragiales*, London 1655 (WING W1846)
—— *The grounds of obedience and government*, London 1655 (WING W1827)
—— *Peripateticall Institutions*, London 1656 (WING W1839)
—— *Euclides Physicus, sive de Principiis Naturae*, London 1657 (WING W1822)
—— *Euclides Metaphysicus, sive de Principiis Sapientiae*, London 1658 (WING W1821)
—— *The middle state of souls*, London 1659 (WING W1836)
—— *A letter to a person of honour written by Mr. Thomas White*, s.l. 1659 (WING W1832)
—— *Religion and reason mutually corresponding and assisting each other*, Paris 1660 (WING W1840)
—— *Apologia pro doctrina sua*, London 1661 (WING W1808)
—— *Devotion and reason. Wherein modern devotion for the dead is brought to solid principles and made rational*, Paris 1661 (WING W1818)
—— *Muscarium ad Immissos a Jona Thamone Calumniarum Crabrones et Sophismatum Scarabeos Censurae Duacenae Vindices Abigendos*, London 1661 (WING W1837)
WOOD, A.: *Athenae Oxonienses*, ed. London 1813–1820 (4 vols.)

Secondary Literature

ANDRIESSE, C.D.: *Huygens. The Man behind the Principle*, Cambridge 2005
ALLISON, A.F.: 'An English Gallican: Henry Holden, (1596/7–1662), Part I (to 1648)', *Recusant History*, n. 22 (1995), pp. 319–349
ALTIERI-BIAGI, M.L.-BASILE, B. (eds.): *Scienziati del Seicento*, Milano 1980
ASHTON, R.: *Counter-Revolution: the second Civil War and its origins, 1646–8*, New Haven 1994
ASHWORTH, W.B. Jr.: 'Catholicism and Early Modern Science', in D.C. Lindberg and R.L. Numbers (eds.), *God and Nature. Historical Essays on the Encounter between Christianity and Science*, Berkeley 1986, pp. 136–166
BERTI, D.: *Il processo originale di Galileo Galilei*, Rome 1876
BIRRELL, T.A.: 'English Catholics without a Bishop, 1655–1672', *Recusant History*, vol. IV (1958), pp. 142–178

SELECTED BIBLIOGRAPHY

BLYTHE, J.M.: *Ideal Government and the mixed constitution in the Middle Ages*, Princeton 1992

BLOCH, O.R.: 'Gassendi critique de Descartes', *Revue philosophique de la France et de l'ètranger*, vol. 91 (1966), pp. 217–236

BOSSY, J.: 'The character of Elizabethan Catholicism, *Past and Present* n. 21 (1962), pp. 39–59

—— *The English Catholic Community 1570–1850*, Oxford 1976 (1975)

BOUSWMA, W.J.: 'Gallicanism and the Nature of Christendom', in A. Molho and J.A. Tedeschi (eds.), *Renaissance. Studies in Honor of Hans Baron*, Florence 1970, pp. 809–830

BRADLEY, R.I.: 'Blacklo and the Counter-Reformation: an inquiry into the strange death of Catholic England', in C.H. CARTER (ed.), *From the Renaissance to the Counter-Reformation. Essays in Honor of Garrett Mattingly*, New York 1965

BROWN, A.J.: 'Anglo-Irish Gallicanism, c.1635–1685' unpublished Ph.D. Thesis, University of Cambridge 2004

BOAS, M.: 'The establishment of the mechanical philosophy', *Osiris*, vol. 10 (1952), pp. 412–541

—— *Robert Boyle and Seventeenth Century Chemistry*, Cambridge 1958

—— *Promoting Experimental Learning. Experiment and the Royal Society 1660–1727*, Cambridge 1991

—— *Henry Oldenburg. Shaping the Royal Society*, Oxford 2002

BRUNDELL, B.: *Pierre Gassendi: From Aristotelianism to a New Natural Philosophy*, Dordrecht 1987

BURNS, J.H. and GOLDIE, M. (eds.): *The Cambridge History of Political Thought, 1450–1700*, Cambridge 1991

—— 'George Buchanan and the anti-monarchomachs', in N. Phillipson-Q. Skinner (eds.), *Political Discourse in Early Modern Britain*, Cambridge 1993, pp. 3–22

CLANCY, T.H.: 'The Jesuits and the Independents: 1647', *Archivum Historicum Societatis Iesu*, vol. xl (1971), 67–89

CLERICUZIO, A.: 'A redefinition of Boyle's chemistry and corpuscular philosophy', *Annals of Science*, vol. 47 (1990), pp. 561–589

COLLINS, J.R.: 'The Church Settlement of Oliver Cromwell', *History*, vol. 87 (2002), pp. 18–40

—— 'Thomas Hobbes and the Blackloist conspiracy of 1649', *Historical Journal*, vol. xlv (2002), pp. 305–331

—— *The Allegiance of Thomas Hobbes*, Oxford 2005

COLLINSON, P: *The religion of Protestants: the Church in English Society, 1559–1624*, Oxford 1982

—— *The Birthpangs of Protestant England: Religion and Cultural Change in Sixteenth and Seventeenth Centuries*, Basingstoke 1988

DARMON, J.C.: 'Les clairs-obscurs d'une critique: quelques enjeux épistémologiques de la querrelle entre Gassendi and Fludd', in F. Greiner (ed.), *Aspects de la tradition alchimique au XVIIe siècle*, Milan-Paris 1998, pp. 67–84

DEAR, P.: *Mersenne and the learning of the schools*, Ithaca 1988
DEASON, G.B.: 'Reformation Theology and the Mechanist Conception of Nature', in D.C. Lindberg and R.L. Numbers (eds.), *God and Nature. Historical essays on the encounter between Christianity and science*, Berkeley 1986, pp. 167–191
DEBUS, A.G.: *Science and Education in the Seventeenth Century. The Webster-Ward Debate*, London and New York 1970
—— *The Chemical philosophy: Paracelsian Science and Medicine in sixteenth and seventeenth century*, 2 vols., New York 1977
—— 'Chemists, Physicians and Changing perspectives', *Isis*, vol. 89 n.1 (1998), pp. 66–81
DOBBS, B.J.T.: 'Studies in the natural philosophy of Sir Kenelm Digby', *Ambix*, vol. XVIII n. 1 (1971), pp. 1–25
—— 'The natural philosophy of Sir Kenelm Digby. Part II. Digby and Alchemy', *Ambix*, vol. xx n.3 (1973), pp. 143–163
—— 'Digby's experimental alchemy: the book of *Secrets*', *Ambix*, vol. XXI n.1 (1974), pp. 1–28
—— *The Janus face of Genius: the role of alchemy in Newton's thought*, Cambridge 1991
DUFFY, E.: *The stripping of the altars: traditional religion in England, c.1400–1580*, New Haven 1992
—— 'William Cardinal Allen, 1532–1594', *Recusant History*, vol. 22 n. 3 (1995), pp. 265–305
EISENACH, E.: 'Hobbes on Church, State, and Religion', *History of Political Thought*, n.3 (1982), pp. 215–243
FEINGOLD, M. (ed.): *Jesuit science and the republic of letters*, Cambridge (Mass.) 2002 —— (ed.) *The new science and Jesuit science: seventeenth century perspectives*, Boston-Dordrecht 2003
FINCHAM, K. and LAKE, P.: 'The ecclesiastical policy of King James I', *Journal of British Studies*, n. 24 (1985), pp. 169–207
FRANK, R.G. Jr.: *Harvey and the Oxford Physiologists. Scientific Ideas and Social Interactions*, Berkeley 1980
FRANKLIN, J.: 'Sovereignty and mixed constitution: Bodin and his critics', in J.H. Burns and M. Goldie (eds.), *The Cambridge History of Political Thought, 1450–1700*, Cambridge 1991, pp. 298–328
GABRIELI, V.: *Sir Kenelm Digby. Un inglese italianato nell'eta'della Controriforma*, Roma 1957
GELDEREN van M. and SKINNER, Q. (eds.): *Republicanism, a shared European heritage*, 2 vols., Cambridge 2002
GIFFORD, J.V.: 'The controversy over the oath of allegiance of 1606', unpublished D.Phil. Thesis, University of Oxford 1971
GOLDIE, M.: 'The Civil Religion of James Harrington', in A. Pagden (ed.), *The Languages of Political Theory in Early-Modern Europe*, Cambridge 1987, pp. 197–222

GOLDSMITH, M.M.: 'Hobbes's Mortal God: is there a fallacy in Hobbes's theory of sovereignty?', *History of Political Thought*, n.1 (1980), pp. 33–50

HAAKONSSEN, K.: 'Repulicanism', R.E. Goodin-P. Pettit (eds.), *A Companion to Contemporary Political Philosophy*, Oxford 1993, pp. 568–574

HAIGH, C.: 'The continuity of Catholicism in the English Reformation', *Past and Present* n. 93 (1981), pp. 37–90

—— *English Reformations. Religion, Politics and Society under the Tudors*, Oxford 1993

HALL, A.R. and BOAS HALL M.: 'The Intellectual Origins of the Royal Society. London and Oxford', *Notes and Records of the Royal Society of London*, vol. 23 n. 2 (1968), pp. 157–168

HENRY, J.: 'Atomism and Eschatology: Catholicism and natural philosophy in the Interregnum', *The British Journal for the History of Science*, vol. XV (1982), pp. 211–239

HILL, C.: *Society and Puritanism in Pre-Revolutionary England*, London 1964

—— *Intellectual Origins of the English Revolution*, Oxford 1965

—— *The world turned upside down. Radical ideas during the English Revolution*, London 1991 (1972)

HILL, K.: 'Neither ancient nor modern: Wallis and Barrow on the Composition of Continua. Part One: Mathematical Styles and the Composition of Continua', *Notes and Records of the Royal Society of London*, vol. 50 n. 2 (1996), pp. 165–178

HINE, W.L.: 'Mersenne Variants', *Isis* vol. 67 n.1 (1976), pp. 98–103

HÖPFL, H.: *Jesuit Political Thought. The Society of Jesus and the State, c.1540–1630*, Cambridge 2004

HOUSTON, A. and PINCUS, S. (eds.): *A Nation transformed. England after the Restoration*, Cambridge 2001

HUGHES, A.: *The Causes of the English Civil War*, New York 1991

HUNT, R.W.-WATSON, A.G.: *Digby Manuscripts*, Oxford 1999

HUNTER, M.: *The Royal Society and its Fellows 1660–1700. The Morphology of an early scientific institution*, Chalfont St. Giles 1982

—— 'Latitudinarianism and the "Ideology" of the early Royal Society: Thomas Sprat's History of the Royal Society (1667) reconsidered', in Id., *Establishing the New Science. The Experience of the early Royal Society*, Woodbridge 1989, pp. 45–71

ISRAEL, J.: *The Dutch Republic. Its Rise, Greatness, and Fall 1477–1806*, Oxford 1995

JACOB, J.R.: *Robert Boyle and the English Revolution: A Study in Social and Intellectual Change*, New York 1977

—— and JACOB, M.C.: 'The Anglican origins of modern science: the metaphysical foundations of the Whig constitution', *Isis*, vol. 71 (1980), pp. 251–267

JACOB, M.C.: *The Newtonians and the English revolution*, Ithaca 1976

JANACECK, B.: 'Catholic Natural Philosophy: Alchemy and the Revivification of Sir Kenelm Digby', in M.J. Osler (ed.) *Rethinking the Scientific Revolution*, Cambridge 2000, pp. 89–118

JESSEPH, D.M.: *Squaring the circle. The War between Hobbes and Wallis*, Chicago 1999

JOHNSON, F.R.: *Astronomical thought in Renaissance England*, Baltimore 1937

JONES, N.L.: *Faith by Statute: Parliament and the settlement of religion, 1559*, London 1982

— *God and the moneylenders: usury and the law in early modern England*, Oxford 1989

JORDAN, R.A.: 'The Blackloists 1640–1668. Ecclesiastical, Theological and Intellectual Authority in English Catholic Polemic', unpublished Ph.D. Thesis, University of Cambridge 1999

KARGON, R.H.: *Atomism in England from Hariot to Newton*, Oxford 1966

KIRK, *Biography of English Catholics in the Eighteenth century*, London 1909

KROLL, R., ASHCRAFT, R., ZAGORIN, P.(eds.): *Philosophy, Science and Religion in England 1640–1700*, Cambridge 1992

KROOK, D.: *John Sergeant and his circle. A study of three seventeenth-century English Aristotelians*, Leiden 1993

LAUDAN, L.: 'The clock metaphor and probabilism: the impact of Descartes on English methodological thought, 1650–65', *Annals of Science*, vol. 22 (1966), pp. 73–104

LAW, T.G.: *The Archpriest controversy*, London 1896–98

LINDBERG, D.C. and NUMBERS, R.L. (eds.): *God and Nature. Historical Essays on the Encounter between Christianity and Science*, Berkeley 1986

LITTLE, P.: Lord Broghill and the Cromwellian union with Ireland and Scotland, Woodbridge 2004

LOOMIE, A.J.: 'A Jacobean crypto-Catholic: Lord Wotton', *The Catholic Historical Review*, vol. III n. 3 (1967), pp. 328–345

MAILLARD, J.F.: 'Descartes et l'alchimie: une tentation conjurée?', in F. Greiner (ed.), *Aspects de la tradition alchimique au XVIIe siècle*, Milan-Paris 1998, pp. 95–109

MANCOSU, P.: *Philosophy of Mathematics and Mathematical Practice in the Seventeenth Century*, Oxford 1996

— and VAILATI, E.: 'Torricelli's Infinitely Long Solid and Its Philosophical Reception in the Seventeenth Century', *Isis* vol. 82 (1991), pp. 50–70

MALCOLM, N.: *Aspects of Hobbes*, Oxford 2002

MALTBY, W.S.: *The Black Legend in England*, Durham (N.C.) 1971

MARTIN, V.: *Le Gallicanisme et la réforme catholique*, Paris 1919

— *Les origines du Gallicanisme*, Paris 1939

MARTIMORT, A.G.: *Le Gallicanisme de Bossuet*, Paris 1953

MARTINICH, A.P.: *The Two Gods of Leviathan: Thomas Hobbes on Religion and Politics*, Cambridge 1992

MASETTI-ZANNINI, G.L.: *La vita di Benedetto Castelli*, Brescia 1961

MATTON, S.: 'Cartisianisme et alchimie: a propos d'un termoignage ignore sur les travaux alchimiques de Descartes. Avec une note sur Descartes et Gomez Pereira', in F.Greiner (ed.), *Aspects de la tradition alchimique au XVIIe siècle*, Milan-Paris 1998, pp. 111–184

MCCOOG, T.M.: *'Our way of proceeding'? The Society of Jesus in Ireland, Scotland and England, 1547–1588*, Leiden 1996

MENDELSOHN, J.A.: 'Alchemy and Politics in England 1649–1665', *Past and Present*, n. 135 (1992)

MILTON, A.: *Catholic and Reformed. The Roman and Protestant Churches in English Protestant Thought, 1600–1640*, Cambridge 1995

MORRILL, J.: 'The religious context of the English Civil War', *Transactions of the Royal Historical Society*, n.34 (1984), pp. 155–178

—— 'The Church in England, 1642-9', in Id. (ed.), *Reactions to the English Civil War, 1642–1649*, New York 1988, pp. 89–114

NEWMAN, W.R.: 'Boyle's debt to corpuscular alchemy', in M. Hunter (ed.), *Robert Boyle reconsidered*, Cambridge 1994, pp. 107–118

—— 'The alchemical sources of Robert Boyle's corpuscular philosophy', *Annals of Science*, vol. 53 (1996), pp. 567–585

—— and PRINCIPE, L.R.: *Alchemy tried in the fire. Starkey, Boyle and the fate of Helmontian chymistry*, Chicago and London 2002

OSLER, M.J.: 'Eternal Truths and the Laws of Nature: The Theological Foundations of Descartes' Philosophy of Nature', *Journal of the History of Ideas*, vol. 46 (1985), pp. 359–362

—— *Divine will and the mechanical philosophy. Gassendi and Descartes on contingency and necessity in the created world*, Cambridge 1994

—— (ed.), *Rethinking the scientific revolution*, Cambridge 2000

—— 'The intellectual sources of Robert Boyle's philosophy of nature: Gassendi's voluntarism and Boyle's physico-theological project', in KROLL, R., ASHCRAFT, R., ZAGORIN, P. (eds.): *Philosophy, Science and Religion in England 1640–1700*, Cambridge 1992, pp. 178–191

PETERSSON, R.T.: *Sir Kenelm Digby. The Ornament of England 1603–1665*, London 1956

PELTONEN, M.: *Classical Humanism and Republicanism in English political thought, 1570–1640*, Cambridge 1995

PHILLIPSON, N. and SKINNER, Q. (eds.): *Political Discourse in Early Modern Britain*, Cambridge 1993

PINCUS, S.: 'Neither Machiavellian Moment nor Possessive Individualism: Commercial Society and the Defenders of the English Commonwealth', *The American Historical Review*, vol. 103 n.3 (1998), pp. 705–736

—— 'From holy cause to economic interest: the study of population and the invention of the state', in A. Houston-S. Pincus (eds.), *A Nation transformed. England after the Restoration*, Cambridge 2001, pp. 272–298

POCOCK, J.G.A.: *The Machiavellian Moment: Florentine political thought and the atlantic republican tradition*, Princeton 1975

—— *Virtue, Commerce, and History: essays on political thought and history*, Cambridge 1985

POLLEN, J.H.: *The institution of the Archpriest Blackwell*, London 1916

POPKIN, R.H.: *The history of skepticism from Erasmus to Spinoza*, Berkeley 1979 (1960)

PRINCIPE, L.M.: *The aspiring adept: Robert Boyle's alchemical quest*, Princeton 1998

PROBST, S.: 'Infinity and creation: the origin of the controversy between Thomas Hobbes and the Savilian Professors Seth Ward and John Wallis', *The British Journal for the History of Science*, vol. 26 (1993), pp. 271–9

QUESTIER, M.C.: 'Loyalty, religion and state power in early modern England: English Romanism and the Jacobean Oath of Allegiance', *The Historical Journal*, vol. 40 n. 2 (1997), pp. 311–329

RAHE, P.: 'Antiquity surpassed: the repudiation of classical Republicanism', in WOTTON, D.: (ed.), *Republicanism, Liberty and Commercial Society, 1649–1776*, Stanford 1995, pp. 233–256

ROCHOT, B.: *Les travaux de Gassendi sur Épicure et sur l'atomisme, 1619–1658*, Paris 1944

—— 'Les véritées éternelles dans la querelle entre Descartes et Gassendi', *Revue philosophique de la France et de l'ètranger*, vol. 141 (1951), pp. 288–298

—— 'Gassendi et la "Logique" de Descartes', *Revue philosophique de la France et de l'ètranger*, vol. 80 (1955), pp. 300–308

ROSA, S.: 'Seventeenth-Century Catholic Polemic and the Rise of Cultural Rationalism: An Example from the Empire', *Journal of the History of Ideas*, vol. 17 n.1 (1996), pp. 87–107.

ROSSI, P.: *Francis Bacon: from magic to science*, London 1968 (1957)

RULER van, J.A.: *The crisis of causality. Voetius and Descartes on God, Nature and Change*, Leiden 1995

RUSSELL, C.: *The Causes of the English Civil War*, Oxford 1990

SALMON, J.H.: 'Catholic resistance theory, Ultramontanism and the Royalist Response 1580–1620', in BURNS, J.H. and GOLDIE, M. (eds.): *The Cambridge History of Political Thought, 1450–1700*, Cambridge 1991, pp. 219–250

SARASOHN, L.T.: 'Motion and morality: Pierre Gassendi, Thomas Hobbes and the Mechanical World-View', *Journal of the History of Ideas*, vol. 46 (1985), pp. 363–380

—— *Gassendi's Ethics. Freedom in a mechanist universe*, Cornell 1996

—— 'Thomas Hobbes and the Duke of Newcastle. A study in the mutuality of patronage before the establishment of the Royal Society', *Isis*, vol. 90 (1999), pp. 715–737

SCOTT, J.: 'The rapture of motion: James Harrington's republicanism', in N. Phillipson-Q. Skinner (eds.), *Political Discourse in Early Modern Britain*, Cambridge 1993, pp. 139–163

—— *England's Troubles. Seventeenth-century English political instability in European context*, Cambridge 2000

—— 'Classical Republicanism in Seventeenth-century England and the Netherlands', in M. van Genderen and Q. Skinner (eds.), *Republicanism. A shared European Heritage*, 2 voll., Cambridge 2002, vol. I, pp. 61–81
—— 'What were Commonwealth Principles?', *The Historical Journal*, vol. 47 n. 3 (2004), pp. 591–613
—— *Commonwealth Principles. Republican writing of the English Revolution*, Cambridge 2004
SHAPIN, S. and SCHAEFFER, S.: *The Leviathan and the air pump: Hobbes, Boyle and the experimental life*, Princeton 1986
SHAPIRO, B.J.: *John Wilkins 1614–1672. An Intellectual Biography*, Berkeley 1969
—— *Probability and certainty in seventeenth-century England. A study of the relationships between natural science, religion, history, law, and literature*, Princeton 1983
SOMMERVILLE, J.P.: 'Jacobean political thought and the controversy over the oath of allegiance of 1606, unpublished Ph.D. Thesis, University of Cambridge 1981
—— 'From Suarez to Filmer: A reappraisal', *The Historical Journal*, vol. 25 n. 3 (1982), pp. 525–540
—— 'The "new art of lying": equivocation, mental reservation, and casuistry', in E. Leites (ed.), *Conscience and Casuistry in Early Modern Europe*, Cambridge 1988, pp. 159–184
SOUTHGATE, B.C.: 'Thomas White's *Grounds of obedience and government*: a note on the dating of the first edition', *Notes and Queries*, vol. 28 (1981), pp. 208–9
—— '"That Damned Booke": *The Grounds of Obedience and Government* (1655), and the downfall of Thomas White', *Recusant History*, vol. 17 n. 3 (1985), pp. 238–253
—— '"Cauterising the Tumor of Pyrrhonism": Blackloism versus Skepticism', *Journal of the History of Ideas*, vol. 53 n. 4 (1992), pp. 631–645
—— *'Covetous of Truth'. The life and work of Thomas White, 1593–1676*, Dordrecht-Boston 1993
—— 'Blackloism and Tradition: From Theological Certainty to Historiographical Doubt', *The Journal of the History of Ideas*, vol. 61 n. 1 (2000), pp. 97–114
SPURR, J.: '"Latitudinarianism" and the Restoration Church', *The Historical Journal*, vol. 31 n. 1 (1988), pp. 61–88
—— '"Rational Religion" in Restoration England', *Journal of the History of Ideas*, vol. 49 n.4 (1988), pp. 536–585
SKINNER, Q.: 'Thomas Hobbes and his disciples in France and England', *Comparative Studies in Society and History*, vol. 8 (1965-6), pp. 153–165
—— 'The ideological context of Hobbes's political thought', *The Historical Journal*, vol. IX n.3 (1966), pp. 286–317
—— 'Meaning and understanding in the history of ideas', *History and Theory* vol. 8 n.1 (1969), pp. 3–53

—— 'Conquest and Consent: Thomas Hobbes and the Engagement Controversy', in G.E. Aylmer (ed.), *The Interregnum: the Quest for Settlement, 1646–1660*, Hamden (Conn.) 1972, pp. 79–98
—— *The foundations of modern political thought*, 2 vols, Cambridge 1983 (1978)
STATE, S.A.: 'Text and Context: Skinner, Hobbes and Theistic Natural Law', *The Historical Journal*, vol. 28 n. 1 (1985), pp. 27–50
SUMIDA JOY, L.: *Gassendi the Atomist: advocate of history in an age of science*, Cambridge 1987
THOMAS, K.: *Religion and the Decline of Magic*, London 1971
TREVOR-ROPER, H.: 'The Great Tew Circle', in Id., *Catholics, Anglicans and Puritans. Seventeenth Century Essays*, London 1987, pp. 166–230
TUCK, R.: *Natural rights theories. Their origin and development*, Cambridge 1979
—— *Philosophy and government, 1572–1651*, Cambridge 1993
—— 'The civil religion of Thomas Hobbes', in N. Phillipson-Q. Skinner, *Political Discourse in Early Modern Britain*, Cambridge 1993, pp. 120–138
TUTINO, S.: 'The Catholic Church and the English Civil War: the case of Thomas White', *The Journal of Ecclesiastical History* vol. 58 n. 2 (2007), pp. 232–255
YATES, F.: *Giordano Bruno and the Hermetic Tradition*, Chicago 1964
WALLACE, W.A.: *Galileo, the Jesuits and the Medieval Aristotle*, Hampshire-Brookfield 1991
WEBSTER, C.: 'English Medical Reformers and the Puritan Revolution: A Background to "Society of Chymical Physitians"', *Ambix*, vol. 14 (1967)
—— *From Paracelsus to Newton: magic and the making of modern science*, Cambridge 1982
WESTFALL, R.S.: 'Unpublished Boyle Papers relating to scientific method', *Annals of Science*, vol. 12 n. 2 (1956), pp. 103–117
—— 'The Scientific Revolution Reasserted', in M.J. Osler (ed.), *Rethinking the Scientific Revolution*, Cambridge 2000, pp. 41–55
WOTTON, D.: 'The republican tradition: from commonwealth to commonsense', in Id. (ed.), *Republicanism, Liberty and Commercial Society, 1649–1776*, Stanford 1995, pp. 1–44
ZAGORIN, P.: *A History of Political Thought in the English Revolution*, Bristol 1997 (1954)
—— *Ways of Lying. Dissimulation, Persecution, and Conformity in Early Modern Europe*, Cambridge (Mass.) 1990

Index

alchemy 17, 55
    and atomism 21–2
    Digby's reflections on 139–41
    in Digby's *Two Treatises* 26–7
    politics, relationship 27–8
Allen, Thomas 7, 17, 138
Allen, William 5
Allison, A.F. 58
Anne, Queen, regent of France 104
Aristotelianism 19, 20, 21, 24, 26, 28
    demise of 144
    Digby's 29, 30
    and new science, attempt at synthesis 143
    Oxford Circle discussions 84–5
    revival 95
    vs Cartesianism 131–2
    vs Epicureanism 94–5
    vs materialism 95
    White's 29–30, 91, 93
Aristotle 158
    as atomist 24–5
    De anima 26
    on slavery 67
Arminianism 132
Arnauld, Antoine 119
Assheton, William
    Evangelium Armatum 75
    White, critique of 75–6, 133, 138
atomism 16
    and alchemy 21–2
    Digby's 22, 102
    in England 17, 20–1, 30
    in France 17–18, 20, 21
    Gassendi's 17–18, 19–20, 86
    White's 28–9, 91–2
atomist, Aristotle as 24–5
atomists, classical 16–17
Austin, John 76
Avicenna 25

Bacon, Francis 1, 21
    Novum Organum 17
Ball, William, critique of White 80–1

Bampsfield, Joseph 103
Barclay, William 76
Bathurst, Ralph 86
Baxter, Richard
    Holy Commonwealth 76
    White, critique of 77
Bellarmine, Robert 32, 71, 76
Bishop, William, Bishop of Chalcedon 4
Blackloists 4, 97, 109, 110
    Bishops proposal 45
    Catholicism 120–1, 138
    Cromwell
        negotiations with 49
        support for 121
    Erastianism 78
    Independents, Oath proposal 44–5, 46, 49, 52–3
    influence 144
    and Irish Catholics 105
    Jesuit opposition 125
    natural philosophy, contribution 143
    and Papal infallibility 44
    politics 43–63
    'rational' Catholicism xiii–xiv, 113
    Ward on 95
    see also Digby; Holden; White
Blackwell, George, Archpriest 3
Book of Common Prayer 1
Bossy, John 2, 4, 45
Bouswma, W.J., Gallicanism, definition 48
Boyle, Robert 21, 30, 32, 83, 85, 86, 139
Bracciolini, Poggio 17
Brown, Anthony 78
Bruno, Giordano 21
Buchanan, David 130

Campion, Edmund 2
Carrier, Benjamin 9
Cartesianism, vs Aristotelianism 131–2
Cary, Lucius, *Discourse on Infallibility* 37, 101
    White's critique 37–8
Catholicism

Blackloists 120–1, 138
  Digby's 54, 55–6, 137
  Jesuitical 137
  and natural philosophy 39–41
  see also English Catholic Church
Cavendish, Sir Charles 17
Cavendish, William (Duke of Newcastle) 15
Charles I, King 110
Charles II, King 87, 104, 137
chemistry
  and alchemy 22
  development of 86
Church, State, Gallican model 48
Church of England, 'Roman' elements 1
Clancy, Thomas 46
Clayton, Thomas Jr 85
Clifford, Hugh 144
Coke, Roger
  Justice Vindicated 73–4
  on knowledge 74
  on Law of Nature 74
  White, critique of 74–5
Collins, Jeffrey 16, 49, 78
common good
  vs common interest 80
  White on 67–8, 78–9, 132–3, 164–7
common reason, Holden on 109, 110, 111
commonwealth, foundations, Holden on 108
Congregation of the Index 119
  condemns White's *De medio statu animarum* 135
consent theory iii, 70, 73, 77, 81
Copernicanism 6, 17
Counter-Reformation xiv
Courtney, Thomas 50, 127, 128
Cromwell, Oliver
  Digby, relationship 103–6
  negotiations with Blackloists 49
  support
    by Blackloists 121
    by White 72–3, 128

De Lugo, Cardinal 47–8
Deason, Gary 39
Dee, John 17
Democritus 16
Descartes, René
  Discourse on Method 16

  mechanical theory of matter 20
  view of White's *De Mundo* 129
  see also Cartesianism
Digby, George 137
Digby, John 7
Digby, Kenelm xiii, 10–11, 49–56, 60, 65, 101–6, 136–41
  Accademia dei Filomati, lecture 7, 140
  alchemy, reflections on 26–7, 139–41
  Aristotelianism 29, 30
  atomism 22, 102
  Catholicism
    brand of 54, 55–6, 137–8
    conversion 8, 10
    and loyalty to King 10, 12, 13, 138
    post-Restoration 137
  Charles II, petition 137
  Cromwell, relationship 103–6
  education 7
  exile and return 53, 102–3
  experimentalism 139–40
  family background 7
  Fellow of the Royal Society 138
  France, reputation in 102
  on Galileo 23–4
  Gentleman to the Privy Council 8
  Hakewill, correspondence 9, 12
  on Hakewill's *An Apologie...* 9
  Henrietta Maria
    Chancellor for 12, 137
    Rome Agent for 8, 49–52, 53
  Hobbes, contact 15–16
  on immortality of the soul 25–6, 29
  influence, loss of 117, 138
  Laud, correspondence 10
  on life after death 22–3
  natural philosophy, work on 138–9
  Oxford Circle, contribution 101
  papacy, distrust of 53–4
  Parisian Circle 15–16
  political activities 102–4
  political treatise, proposed 54–5
  Ponce's attack 105
  proselytism, accusation of 11–12
  on public/private sphere 11–12
  on quantity 23
  The Queens closet opened, contribution to 139
  religious affiliations 28

on resurrection of bodies 140–1
Wallis, correspondence 93–4
White, assistance to 128–9
works
  Chymical Secrets 139
  Discourse... 101–2
  Two Treatises 22–5, 101, 141
    alchemy in 26–7
on written vs spoken language 7–8
Digges, Thomas 17
Dobbs, Betty Jo 32, 139, 140
Douai, English College
  aim 5
  Jesuit takeover 5
  Leyburn, President 4, 100
  Scholasticism 6
Du Perron, Cardinal 112
Dutton, John 11, 12

ecclesiology, White's 36–7
ecumenism, White's 36
four elements 28–9, 31–2, 89
Elizabeth I, Queen, excommunication 2, 48
Elizabethan Settlement (1559) 1
England, Ireland, conflict 60–1
English Catholic Church 1, 3, 128
  dangers to 123–4
English Catholics 10, 98
  bid for toleration 44, 46–7
  diversity 62
  in English politics 109–10
  loyalty assurances 45, 51–2
  see also Blackloists
English Chapter 4, 43
  censure of Leyburn 99–100, 121
  conflicts in 127
  Papal confirmation sought 49, 54
  White
    opposition to 97
    support for 100–1, 117, 118
English Civil War 44
English Reformation 1
English republicanism, and natural law 79–81
Epicureanism, vs Aristotelianism 94–5
Epicurus 19
Erastianism
  Blackloists 78
  Harrington's 78
  Hobbes's 16, 78

Eucharist doctrine 1
experimentalism, Digby's 139–40
Fermat, Pierre 93
Fitton, Peter 44, 60
free will
  and obedience 66–7, 152–4
  White on 40

Gabrieli, V. 105
Galileo, Digby on 23–4
Gallicanism
  Bouswma's definition 48
  Holden's 58, 59
  significance 59
Gassendi, Pierre 6, 15, 21, 40, 94
  atomism 17–18, 19–20, 86
  on Scholasticism 18
  on the soul's immortality 19–20
  works
    De motu 19
    Exercitationes Paradoxicae 18
    Syntagma Philosophiae 22
Genesis account, and natural philosophy 31–2, 40
Glanvill, Joseph, *Vanity of Dogmatizing* 136
Glorious Revolution (1688–89) 145
Goddard, Jonathan 83
Goldie, Mark 77
government, Holden on 108–9
Grant, William 58–9, 113–15
Gunpowder Plot (1605) 3, 7, 137

Hakewill, George 8–9
  An Apologie... 9
  Digby, correspondence 9, 12
Hammond, Henry, *Treatise of Schism*, Holden's critique 113
Harlay de Champvallon, François de, Archbishop of Rouen 43, 57
Harrington, James
  Erastianism 78
  Oceana 76, 77
Hartlib, Samuel 139
  laboratory 27, 103
Harvey, Gabriel 87
  De motu cordis 85
  medical discoveries 85
heliocentrism, White on 31
Hendrik, Frederik 129, 131
Henrietta Maria, Queen 49, 51–2, 53, 55

recipes 139
Henry, John 30, 36
Highmore, Nathaniel 86
Hill, Christopher 27, 38
Hobbes, Thomas xiv, 6, 15
    anti-monarchism, accusation of 76
    Digby, contact 15–16
    Erastianism 16, 78
    materialism 20–1, 90, 92
    on origin of government 78
    Wallis, dispute 89–90, 92–3
    White
        debates with 136
        theories, links 73–4, 78
    works
        De Corpore 89
        Leviathan 76
            censured by Parliament 135
Holden, Henry xiii, 13, 45, 56–9, 60, 106–15
    Analysis Divinae Fidei 59, 106–7, 119
    aim 111–12, 113
    'appendix of Schisme' 107
    audience 111
        dedication to William Grant 113
        English/Latin versions, differences 110–11
    Bishops' role, view of 57
    on common reason 109, 110, 111
    on commonwealth foundations 108
    death 43, 126
    Gallicanism 58, 59
    on government 108–9
    on obedience 108–9
    papal authority, view of 44, 57
    on Papal infallibility 107, 112–13
    in Rome 43, 44
    on tradition 107
    White
        defence of 118, 119–20
        influence of 43–4
Huygens, Christiaan 129
Huygens, Constantijn 129

Independents 130
    Blackloists, Oath proposal 44–5, 46, 49, 52–3
    Presbyterians, rift 51
infinitesimal concept, Wallis 90–1
infinity concept, White on 88

Injunctions 1
Innocent X, Pope 57
Inquisition 6, 46, 99, 117, 120, 124, 125
    condemns White's *opera omnia* 121, 135
Irish Catholics, and Blackloists 105

Jacob, James 32, 37, 83
Jacob, Margaret 32, 37
James I, King 6
Janacek, Bruce 26
Jansenism 119, 120, 123
Jesuits
    English mission 5
        Catholic opposition to 2–3
        opposition to Blackloists 125
Jordan, Ruth 35, 37

Kargon, Richard 17, 30
Kircher, Athanasius 139
knowledge, Coke on 74

Lane, Joseph 104
latitudinarianism 83–4, 96, 97
Laud, Archbishop William, Digby, correspondence 10
Law of Nature, Coke on 74
Leyburn, George 115, 117, 126
    attacks on White 97–8
    censured by English Chapter 99–100, 121
    President, Douai College 4, 100
Locke, John 30
Lucretius, *De Rerum Natura* 16–17

Mariana, Juan de 72
Marillac, Michel de 43
Marsilius of Padua 78
materialism
    Hobbes's 20–1, 90
    vs Aristotelianism 95
matter, White on 31–2, 88–9
Mazarin, Jules, Cardinal 57, 104
Mendelsohn, J. Andrew 27–8
Mersenne, Marin 15, 19, 21, 129
Montagu, Richard 59
Montague, Walter 10
    attacks on White 98–9
More, Henry 46
Mumford, James, *Remembrance for the Living* 134

natural law, and English republicanism 79–80, 81
natural philosophers 94
natural philosophy
   and Catholicism 39–41
   Digby's 138–9
   and *Genesis* account 31–2, 40
   unifying factor 87
   White's 33–4, 69
   see also Aristotelianism
Newcastle group 17
Newman, William 21
Newton, Isaac 32
Nicholas, Sir Edward 104
Northumberland circle 17, 20

Oath of Allegiance (1606) 3, 48
obedience
   and free will, White on 66–7, 152–4
   Holden on 108–9
Oldenburg, Henry 139
Origen 153
Osler, Margaret 19, 32, 97
Oxford Circle
   Aristotelianism, discussions 84–5
   Digby's contribution 101
   members 83
   religious character 96–7
   role 91
   scientific interests 84
   Wallis's contribution 93
   White's contribution 86, 88, 91, 93–4

Papal authority, Holden's view 44, 57
Papal infallibility 36, 117
   and Blackloists 44
   Holden on 107, 112–13
Paul V, Pope 3
Penry, William (Fr Elisius) 46
Percy, Henry, scientific inquiries 17
Percy, Thomas, Earl of Northumberland 8
Perez, Antonio 47
Persons, Fr Robert 2, 5
Persons, Robert 71
Petersson, R.T. 105
Petty, William 85
Phyrronism 19
Pincus, Steven 80
Platonism 17

Plowden, Edmund 5
politics, alchemy, relationship 27–8
Ponce, John, attack on Digby 105
Pope, refusal to appoint English Bishop 57
Pope, Thomas, Earle of Downe 11
Presbyterians, Independents, rift 51
Protestantism, and science 39
Prynne, William 104
Pugh, Robert 61, 127–8
Purgatory, White on 36, 134–5

quantity
   Digby on 23
   White on 28–9
The Queens closet opened, Digby's contribution 139

religion, science, scientific revolution era 32
resistance, right of
   in English Catholic thought 71
   White on 70–2, 144, 175–8
Restoration (1660) 87, 115, 122, 128, 136
retributive justice 68
Rinuccini, Monsignor, Papal Nuncio 52, 61, 105
Rosa, Susan 37
Rossi, Paolo 21

Sanders, Nicholas 71
Scarburgh, Charles 87
Scholasticism 26, 29, 37, 91
   Gassendi on 18
science
   17th century 96
   and Protestantism 39
   and religion, scientific revolution era 32
   see also Oxford Circle
scientific revolution, transition period 143–4
Scott, Jonathan 77, 79
Sennert, Daniel 21
Sergeant, John 100, 127, 134, 143
   on White 34
Shapiro, Barbara 37, 83–4, 87
skepticism 19, 29–30, 37
Skinner, Quentin 16
slavery

Aristotle on 67
White on 67, 161–4
Smith, Richard, Bishop of Chalcedon 4, 6, 43, 44, 97–8, 100
soul, immortality
   Digby on 25–6, 29
   Gassendi on 19–20
Southgate, Beverley xiii, 30, 143, 144
Spanheim, Friedrick the Elder
   interest in White's *De Mundo* 132
   treatise 129–31
   White, relations 131
Stanley, Venetia 8
State, Church, Gallican model 48

theology, voluntarist 97
Thomas, Keith 27
Thurloe, John 103, 104
tradition
   Holden on 107
   White's defence of 35–6, 38, 43–4, 102, 117
transubstantiation 1
   White on 34–5
Tuck, Richard 79

Urban VIII, pope, White on 72

Voetius, Gisbertus 131–2

Wallis, John 83, 87
   Digby, correspondence 93–4
   Hobbes, dispute 89–90, 92–3
   infinitesimal concept 90–1
   Oxford Circle contribution 93
Walsh, Robert 105
Ward, George 46
Ward, Seth 83, 86
   on Blackloists 95
   In Thomae Hobbii... 94
Warner, Walter 17
Webster, Charles 27
Westfall, Richard 30–1, 32
White, Jerome 5
White, Thomas (Blacklo) xiii, 4, 13, 59–63, 83–101, 117–36
   anti-monarchism, accusation of 76
   Aristotelianism 29–30, 91, 93
   Assheton's critique 75–6, 138
   atomism 28–9, 91–2
   Ball's critique 80–1
   Baxter's critique 77
   Coke's critique 74–5
   on the common good 67–8, 78–9, 132–3, 164–7
   consent theory iii, 70, 73, 77, 81
   critique of Cary's *Discourse on Infallibility* 37–8
   Cromwell, support of 72–3, 128
   death 136
   Digby, assistance from 128–9
   on duty of a Catholic 61–2
   ecclesiology 36–7
   ecumenism 36
   education 5
   English Chapter
      opposition to 97
      support of 100–1, 117, 118
   on free will 40
   on heliocentrism 31
   Hobbes
      debates with 136
      theories, links 73–4, 78
   Holden
      defence by 118, 119–20
      influence on 43
   importance 143
   on infinity concept 88
   influence, loss of 121–4, 127, 128, 135
   on Irish conflict 60–1
   Leyburn's attacks 97–8
   on matter 31–2, 88–9
   model of government 65–6
   Montagu's attacks 98–9
   natural philosophy 33–4, 69
   in Netherlands, post-Restoration 128–9
   on obedience and free will 66–7, 152–4
   Oxford Circle, contribution 86, 88, 91, 93–4
   political theory 121
   on Purgatory 36, 134–5
   on quantity 28–9
   on resistance, right of 70–2, 144, 175–8
   in Rome 6
   royal pardon 133
   Sergeant on 34
   on slavery 67, 161–4
   Spanheim, relations 131

tradition, defence of 35–6, 38, 43–4, 102, 117
on transubstantiation 34–5
on Urban VIII 72
on 'vigilancy' 69–70
works
   Apologia pro Doctrina sua adversus calumniatores 124
   Apology for Rushworth's dialogue 97
   Apology for the Treatise of Obedience and Government 132–3
   De medio statu animarum 134
     censured by Parliament 135
     condemned by Congregation of Index 135
   De Mundo 16, 28
     Descartes' view of 129
     Spanheim's interest in 132
   Devotion and Reason 134–5, 135–6
   Euclides Metaphysicus 86, 87, 91, 93, 96
   Euclides Physicus 86, 88, 91
   The Grounds of Obedience and Government
     analysis 65–73, 138, 144
     context 73–81
     dedication 147
     second edition 144
     text 147–94
   Institutionum Peripateticarum 28, 32–3, 40, 60, 86
     prohibited by Rome 119
     'Theological Appendix' 31
   opera omnia, condemned by Inquisition 121, 135
   Religion and reason 134
   Sonus Buccinae 97, 99
     condemned by Inquisition 117
   Tabulae Suffragiales 97
     condemned by Rome 118–19
   Villicationis... 97
Wilkins, John, Oxford Circle leader 83, 84, 85
Wootton, Lord 3
Wren, Christopher 83

Xenophon, *Cyropaedia* 65, 148

Yates, Frances 21

Zagorin, Perez 67